Forensic Focus 22

Violen e and Mental Disorder

A Cr ical Aid to the Assessment and Management of Risk

Stephen Blumenthal and Tony Lavender

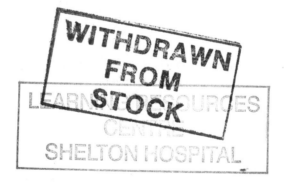

Jessica Kingsley Publishers
London and Philadelphia

First published in the United Kingdom in 2000 by
The Zito Trust

Published in the United Kingdom in 2001 by
Jessica Kingsley Publishers Ltd,
116 Pentonville Road, London
N1 9JB, England
and
325 Chestnut Street,
Philadelphia PA 19106, USA.

www.jkp.com

© Copyright 2000 Stephen Blumenthal and Tony Lavender
Foreword © Copyright 2000 John Monahan

Library of Congress Cataloging in Publication Data
A CIP catalog record for this book is available from the Library of Congress

British Library Cataloguing in Publication Data
A CIP catalogue record for this book is available from the British Library

ISBN 1 84310 035 5

Printed and Bound in Great Britain by
Athenaeum Press, Gateshead, Tyne and Wear

CONTENTS

ACKNOWLEDGEMENTS

We would like to thank Michael Howlett, Director of The Zito Trust, for commissioning and publishing this review and for his helpful comments. We are grateful to Professor John Monahan, Dr Deborah Brooke and Dr James Anderson for reading and commenting on earlier drafts and to Natasha Broad for proof-reading the initial drafts of the manuscript. Thank you to Jane, Ellen and Sarah Lavender for their support.

Stephen Blumenthal
Tony Lavender

The Zito Trust would like to thank The Baily Thomas Charitable Foundation for its financial support towards the cost of this publication.

HOW TO USE THIS BOOK

We have carried out a wide-ranging review of the literature on violence and mental disorder which is intended for a broad audience, including clinicians, researchers and policy-makers working in this area. It is intended as a reference book for mental health professionals, whose day-to-day work involves assessing and managing those thought to be at risk of engaging in violence. We provide a guide to the clinical, research and policy issues in the field. It is also intended as an up-to-date academic review of the literature, detailing research and commentary to assist academic researchers.

Some readers may wish to study the research findings in detail, whereas others will be content with a summary of the findings. Each section, therefore, is accompanied by a summary which is highlighted in a grey box. If readers want more information about a particular issue, they will find more detail in that section. Chapter 1 is a general introduction where various issues are outlined, including the way in which mental disorder has been defined throughout this work; clinical versus actuarial prediction of risk; the context of the mental health services in the UK, and mental health homicide inquiry reports. In Chapter 2 we examine research linking violence and mental disorder, and outline the various types of studies, including those looking at violence in the mentally disordered, and mental disorder in the violent. The detail in Chapter 2 is not necessary for the non-academic reader. We review the evidence for and against various factors which have been identified by research to be associated with violence in Chapter 3. Once again, there is considerably more detail than may be required and the grey box summarises each section within the chapter. Chapter 4 concerns the more psychological aspects of risk assessment and management. In this section, we focus on important clinical and developmental aspects of risk and the internal world of the violent offender. We discuss background factors such as childhood experiences, peer relationships and attachment theory. In Chapter 5 we describe three risk assessment instruments. These are based on empirical research and offer a means of rating risk according to the presence or absence of various factors. We evaluate the literature in Chapter 6, and in Chapter 7 we conclude the review with a discussion of the implications of the literature on violence and mental disorder on public policy, clinical practice and future research.

All technical expressions used in the text are defined in the Glossary on page 139.

FOREWORD

John Monahan
Doherty Professor of Law
University of Virginia

If there is one issue in mental health law of truly international importance at the beginning of the 21st century, it is how to identify which people with mental disorder present an undue risk of violence. Dr. Stephen Blumenthal and Professor Tony Lavender have written the most comprehensive, up-to-date, readable, and balanced assessment of the huge research and clinical literatures on violence risk assessment of which I am aware. They have, in the process, made a significant contribution to our understanding of the relationship of mental disorder to violence, a contribution whose relevance extends far beyond the shores of the United Kingdom.

The general public, of course – and politicians ever attuned to their desires – has always and everywhere been of the view that there is a non-coincidental link between disorder and danger. Ancient examples abound. In the *Republic*, for example, Socrates debated with a friend about whether justice required a person to repay all debts, without exception. The friend believed this to be the case, but Socrates argued otherwise: 'Ought I, for example, to put back into the hands of my friend, who has gone mad, the sword which I borrowed of him when he was in his right mind?' (Jowett, 1953, p. 13).

Yet even in ancient times, no one believed that *all* people with mental disorder were at increased risk of violent behavior, only some of them. For example, the Roman philosopher Philo Judaeus divided people with mental disorder into two groups, one of which consisted of those 'of the easy-going gentle style', and the other of which consisted of people 'whose madness was ... of the fierce and savage kind, which is dangerous both to the madmen themselves and to those who approach them' (quoted in Rosen, 1968, p. 89). Almost two millennia later, making this distinction accurately is still a vexing issue in mental health law and policy around the world.

The American Bar Association, along these lines, recently published a *National Benchbook on Psychiatric and Psychological Evidence and Testimony* (1998) for use by state and federal judges. The *Benchbook* states that courts rely on information from psychiatrists and psychologists in the form of violence risk assessments when making decisions about hospitalisation 'because courts are ultimately responsible for making these decisions and though the information may remain open to challenge, it is the best information available. The alternative is to deprive fact finders, judges and jurors of the guidance and understanding that psychiatrists and psychologists can provide' (p. 49).

It is not only as a standard for involuntary hospitalisation that risk of violence is pivotal, however. Community treatment orders ('outpatient commitment') − controversial throughout the world − often use dangerousness as a threshold standard as well. For example, in the summer of 1999, New York State enacted 'Kendra's Law', named after a woman pushed in front of a subway by a man with an untreated mental disorder. This law permits the mandatory treatment in the community of those persons with a mental disorder who have a 'history of lack of compliance with treatment that has caused either two hospitalisations within the last 36 months or one or more past acts of violence.'

Finally, less legally formal procedures for assertive community treatment in the form of 'community supervision and monitoring' and the intensive administration of mental health services are often predicated on a perceived risk of violence.

As Blumenthal and Lavender point out, the field of violence risk assessment has seen a dramatic shift in recent years away from studies attempting to understand clinical decision- making or to validate the accuracy of clinical predictions and toward studies attempting to isolate specific risk factors that are actuarially associated with violence. As Borum (1996) has noted, a wide range of instruments can be subsumed under the rubric of 'actuarial':

'At a minimum, these devices can serve as a checklist for clinicians to ensure that essential areas of inquiry are recalled and evaluated. At best, they may be able to provide hard actuarial data on the probability of violence among people (and environments) with a given set of characteristics, circumstances, or both' (p. 948).

The Zito Trust is to be congratulated for having sponsored such a first-rate and non-ideological review of such a contested topic. I know of few advocacy organisations in the United States that would have chosen to commission so objective a report. One can only hope that The Zito Trust will see the wisdom of sponsoring periodic updates of *Violence and Mental Disorder*. After a long period of quiescence, violence risk assessment, as Blumenthal and Lavender make abundantly clear, is a field on the move.

References

American Bar Association (1998). *National benchbook on psychiatric and psychological evidence and testimony*. Washington, D.C.: American Bar Association.

Borum, R. (1996). Improving the clinical practice of violence risk assessment: Technology, guidelines, and training. *American Psychologist, 51,* 945–956.

Jowett, B. (Ed.). (1953), *The dialogues of Plato* (4th ed.). Oxford: Oxford University Press.

Rosen, G. (1968). *Madness in society: Chapters in the historical sociology of mental illness.* Chicago: University of Chicago Press.

CHAPTER 1

INTRODUCTION: DEFINITIONS AND CONTEXT OF THE REVIEW

In this chapter we set the context of the review by outlining key issues relating to the field of violence and mental disorder. We define the terms and offer a critique of the taxonomic approach to mental disorder. We discuss clinical and actuarial approaches to risk assessment, risk management in the context of shaping mental health services, mental health inquiry reports, and perceptions of the public and the scientific community

The question of whether individuals suffering from a mental disorder have a greater propensity to violence than the general population has been controversial. Early research found that psychiatric patients were no more likely to be violent than the rest of the population, but recent studies have established a consistent, albeit modest, relationship. These recent developments are thought to be the result of increased methodological sophistication of studies, as well as changes in patient populations as a consequence of deinstitutionalisation (Stueve & Link, 1997). Despite controversy, and only recent convergence of views, legislators have long assumed a link, and people suffering from mental disorder have been the only individuals in democratic societies who can be detained involuntarily because of their potential for violence. Until the 1960s there was little impetus to predict dangerousness because of very conservative policies governing the management of people with mental disorder, particularly in forensic establishments (Quinsey, Harris, Rice & Cormier, 1998). Changes in policy leading to the closure of large institutions for the mentally ill, and concerns about the civil liberties of mentally disordered offenders, led to more contact between the mentally disordered and society at large, and consequently necessitated improvements in the prediction of the risk of violence by these individuals. Risk assessment has steadily increased in importance since then, and this has been accompanied by methodological improvements, particularly in the past decade.

Following a series of high profile cases involving homicides by individuals suffering from severe mental disorders, the 'care in the community' of such people has been the subject of public criticism in the UK. Policy initiatives, centring on the Care Programme Approach (CPA), provide a framework for improvements in community care. This has involved the allocation of individuals with severe mental disorder to levels of care according to their needs, and the identification of those with particularly high levels of needs (Department of Health, 1990). Supervision registers distinguish those patients at high risk of harm to self or others (Department of Health, 1994a). More recently, public debate about violence and mental disorder has turned to the risk posed by individuals with the more elusive diagnosis of personality disorder. The assessment of the risk of violence posed by individuals with mental health problems (both those suffering from mental illness and personality disorder) has become a central issue in mental health services. Mental health professionals now work in what might be termed a culture of risk assessment. In some respects, the prediction of dangerousness has been adopted uncritically, and an exclusive focus on risk detracts from effective treatment and care. Our purpose in this review is to provide a critical appraisal of the literature on violence and mental disorder.

There has been a substantial literature on the subject of violence and mental disorder which has focused mainly on mental illness and violence, with a rather tertiary interest in developmental and interpersonal issues associated with personality disorder. Reviews to date have also concerned themselves mainly with mental illness and have tended to be brief, examining only the main studies. This current analysis is, however, a detailed and comprehensive review of the literature. Violence perpetrated by individuals suffering from severe mental disorder tends to be related to an acute mental state, whereas violence perpetrated by those with personality disorder is characterised by more enduring personality traits. Personality – and its disorder– requires a detailed examination of psychological issues related to development and interpersonal issues. In addition to a critical discussion of factors typically identified by research as being related to violence, this review focuses on these developmental and interpersonal issues and their relationship with violence. As will be seen, the inclusion of personality disorder as a form of mental disorder raises a host of questions about risk assessment and management.

The first question we address is that of definition. We propose that the way in which 'mental disorder' (and to a lesser extent 'violence') has been defined reflects a particular paradigm, a particular way in which discourses of violence and mental disorder have been organised. The definition of mental disorder therefore reflects specific interests within society, and is important because it shapes the way in which research has been undertaken and the clinical application of that research to the assessment of risk. The way in which mental disorder and the potential for violence are conceptualised, and consequently the practice of risk assessment, is highly dependent on the social construction of violence and, especially, of mental disorder.

1.1. Defining Violence and Mental Disorder

- *Violence and mental disorder are defined*
- *We argue that the way in which mental disorder has been defined reflects a specific paradigm which has shaped research and the clinical practice of risk assessment*
- *This definition, based on the medical model, focuses on psychotic disorders, rather than personality disorder. We include personality disorder in our definition of mental disorder*

Violence. We have found Glasser's (1998) definition of violence, 'as a bodily response with the intended infliction of bodily harm on another person', as a simple and useful one. De Zulueta (1993) views violence as an essentially human characteristic related to the meaning we give to destructive forms of interpersonal or personal behaviour, the meaning being determined by social context. She distinguishes it from aggression, which has been used by ethologists to describe a form of social behaviour human beings share with other animals. With reference to Megargee (1982), Hollin and Howells (1989) define aggression as 'the intention to hurt or gain advantage over other people, without necessarily involving physical injury', whereas violence 'involves use of strong physical force against another person, sometimes impelled by aggressive motivation' (p3). Perelberg (1999) distinguishes between aggression and violence in a similar way: 'While aggression is potentially built into human beings by biology, as a reaction to danger, violence is the bodily actualisation of aggression which aims to negate the danger' (p37). For the purposes of this review, violence is limited to acts against others and excludes acts of violence against the self in the form of self-harm and suicide. Sexual offending is only covered in a general way, and is not discussed as a separate issue.

Mental Disorder. The definition of mental disorder is more complex in the context of this review and raises a host of philosophical, ideological and conceptual issues which have had a profound effect on the way in which research and clinical practice have been conducted in the field. Susan Sontag (1978) has illustrated the way in which illness is imbued with mythology, and nowhere is the social construction of illness more clearly epitomised than in the area of mental disorder. In Sontag's words 'Any important disease whose causality is murky…tends to be awash with significance… The subjects of deepest dread are associated with the disease. The disease itself becomes a metaphor' (p58).

On one level, mental disorder includes those 'major' disorders of affect and thought which form a subgroup of Axis I disorders in the Diagnostic and Statistical Manual of Mental Disorder (4th Edition; DSM-IV) (American Psychiatric Association, 1994). However, the inclusion of personality disorder as a form of mental disorder has been a controversial issue, as evidenced by the current debate over the inclusion of psychopathic disorder in the Mental Health Act (1983) in England and Wales.

The law requires that two questions be asked. The first is to determine whether the individual is guilty of the act, the *actus reus*, and the second requires the judgement of whether the individual is capable of guilt, that in committing the crime the individual has an 'evil mind', the *mens rea*. The line between badness and madness is undergoing a constant process of redefinition. In the UK, the question of whether personality disorder is a mental disorder, and whether it is treatable, is currently the subject of heated debate. In a letter to The Times on 31 October 1998, The Home Secretary, Jack Straw, observed that the proportion of restricted patients admitted under the Mental Health Act 1983 with the diagnosis of psychopathic disorder has declined from 14% in 1984 to 3.6% in 1997. The issue of treatability is central to this debate and the decline in the proportion of personality disordered individuals who become patients rather than prisoners reflects the way in which attitudes are changing about the treatment of this group. For many psychiatrists the issue of what constitutes mental 'disorder' is often simplified by defining it solely as those disorders which are considered to respond routinely to psychotropic medication.

The issue of responsibility for psychiatric care is intrinsic to the problem of definition. Since psychiatrists often take lead responsibility for the treatment of people with mental disorder, it is understandable that there is a tendency to avoid assuming this responsibility for the whole spectrum of mental disorders, including personality disorder, if the nature of the disorder is not perceived to be treatable with medication. The consequence is a definition of mental disorder which focuses on the psychotic end of the spectrum. Current discussions about changes to mental health legislation to detain people with personality disorder highlight inherent and unresolvable tensions. As psychological and social-psychological interventions for severe personality disorder (and indeed psychosis) become more sophisticated, and personality disorder becomes better understood, the notion of mental disorder is being stretched beyond that which is treatable with medication.

For the purposes of this review the term mental disorder includes those 'major' disorders of affect and thought which form a subgroup of Axis I disorders in the DSM-IV, including schizophrenia, schizo-affective disorder and manic depression, as well as Axis II personality disorders. We will refer to the former group as psychotic disorders, or major mental disorders, and to the latter group as personality disorders. The inclusive term 'mental disorder' will be used to refer to both. When reference is made to studies of 'psychiatric patients', this usually refers to individuals with a major mental disorder rather than a personality disorder. Some studies also refer to 'mental illness' or 'severe mental disorder' and this generally refers to major mental disorder or psychotic disorders.

1.2. Critique of Taxonomic Approaches to Mental Disorder

- *We expand upon our critical approach to the definition of mental disorder and the way in which the boundary between sanity and insanity is constantly drawn and redrawn*
- *The classical diagnostic approach is contrasted with an approach which is focused on symptoms rather than on categories of disorder*
- *The definition of personality disorder is particularly problematic in the context of the diagnostic approach, with much overlap between disorders, as well as between personality disorder and criminality*

The following review maintains a critical perspective on the definitional problems with mental disorder, and in particular, the way in which the boundaries between sanity and insanity are drawn and redrawn. As will be seen, research on violence and mental disorder has predominantly used as a definition those 'major' psychotic disorders which form a subgroup of Axis I disorders in the DSM-IV (American Psychiatric Association, 1994).

Bass and Murphy (1995) are critical of the nosology of DSM-IV and the ICD-10 (World Health Organisation, 1992) which define mental disorders as discrete syndromes with natural boundaries. An individual's symptoms frequently match several diagnostic categories resulting in a 'mixed picture' rather than 'pure' cases. The diagnosis thus often gives the false impression of understanding, but conveys little information about the individual's underlying psychopathology. Bass and Murphy (1995) call this the *classical approach* and by no means dismiss it, pointing out that in the interests of cognitive economy, we require a system of classification which summarises large quantities of information in order to conceptualise problems and communicate. However, problems arise when psychiatric classification is rigidly adhered to, and when a category is given the characteristics of an object in the real world.

Related, but more powerful, criticisms of aspects of the diagnostic system have been made by, for example, Boyle (1990) and Bentall, Jackson & Pilgrim (1988) who argue that the concept of schizophrenia is invalid scientifically. Their arguments state, first, that the symptoms in the syndrome can also be found in people with other psychiatric conditions (e.g. thought disorder is common among people suffering with mania and delusions are found in affective disorders). Second, it is not possible to predict the onset, course or response to treatment from a diagnosis of schizophrenia. As Ciompi (1980) found in his study of 228 individuals with schizophrenia over a period of 35 years, the onset was either acute or, conversely, insidious in approximately half the cases. With regard to the course of the condition, equal numbers had episodic and continuous courses. With regard to outcome (that is, symptomatology), only half were left with a moderate or severe disability and more than a quarter showed full recovery. Other studies attempting to predict outcome have proved equally inconclusive (Kendell, Brockington & Leff, 1976). In addition, Strauss and Carpenter (1977) found that social factors, including work performance and social contacts, were better predictors of outcome than symptomatology. Similarly, Vaughn & Leff (1976) and Ciompi (1984) have found family variables (see later discussion) to be good predictors of relapse. Indeed Bentall et al. (1988) argue that 'it is possible that these factors are all sufficient to account for the marginal differences in outcome'. Third, thus far it has still proved impossible to find a clear relationship between diagnosis and aetiology (i.e. the cause of schizophrenia). All possible contenders – genetic, biochemical, neurological, cognitive, familial (systemic and psychoanalytic) – have been proposed, but no clear cause identified. Indeed, there is now widespread acceptance that a complex stress vulnerability model is probably required to explain the major symptoms of schizophrenia (Zubin & Spring, 1977; Nuechterlein, 1987; Clements & Turpin, 1992; Warner, 1994). Such criticism potentially undermines the usefulness of relating violence to categories of mental disorder and generally advocates a more symptom or psychological phenomena based approach (Bentall, 1990).

The definition of personality disorder is particularly problematic in this context. Diagnostic criteria for particular personality disorders are so overinclusive as to include potentially a wide range of individuals. There is a high degree of overlap between disorders, as well as an overlap between criminality and personality disorder. In particular, antisocial personality disorder (ASPD) and psychopathy represent a medicalisation of deviance.

Stevens (1993) likens the search for ASPD in prisons to 'looking for hay in a haystack'. While useful at times, terms such as psychopathy and ASPD are tautological. It is unsurprising to find high levels of offending among a group of individuals when part of the definition of group membership is criminal behaviour itself.

Bass and Murphy (1995) describe an alternative approach to the definition of mental disorder by invoking *prototype theory*. A prototype is the most typical instance of a category or class. It is an abstraction based on shared features of members of that category. Bass and Murphy refer to Wittgenstein's (1953) critique of the classical approach by his analysis of the category 'games'. Wittgenstein demonstrated that despite there being no set of properties that all games share and no fixed boundaries to the category, we all recognise football, chess and pat-a-cake as games. Games share 'family resemblances' rather than common properties; thus chess and football are both competitive, whereas pat-a-cake is not; football and rugby are both team games, chess and draughts are board games, and so forth. Rosch (1978) developed this alternative to the classical approach to taxonomy into prototype theory, which holds that there are grades of category membership which make some members better examples of the category than others. This would not be the case if categories were defined solely by the properties that all members have in common. From an empirical point of view, individuals tend to have high inter-rater reliability in their judgements of a good example of a particular category, despite having less agreement on the boundaries of the category. The best examples of a category are prototypes.

Prototype theory has influenced taxonomy by the development of *polythetic classification*. While monothetic classification is based upon distinguishing between categories on the basis of a single principle, the polythetic approach holds that members of a category have features in common with other members, but there is no essential feature which distinguishes category membership (Rosch, 1978).

The diagnostic approaches in DSM-IV (American Psychiatric Association, 1994) and ICD-10 (World Health Organisation, 1992) are polythetic systems. Bass and Murphy (1995) argue that two consequences of this are that categories defy precise definition and there is significant overlap in their properties. They argue that these systems are often used by practitioners and psychiatric taxonomists as monothetic systems. Attempts to accomplish increased diagnostic reliability are undertaken by defining the boundaries of disorder more clearly and minimising overlap. However, polythetic classification suggests the opposite; i.e. the use of family resemblances and internal heterogeneity with central prototypes, these being abstractions rather than concrete examples. Artificial boundaries between diagnostic categories have led to particular assumptions in the research which have then led to risk assessment being undertaken in a particular way.

The problem of defining particular categories of disorder is particularly acute with psychopathy and personality disorder. These difficulties are exemplified by Sir Aubrey Lewis who commented 'The diagnostic sub-groupings of psychiatry seldom have sharp and definite limits. Some are worse than others in this respect. Worst of all is psychopathic personality, with its wavering outlines' (Lewis, 1974, p139). Although considerable advances have been made in defining psychopathy in the last 25 years, uncertainty remains about the boundaries of personality disorder.

1.3. Clinical and Actuarial Approaches to Risk Assessment

- *Until fairly recently, prediction of violence was based on subjective judgement rather than empirical research*
- *Most research has found subjective judgement to be inaccurate compared to the use of actuarial information based on empirical research*
- *Risk assessment requires expert clinical judgement about factors which have been identified as being related to risk by empirical research. The assessment and management of risk requires a combination of actuarial and clinical expertise*

The risk of violence is used extensively as a rationale for involuntary detention, yet there is a substantial body of research which shows that the accuracy with which clinicians assess dangerousness is limited (Steadman, Monahan, Robbins, Appelbaum, Grisso, Klassen, Mulvey, & Roth; 1993), and consequently there is a requirement for a more empirical approach to risk assessment (McNiel, 1997). In 1980 Steadman asserted that predictions about risk were 'most consistent in that even among what are generally considered extremely high risk groups, clinical estimations rarely exceeded that which was obtained by chance' (Steadman, 1980). Some of the problems with risk assessment are due to the poor accuracy of clinical prediction (Cocozza & Steadman, 1978), and the errors usually made are in the over-prediction of violence (Steadman & Morrissey, 1981). In 1981 Monahan stated that psychiatrists and psychologists tended to be wrong at least twice as often as they were right in their prediction of violence (cited in Monahan, 2000). He coined the purely descriptive approach to prediction of risk the first generation of research and advised that the second generation should incorporate actuarial methods. The actuarial approach is based upon the use of empirical research into particular factors predictive of violence and its application in the assessment of risk. In arguing for a statistical approach to the prediction of dangerousness, Klassen & O'Connor's (1988a) estimate of false-positive rates range from 65% to 86%, and these appear unacceptably high when considering the civil liberties implications (DeJong, Virkkunen, & Linnoila, 1992).

Only one study was published between 1979 and 1993 which assessed the validity of clinicians' judgements in the community (Monahan, 2000). Sepejak, Menzies, Webster, & Jensen (1983) found that 39% of defendants rated as having a 'medium' or 'high' risk of dangerousness to others committed a violent act during a two year follow-up. Lidz, Mulvey, & Gardner (1993) have more recently argued that clinical judgement has been undervalued since recent research indicates clinical judgements to be more accurate in predicting violence than previously thought. Lidz et al. (1993) followed up psychiatric patients who had been examined in an acute psychiatric clinic. Psychiatrists and nurses were asked to determine the risk of potential violence posed by patients over a six month period. Violence was assessed by official records, patient self-report and the reports of informants in the community, such as a family member. In those cases which raised the concern of mental health professionals, patients were significantly more likely to be violent in the follow-up period (53%), compared with patients who had not raised concern (36%). Clinicians were able to make significant predictions of male violence even when there was no previous history of violence, but they were unable to predict female violence better than chance, despite the rate of female violence in this study being slightly greater than male violence. Monahan (2000) points out that the difficulties in predicting violence in women appeared to be a result of clinicians underestimating the base rate of violence among women with a mental disorder. McNeil & Binder (1991) found that staff were able to predict inpatient violence in patients significantly better than chance. Only 10% of patients rated by nurses as being a low risk committed a violent act, whereas 40% of a high risk group were rated as having acted in a violent manner.

In a further study, McNeil, Sandberg & Binder (1998) investigated the relationship between confidence and accuracy in clinicians' assessment of risk of violence among psychiatric inpatients. Seventy-eight physicians estimated the likelihood of inpatient violence during the first week of admission in 317 patients. They also rated the degree of confidence they had in their estimation of the risk. Findings indicated that when confidence was high, risk evaluations were strongly related to whether or not patients were violent. On the other hand, when confidence was low, clinical assessment of risk was inaccurate. This suggests that the assessor's level of confidence is an important variable in the predictive validity of clinical assessments of risk.

Gardner, Lidz, Mulvey, & Shaw (1996a) compared the accuracy of clinical ratings of concern about patients' violence with an actuarial procedure for predicting community violence by psychiatric patients following their being seen in a psychiatric emergency clinic, and followed up over a period of six months. They found that actuarial methods had lower rates of predicting that individuals would be violent when they were not (false positive), and not predicting violence in individuals who later were (false negative), when compared with clinical prediction. Clinical and actuarial methods were similar in the identification of the seriousness of violence.

Quinsey et al. (1998) have recently compiled an extensive body of research they have conducted over the past 25 years at Oak Ridge maximum security psychiatric hospital in Ontario, Canada. While they previously advocated combining clinical and actuarial methods of risk assessment, they have recently modified their position and now recommend that risk assessment be based on empirical methods alone. They review research findings which show that the amount of clinical training and experience is unrelated to accuracy of prediction. Moreover, the amount of information available to the clinician was strongly related to confidence in judgement, but was not related to accuracy (Goldberg, 1968). In one study (Rice, Harris & Quinsey, 1996), forensic clinicians were asked to make recommendations about the release of forensic psychiatric patients and requested to indicate what community supervision would be necessary to maintain their safety in the community. They found that clinicians were most likely to recommend releasing without supervision those patients who were at highest risk of violent recidivism, and to retain or suggest intensive supervision to the least dangerous individuals. They state that this occurred because clinicians tended to focus on symptoms which were not accurate predictors. Quinsey et al. (1998) state that the main reason why subjective judgement is inferior to actuarial methods is because judges are insensitive to differing base rates under various conditions. Base rates refer to the occurrence of a given behaviour in particular population. Thus where there is a 10% likelihood of violence in one population, and a 50% chance in another, assessors are known not to make this differentiation, and tend to judge both populations in the same way.

The terms 'clinical' and 'subjective judgement' have been used interchangeably and inaccurately. Risk assessment requires expert clinical judgement about factors which have been identified as being related to risk by empirical research. Risk management also requires competent clinical decisions. The assessment and management of risk, therefore, demands a combination of actuarial and clinical expertise.

1.4. Risk Assessment and Management: Inquiries and Mental Health Services

- *Mental health inquiry reports follow cases of homicide by individuals with a mental disorder. We address the way in which they have influenced clinical practice and the policies which have been adopted as a result of these reports*
- *Inquiry reports have produced a large amount of information in the form of recommendations to improve practice*
- *In some cases, methods of assessment and management have fallen short of good practice, but rarely could the homicide have been predicted*
- *There is a danger of allowing policy and legislation to be driven by trends and opinions rather than scientific findings*

Mulvey & Lidz (1995) have commented that the issues of dangerousness and risk assessment have become more salient as a shift has occurred in the type of patients being served by mental health services, which has made violence more of a practical concern. The use of dangerousness as a criterion for entry to services has increased the likelihood that high risk individuals will be served by the system. Simultaneously the policy of de-institutionalisation, and accompanying civil liberties issues, has meant that it has become less likely that people considered dangerous can be managed by confining them.

The 1990s saw attention focused on homicides committed by individuals who have had contact with psychiatric services. In some cases methods of assessment and management have fallen far short of good practice, but attention arising from public concerns about community care and a number of tragic deaths has resulted in media attention, some of it alarmist, which has tended to obscure the facts (Prins, 1998). Prins argues that 'fashions' in criminal, social and mental health policies come and go, and there is a danger of allowing policy and legislation to be driven by trends rather than scientific findings.

Notwithstanding the sometimes strong media responses, there have been very real attempts to 'learn the lessons' when 'things go wrong' (Sheppard, 1996). Independent homicide inquiries have been used to determine the reasons why significant problems have arisen in psychiatric services since the late 1960s (Sheppard, 1996), although up until the late 1980s these had largely been concerned with bad practice in long stay psychiatric hospitals and 'mental handicap' hospitals (Reith, 1998). In more recent years inquiries have been used to investigate homicides involving people with mental health problems. Indeed, since 1994 the NHS Executive has required that independent inquiries in cases of homicide must always be established (Department of Health, 1994b). Between 1994 and 2000 there have been 60 independent inquiry reports published, with a further 30 underway; and in 1992 the Department of Health commissioned the Royal College of Psychiatrists to conduct a national investigation into homicides committed by people with a history of mental health problems. This was later extended to suicides (Steering Committee of the Confidential Inquiry, 1994; Boyd, 1996; Appleby, Shaw, Amos & McDonnell 1999). While there is considerable debate about whether this continues to be the best way to deal with these problems, the inquiry reports have produced a mass of detailed analysis and recommendations. Perhaps the most serious concerns about inquiries involve the relative lack of impact on practice (Reith, 1998).

These inquiries are an important part of the literature and, in many ways, have used procedures similar to those used within qualitative research to discover what went wrong and to generate recommendations for future practice. These recommendations have provided an information source for the plethora of guidance issued by the Department of Health and the Home Office concerned with the assessment and management of risk of harming others, both by mentally disordered and non-mentally disordered individuals (Prins, 1998). For example, the *National Standards* (Home Office, Department of Health and Welsh Office, 1995) was a revised code of practice; the Association of Chief Officers of Probation issued guidelines on risk assessment and management for probation officers (Association of Chief Officers of Probation, 1994), and the Department of Health published guidelines concerned with the management of mentally disordered people thought to be at risk of harming others (Department of Health, 1994b). More recently, the report from the National Confidential Inquiry into Suicide & Homicide by People with Mental Illness (Appleby et al., 1999) has provided detailed recommendations about staff training, patient documentation, the range of treatments that should be available and dealing with non-compliance with medication. These recommendations will be considered in some detail in chapter 7.

So what are the conclusions from the above guidance and from the independent inquiries into individual cases of homicide for risk assessment and management? Many of the inquiries pay particular attention to these issues, including those of Armstrong (Freeman, Brown, Dunleavy & Graham, 1996), Clunis (Ritchie, Dick, & Lingham, 1994), Grey (Mishcon, Dick, Welch, Sheehan & Mackay, 1995), Hampshire (Mishcon, Dick, Milne, & Beard, 1996), Kirkman (Dick, Shuttleworth & Charlton, 1991), Robinson (Blom-Cooper, Hally & Murphy, 1995), Stoker (Brown, Harrop, Cronin & Harman, 1996) and Laudat (Woodley, Dixon, Lindow, Oyebode, Sandford & Simlet, 1995). These reports point to the importance of a number of key aspects of practice which often 'go wrong'. Sheppard (1996) has provided a detailed listing of the recommendations concerned with risk, and Reith (1998) a more critical analysis of the important issues to emerge about risk assessment. Indeed, the recent National Confidential Inquiry Report (Appleby et al., 1999) reiterates many of the recommendations from these earlier works. The major themes to emerge are first, the need to obtain a detailed and accurate recording of the individual's development and history, without which it is impossible to produce an effective understanding of risk. Particularly important is the accurate recording of incidents of violence and the situations that generated these incidents, especially given the importance of past behaviour in predicting future behaviour. The use of a number of sources (e.g. relatives and staff) and methods (e.g. interviews and notes) to identify these incidents of violence are also important in establishing the facts, and parallels the procedures recommended in 'triangulation' in qualitative research (Smith, 1996).

Second, high quality team working and interagency co-operation and liaison is crucial. Ensuring a flow of information between team members and across agencies is needed, both to assess risk accurately and to co-ordinate the management of that risk. Shaw, Appleby, Amos, McDonnell, Harris, McCann, Kiernan, Davies, Bickley & Parsons (1999) writing about the survey from the National Confidential Inquiry, stress the importance of preventing the patient losing contact with services. This can require a high level of co-ordination, particularly when the patient may be moving across service areas and therefore across several multi-disciplinary teams. Onyett (1999a) and Shepherd (1995) also point out the difficulties in getting mental health teams within Trusts to work effectively. The care of individuals with serious mental disorder and a potential for serious violence is simply too complicated to be undertaken by one individual. Effective teamwork is the only means whereby the range of necessary skills to address the problems can be brought together. As Reith (1998) emphasises, this involves, within teams, paying close attention to the views and observations of junior members of staff as these are often overlooked in comparison with the views of senior colleagues.

Third, the involvement and assessment of the views of the people closest to the person has frequently been overlooked. There can be particular ethical, professional and practical difficulties involved in undertaking such assessments when either the patient does not want staff to contact the relative (Harbour, Brunning, Bolter, & Hally, 1996) or the relative is unwilling to see staff. What is clear, however, is that without such information it is impossible to assess risk accurately. This was not addressed, with tragic consequences, in the cases of Hampshire (Mishcon, et al., 1996) and Viner (Harbour, et al., 1996).

Fourth, the importance of staff being adequately trained to undertake risk assessment is reiterated in most reports, including the National Confidential Inquiry (Appleby et al.,1999). The importance of staff training and retraining is emphasised as more knowledge about predictors of risk and the skills required to assess that risk comes to light. The importance of both clinical governance and lifelong learning, which receives great emphasis in current policy initiatives (Department of Health, 1998a) is perhaps nowhere more important than in the area of risk assessment.

It is, however, important not to overstate the accuracy with which it is possible to predict violence. Indeed, the overall conclusions from the inquiries is that hindsight would only rarely lead to the conclusion that the homicide in question was predictable (Holloway, 1998), although there always appear to be actions available which may have made them preventable. It is relatively recently that the science of risk assessment has developed sufficiently to claim a level of accuracy which makes it useful and it is these predictive factors which are considered in the following chapters.

1.5. Mental Disorder, Violence, Public Perception and the Media

- *Beliefs about the link between mental disorder and violence are important because public perceptions drive formal legislation. Public views often serve particular interest groups and are frequently at odds with empirical research*
- *Some surveys of the general public show that the mentally ill tend to be feared, while others indicate less stigmatised views*
- *Violent crimes committed by people suffering from mental disorder tend to receive disproportionate and elaborate news coverage*

Beliefs about the link between mental disorder and violence are important both because beliefs and public perceptions drive formal legislation designed to control the behaviour of people suffering from a mental disorder, and because they determine our informal responses and modes of interacting with those who are classed as mentally ill (Monahan, 1992). Public attitudes therefore have a profound effect on the lives of individuals labelled with a mental disorder irrespective of whether or not they have a history of violence. On the one hand, those suffering from mental disorder often become the scapegoat for blame in communities where violence is extensive (Campbell, Stefan, & Loder, 1994), and on the other, advocates for the mentally disordered argue that there is no basis for public fears about violence. For example, the National Mental Health Association in the USA has stated, 'People with mental illness pose no more of a crime threat than do other members of the general population' (National Mental Health Association, 1987). Thus objective scientific attention to the issue of risk is important because public attitudes which drive policy are shaped by media perceptions which may be distorted by particular interest groups.

Some surveys of the general public show that the mentally ill tend to be feared (Rabkin, 1972) and the general public assume that mental disorder is associated with a high risk of violence (Rabkin, 1974; Link & Stueve, 1994). The Field Institute (1984) found that 61% of 1,500 people surveyed agreed with the statement 'A person diagnosed as schizophrenic is more likely to commit a violent crime than a normal person'. In an unpublished survey in 1990, Link found that 80% of the American public endorsed one of the following statements: 'mentally ill people are more likely to commit violent crimes than other people', 'it is natural to be afraid of someone who is mentally ill', or 'it is important to remember that former mental patients may be dangerous' (cited in Link & Stueve, 1995).

Other studies of public attitudes have indicated less stigmatised views of the mentally ill. The DYG Corporation (1990) in the USA found that only 24% of respondents in their survey agreed with the statement 'People with chronic mental illness are, by far, more dangerous than the general population', and 48% endorsed the statement, 'The mentally ill are far less of a danger than most people believe'. A more recent American survey found that individuals with mental disorder are perceived to be more likely to harm themselves than others, although 80% stated that those with alcohol and drug problems and 60% with schizophrenia are likely to do something violent toward others. Ninety per cent of the survey sample were willing to use coercive means if individuals are viewed as dangerous to themselves or others (Pescosolido, Monahan, Link, Stueve, & Kikuzawa, in press). A recent MORI poll of 1,804 adults in the United Kingdom found that 72% of the survey sample thought that people with schizophrenia could live successfully in the community with the aid of careful support and treatment, and only 12% took the view that people with mental illness should live in institutions. Only 18%, however, were willing to work alongside someone with schizophrenia (MORI, 1997).

Link, Cullen, Frank, & Wozniak (1987) examined the way in which an individual's status as an ex-patient encouraged social distancing by others, by asking respondents about their willingness to have as a co-worker or neighbour someone who was described in a vignette as previously having been a patient in a psychiatric hospital. Participants also rated themselves on a 'perceived dangerousness scale' which determined whether they believed mental disorder and violence was linked. The researchers found that those who believed there was no link were more inclined to have as co-worker or neighbour an ex-psychiatric patient than someone who had never been hospitalised, whereas those who believed there was a link tended to distance themselves socially.

Violent crimes committed by people suffering from mental disorder sometimes tend to receive disproportionate and elaborate news coverage (Mayer & Barry, 1992). Content analyses of television dramas indicate that mental illness tends to be stigmatised and people suffering from mental disorder tend to be portrayed as violent (Signorielli, 1989). Shain & Phillips (1991) examined stories from the United Press International database and found that in 86% of print stories dealing with ex-psychiatric patients, a violent crime was the focus of the article. Gerbner, Gross, Morgan, & Signorielli (1981) studied television programmes in the USA and found that mental illness was shown in 17% of dramas. In 73% of cases this characterisation included violence, and in 23% homicidal acts. There did, however, seem to be a shift in attitude during the 1980s, in that fewer stories appeared about violence committed by people with a mental disorder and more emphasis was placed on homelessness, lack of care and vulnerability (Shain & Phillips, 1991).

Philo, Henderson, & McLaughlin (1994) conducted an extensive review of print and electronic media in Britain during April 1993. They found that news stories tended to report stories of harm to others as by far the most frequent activity of the mentally disordered, whereas sympathetic accounts were less frequent. Fictional stories of mental disorder were again dominated by harm to others, with occasional sympathetic portrayals. The researchers investigated the relationship between media depictions and the personal experience of the general public. They found that media themes were frequently used as evidence for the public's view of dangerousness, rather than actual experience.

1.6. Perspectives in the Scientific Community

- *Views about the relationship between violence and mental disorder among the scientific community have changed significantly*
- *The previous lack of a coherent body of research stating a clear position about the relationship between violence and mental disorder was at odds with the requirement to provide predictions of risk*
- *About ten years ago, the view that individuals suffering from mental disorder were at no greater risk of committing violence than the general public altered dramatically*
- *Recent research has indicated a modest but consistent relationship between violence and mental disorder*

Link & Stueve (1995) distinguish four perspectives on the association between violence and mental disorder in the research community. First, that there is no association. Second, an association is acknowledged, but it is claimed to be spurious or artefactual. Third, that there is a link, and mental disorder is causal. Fourth, that there is a causal link, but the strength of it is contingent on the social context. As research evidence has accumulated, there has been increasing support for the third and fourth positions, but this has been a fairly recent phenomenon. In 1983, Monahan and Steadman (1983) reviewed the literature and reached the conclusion that:

'...the relation between crime and mental disorder can be accounted for largely by demographic and historical characteristics that the two groups share. When appropriate statistical controls are applied for factors such as age, gender, race, social class, and previous institutionalisation, whatever relations between crime and mental disorder are reported tend to disappear' (p152).

This placed mental health professionals in a problematic position. On the one hand, in 1983 members of the American Psychiatric Association disavowed themselves of the competence to provide useful predictions of dangerousness on the basis of psychiatric expertise, yet there was a simultaneous expectation and demand for mental health professionals to make predictions and protect the public (Mullen, 1997). In the USA this expectation was reinforced by the Tarasoff decision (Tarasoff v. Regents of the University of California, 1976). The California Supreme Court held that psychotherapists who know or should know about the possibility of their patients inflicting harm on another identifiable individual have an obligation to take reasonable steps to protect a potential victim. This was initially vilified by mental health professionals, but has now become part of accepted practice and in some cases has been extended to include non-identifiable victims (Monahan, 1996). Since then courts and parole boards increasingly made use of psychiatric opinion, at times misusing them, most flagrantly in the case of death sentence hearings (Mullen, 1997). Mental health workers in the UK continue to maintain their independence in relation to the criminal justice system, but the political climate is increasingly approaching this position and many professional bodies require that their members breach confidentiality if someone is thought to be at risk.

In 1992, Monahan stated that the conclusion that individuals suffering from mental disorder were at no greater risk of committing violence than the general public was premature and possibly incorrect (Monahan, 1992). This was because controlling for factors such as social class, which are related to mental disorder, is problematic since low socio-economic status may either be a cause or a consequence of mental disorder according to Monahan. More recent research (described later) which was more methodologically rigorous indicated a modest, but consistent relationship. In the past 10 to 15 years a growing literature on the subject has investigated the nature of this relationship in greater detail. This research is the main focus of the rest of this review.

CHAPTER 2

EVIDENCE FOR A RELATIONSHIP: PREVALENCE

This chapter addresses evidence for the relationship between violence and mental disorder. This involves a detailed exposition of the academic literature. We examine the various types of studies investigating the link between violence and mental disorder. The chapter begins with a discussion of methodological issues. We then describe studies examining violence among the mentally disordered prior to, during and after hospital admission. This is followed by a discussion of studies of mental disorder among the violent

2.1. Methodological Issues

Four weaknesses of research are discussed:
- *inadequacy of cues or factors selected to predict the likelihood of violence*
- *weak criterion variables*
- *constricted validation sample*
- *and unsynchronised research efforts*

There are a number of methodological issues in the study of the relationship between violence and mental disorder which will arise throughout the following discussion. These relate mainly to the selection of experimental and control groups and the setting in which research is conducted. Prior to the review of the literature, however, we would like to consider four methodological issues raised by Monahan (Monahan, 1988; Monahan & Steadman, 1994) which have plagued actuarial research on risk assessment. These are as follows: inadequacy of cues or factors selected to predict the likelihood of violence; weak criterion variables; constricted validation samples; and unsynchronised research efforts. These issues are discussed in turn below.

2.1.1. Inadequacy of Predictors

Violence is clearly a complex phenomenon involving a variety of social, psychological and biological factors. Despite this, according to Monahan & Steadman (1994), research has focused on a narrow range of predictor variables (such as diagnosis, substance abuse and history of violence) which have been selected without regard for any theoretical framework for either violence or mental disorder. The more complex causes of violence are therefore not addressed.

2.1.2. Weak Criterion Variables

Criterion variables refer to the particular outcome that is being investigated, in this case violence. Violence has been measured both by using official data on arrests and convictions and by utilising information on violence regardless of whether they have resulted in arrests and convictions. Official data has the advantage of not being subject to reporting biases which are inherent in studies relying on self-reporting socially undesirable behaviours. However, arrest and conviction rates are themselves subject to bias and do not reflect true rates of violence (Link & Stueve, 1995). Mullen (1997) also points out that behaviour which induces fear is important even though it may not involve physical violence, since relatives and carers frequently complain of the fear and distress caused by the behaviour of individuals with mental health problems.

A related issue is the temporal relationship between violence and mental disorder. Some studies have addressed the question of whether an individual has ever been violent in their lifetime. This answers a very different, retrospective question about risk from the question of whether someone will be violent in the future: in a population which *currently* meets the criteria for mental disorder, what chance is there that they have *ever* been violent? While interesting, this does not allow the inference of a temporal connection between violence and mental disorder (Swanson, 1994).

2.1.3. Constricted Validation Samples

Constricted validation samples refers to the relatively few characteristics of the groups that have been studied. Participants have tended to be highly selected, in that they have come from very particular groups which are not representative of the general population.

Research has taken place in a variety of contexts, broadly speaking either within institutions or in the community. Monahan (2000) has pointed out that research on inpatient violence is influenced by the structured environment of the institution and the therapeutic effects of interventions which are likely to reduce the base rates of violence. On the other hand, community-based research is influenced by different factors. Part of the decision to discharge patients into the community is based upon their risk of violence, thus resulting in a distortion of the 'real' likelihood of violence. This makes generalisability problematic and therefore sample selection is crucial. Monahan & Steadman (1994) recommend enrolling a broadly representative sample with and without a history of violence, and the use of large sample sizes.

2.1.4. Unsynchronised Research Efforts

Monahan & Steadman (1994) point out that lack of communication and co-ordination of research efforts is particularly acute in research on violence and mental disorder. This results in predictor and criterion variables being idiosyncratically defined. This makes it difficult to compare findings.

2.2. Typology of Studies

> - *The prevalence of mental disorder has been studied among the violent, and it has been studied among the mentally disordered*
> - *The main source of information on the link between violence and mental disorder has come from studies examining violence among psychiatric patients*
> - *Three types of study result from this category. Prevalence of violence has been examined prior to hospital admission, during hospitalisation and post discharge. Thus research has taken place within psychiatric establishments, and it has taken place in the community*
> - *Studies on mental disorder among the violent have taken place in prison establishments*

Several types of study designs have been used to examine the relationship between violence and mental disorder. While some designs are inherently more robust than others, no single design, in and of itself, is ideal for determining the nature of the relationship. However, when studies are considered in conjunction with one another, the combined strengths and weight of research do allow conclusions to be drawn on the nature of the relationship (Link & Stueve, 1995).

There are two ways of determining whether there is a relationship between violence and mental disorder and, if this is established, ascertaining the strength of the association. The first is to examine whether being mentally disordered increases the likelihood that the individual will commit a violent act; in other words, is the prevalence of violence higher among the mentally disordered compared with the non-disordered? The second is to determine the prevalence of mental disorder among people

who have committed violent acts. Within each of these categories, two types of research have been undertaken. Type 1 includes those who are being treated for mental disorder (in hospitals) or violent behaviour (in prisons). Type 2 involves people who are unselected for treatment status and are studied in the open community (Monahan, 1992). Four categories of study result (Table 1).

1. Prevalence of violent behaviour among individuals with mental disorder: a. among identified psychiatric patients   b. among random community samples   2. Prevalence of mental disorder among individuals committing violent behaviour: a. among identified criminal offenders   b. among random community samples

TABLE 1: TYPES OF PREVALENCE STUDIES (FROM MONAHAN, 1992)

2.3. Violence Among the Mentally Disordered: Identified Psychiatric Patients

- *We discuss the three types of studies which have been undertaken with psychiatric patients: prior to admission, during hospitalisation, and post discharge*
- *Data from each type of study has its use, although the first two are beset by more significant methodological problems*
- *Post discharge studies are the main source of information for the assessment and management of risk in the community*

In the first category of the prevalence of violence in individuals with mental disorder in hospital (1a in Table 1), three types of study exist. The first assesses prevalence of violence before entry into hospital; the second, during their hospital stay, and the third, following discharge from hospital. According to Monahan (1992), each of these studies has important implications for policy and practice. Studies on violence prior to admission provide information on the workings of mental health law and the interface between mental health and criminal justice. Research on violence during admission provides data on the need for the level of security required in an establishment and staff training requirements in managing aggression (Binder & McNeil, 1988). Studies on violence following discharge are used to make risk assessments and assist planning the discharge and care plans for life in the community. However, studies of violence before and during hospitalisation result in the violence being a primary selection criteria for admission and are therefore more limited in their usefulness (Torrey, 1994). These studies are mainly, but not exclusively, concerned with psychotic disorders rather than personality disorders.

2.3.1. Studies Prior to Admission

- *Results of studies prior to admission indicate that between 10% and 40% of patients are assaultative before entry into hospital*
- *However, violence is often a key criterion for admission, and admission is frequently accompanied by tensions which may result in provoking threats or assault by a fearful patient*

Johnston, Crow, Johnston, & Macmillan (1986) examined the disturbed and threatening behaviour of patients in the month preceding their first admission and found that 19% had behaved in a way which placed others at risk. Binder & McNeil (1988) found that 26% of acute psychiatric admissions had been assaultative in the previous six months and the behaviour of a further 36% had caused fear in others. Rossi et al. (1986) reviewed the case notes of 1,687 patients and found that 12% had been identified as having acted violently and 8% had acted in a threatening manner in the two days leading up to admission. Reviewing this research, Monahan (1992) reports 11 studies on the prevalence of violent behaviour in those who eventually became psychiatric patients. The time period prior to hospitalisation was typically two weeks. Results across the studies varied but between 10% and 40% (median rate 15%) committed a physical assault shortly before admission.

In a number of studies examining violence prior to admission, a specific association with schizophrenia was established. Lagos, Perlmutter, & Saexinger (1977) examined the hospital records of 321 mentally disordered patients (excluding individuals with personality disorder and substance abuse diagnoses) for violence leading to hospital admission. Thirty-six per cent of admissions were preceded by some form of violence. Tardiff & Sweillam (1980) retrospectively studied 9,000 admissions and found that 10% had been violent prior to admission. Other studies report similar rates of violence before admission (Craig, 1982; Johnston et al., 1986). The range of 10%-36% suggests that results depend on the particular characteristics of the sample and the context in which research has taken place.

Since violence is often a key criterion for admission, it is hardly surprising that high levels of violence should be reported in these studies.

Furthermore, as Mullen (1997) points out, hospital admission is frequently accompanied by tensions which may have the consequence of provoking threats or assault by a fearful patient.

2.3.2. Inpatient Violence

- *Rates of inpatient violence are highly variable and depend on a number of factors including the definition of violence and the setting, culture and patient group. This makes it difficult to compare studies*
- *Prevalence rates range from 10% to 40%. These rates tend to be higher in the US than the UK*
- *Important findings include: a small number of patients are responsible for a large number of assaults; violence is related to individual factors such as illness, age, substance abuse, history of violence, symptom severity, and situational factors such as overcrowding and nursing practices*
- *Nurses are most frequently the victims of assault in inpatient settings. However, the circumstances of many inpatient settings may provoke violence and therefore little can be concluded from these studies*

Violence was recognised as a problem in inpatient psychiatric settings much earlier than violence in other settings and thus many more studies of inpatient violence have been conducted (Wittington, 1994). Shah (1993) estimated that between 1980 and 1993 over 100 studies were published on the subject. Although riddled with methodological problems which make it difficult to draw conclusions about the relationship between violence and mental disorder, these have generally supported relatively high rates of violence among psychiatric inpatients. Only a selection of studies are therefore reported here. The studies are difficult to compare because of the varying definitions of violence and the variety of settings in which research has been conducted, ranging from general to forensic hospitals (Davis, 1991).

Reid, Bollinger, & Edwards (1985) surveyed a number of psychiatric hospitals in the US and reported an average of 2.54 assaults per bed per year, very few of these leading to serious injury. There was a large variation in assaults from one hospital to another. Kay, Wolkenfeld, & Murrill (1988) reviewed several surveys in the New York City area and reported an average of 7–10% of patients being involved in assaults in a one to three month observational period. In a review of British studies on assaults on staff, Wittington (1994) states that the average rate for hospitals is one assault every 6 days and for individual units this is one every 11 days. Urban hospitals tended to have higher rates than rural hospitals. He found the incidence of serious assault to be low.

Several researchers have found that few patients are responsible for the majority of assaultative behaviour. For example, Barber, Hundley, Kellogg & Glick (1988) found that 15 patients (3.3%) in a state hospital accounted for 48.6% of assaults in a one year period. These individuals tended to be relatively young, displayed severe symptomatology which was generally unresponsive to treatment, and had been hospitalised continuously for more than four years. Owen, Tarantello, Jones, & Tennant (1998a) conducted a prospective study of violent incidents in five psychiatric units in Sydney, Australia. They found that of 174 patients involved in violent incidents, 12% were recidivists (defined as responsible for 20 or more incidents). These individuals were responsible for 69% of 752 violent incidents.

A trend in the literature is that rates of violence tend to be higher in the US than the UK (Davis, 1991), one study indicating them to be four times higher (Edwards, Jones, & Reid, 1988). A number of British studies have indicated that rates of violence have increased from one year to another (Hodgkinson, McIvor, & Phillips, 1985; Noble & Rodger, 1989; James, Fineberg, & Shah, 1990). For example, Noble & Rodger (1989) conducted a large longitudinal survey of incidents in the UK over 13 years which indicated that the average number of violent incidents in the 1980s was three times that of the latter part of the 1970s. However, Wittington (1994) points out that this may be due to perception, in that staff have become increasingly sensitive and less tolerant of violence over the past 20 years and therefore report it more often.

Monahan (1992) reports 12 studies on the prevalence of inpatient violence. These findings ranged from 10% to 40% (median rate 25%). However, the circumstances of many inpatient settings may provoke violence and therefore little can be concluded from these studies. The patient's state of mind is not the only factor in provoking violence, but reflects reactions to restrictions and provocations from other patients and visitors (Powell, Cann, & Crowe, 1994). For example, Sheridan, Henrion, Robinson, & Baxter (1990) state that external factors are more important than the state of mind of the individual, the most common precipitants of violence being the enforcement of rules and denying patients' requests. Wittington (1994) stresses the importance of environmental and interpersonal factors. Davis' (1991) review found evidence for a link between inpatient violence and individual factors such as acute illness, psychosis, drug abuse and history of violence; situational factors such as overcrowding, provocation, staff inexperience and management practices, and structural factors such as changes in mental health policy. Wittington's (1994) review produced a very similar list of significant factors. McNeil & Binder (1994) compiled an actuarial scale for predicting violence among inpatients. They used five variables, scored zero or one depending whether the variable was present or not. Patients who scored three or more were categorised as being high risk and those scoring two or less were considered low risk. Variables included history of violence and/or fear-inducing behaviour within two weeks before admission, *absence* of suicidal behaviour, diagnosis of schizophrenia or mania, male gender, and being currently married or living together.

In health care settings, nurses are by far the most frequent victims of assaults on staff (Wittington, 1994; Owen, Tarantello, Jones, & Tennant, 1998b), and assault related injuries are most common among nursing personnel (Lehmann, McCormick & Kizer, 1999). Reviewing evidence for those staff more likely to be assaulted, Wittington & Wykes (1994) state that risk increases if staff have to cause a patient frustration, demand them to engage in an .activity, and criticise or physically intrude upon them. Owen, et al. (1998b) found that the relative risk of violence on inpatient units increased with increased numbers of nursing staff, more non-nursing staff on leave and older nursing staff. However, expenditure on staffing has been found to be inversely related to frequency of assault (Lehmann, McCormick & Kizer, 1999). Katz & Kirkland (1990) found that there were higher levels of violence on wards where staff were uncertain about their role. Coercive nursing practices have also been linked to inpatient violence (Morrison, 1994). Shepherd & Lavender (1999) examined contextual factors to inpatient violence. They found that staff victims were more likely to be male than female. Incidents were more likely to be preceded by external antecedents (interpersonal factors) rather than internal factors (attributed to the perpetrator's mental state).

2.3.3. Violence Post Discharge

- *Early studies on discharged psychiatric patients concluded that they were no more likely to be violent than the rest of the population*
- *This finding was probably a result of the research taking place in a period when the majority of seriously mentally ill were confined to hospital*
- *Studies made after the introduction of accelerated deinstitutionalisation found that patients were more likely to be arrested or convicted for violent offences*
- *A number of methodological flaws make interpretation of these findings difficult*

The literature on violent behaviour of psychiatric patients following their discharge from hospital is extensive and goes back to the 1920s (Rabkin, 1979). Rabkin conducted a comprehensive review of the research up to 1979. She noted that studies conducted prior to 1965 indicated that discharged psychiatric patients were less likely to be arrested than the general public. This led to the conclusion that mentally ill individuals, that is people with psychotic disorders, were no more dangerous than the rest of the population. One reason for this belief was that studies took place during a period when the majority of severely mentally ill people were confined to psychiatric hospitals (Torrey, 1994). In studies conducted after 1965, however, the opposite result emerged, with patients being *more* likely to be arrested. The magnitude of the arrest ratio varied from 15 ex-patients for each member of the public (Sosowsky, 1974), although some studies found no difference (Zitrin, Hardesty, Burdock, & Drossman, 1976). Rabkin noted that these results were not confined to minor offences, but that differences were particularly pronounced in violent crime. Rabkin found that people with a mental disorder perpetrated violent crime significantly more than the general population.

Studies conducted since Rabkin's review have indicated higher arrest rates for psychiatric patients compared to the general population (Shore, Filson, & Rae, 1980; Schuerman & Kobrin, 1984; Holcomb & Ahr, 1988; McFarland, Faulkner, Bloom, Hallaux, & Bray, 1989). Only one study showed a reduced rate of arrest for ex-patients (Harry & Steadman, 1988). The median ratio of patient/public arrest rates for studies conducted since 1965 is 3.05:1 (Link, Andrews, & Cullen, 1992).

Klassen and O'Connor (1988b; 1990) followed up 304 male patients, who were selected on the basis of being considered as being at high risk of committing violence. They found that 25%-30% with a record of at least one violent incident in the past were violent within the first year of discharge from hospital. Although the sample was highly selected, it is nevertheless a relevant group. Findings from the MacArthur Risk Assessment Study indicate that 27.5% of discharged psychiatric patients committed at least one violent act within a year of discharge (Steadman, Mulvey, Monahan, Robbins, Appelbaum, Grisso, Roth, & Silver; 1998).

In a study of 133 psychiatric outpatients with a diagnosis of schizophrenia, Bartels, Drake, Wallach, & Freeman (1991) rated patients on a five point scale according to their hostility. Three were rated as being assaultative with potential or actual harm, 14 were rated as either destructive to property or assaultative without causing harm, 24 as verbally threatening or displaying mild aggression to objects, 28 as irritable and argumentative and 64 as showing no hostility. They found a strong correlation between hostility and lack of compliance with medication. Of those rated as assaultative or destructive to property, 71% had problems with medication compliance compared with only 17% of those rated as showing no hostility. They also found that higher levels of hostility were strongly predictive of rehospitalisation within a year.

In a specific study of individuals discharged from high security special hospitals in the UK, Buchanan (1998) examined the criminal convictions of a cohort of 425 ex-patients. After a period of ten and a half years, 34% of the sample had been convicted of at least one offence (not necessarily violent) and 14% had received a conviction for a violent offence. Interestingly, variables examined in the study (such as gender) had a low predictive power, suggesting that actuarial methods may be of limited utility with this particular group of patients. Compared with previous studies, the rates of conviction for ex-special hospital patients was substantially lower.

2.4. Critique of Studies Before, During and After Hospitalisation

Methodological problems associated with studies reviewed so far include:
- *The criminalisation of the mentally ill. This refers to the view that the mentally ill are more likely to be arrested than the general population*
- *The medicalisation of deviance. This refers to the view that individuals who are violent are more likely to be labelled as psychiatric patients*
- *The nature of the comparison groups these studies used. This refers to the use of general population comparison groups which are inappropriate, since patients have demographic characteristics which are different from those of the general population, which are themselves predictors of violence, such as socioeconomic status*

Let us pause for a moment to consider the limitations of the studies reviewed so far which rely on one particular source of information for the outcome measure of violence. These limitations include: the criminalising of the mentally disordered, the medicalising of deviance, and the nature of comparison groups.

The criminalisation of the mentally ill perspective (Teplin, 1984) argues that differences in arrest rates between the general public and the mentally disordered tell us more about the association between mental disorder and the arrest process than it does about the relationship between violence and mental disorder (Link & Stueve, 1995). Teplin (1984) assigned clinical psychology students to go on patrol with police officers in a large American city. Encounters with the public were coded according to whether the individual showed evidence of a mental disorder, the type of offence committed and whether the individual was arrested. Those who were mentally disordered (47%) were more likely to be arrested than individuals who were not (28%), even when the type of offence was the same.

The medicalisation of deviance perspective (Monahan, 1973; Steadman, Cocozza, & Melick, 1978; Melick, Steadman, & Cocozza, 1979) holds that an increased range of behaviours, including violent behaviours, are becoming the province of psychiatry and therefore more people who are likely to be violent are becoming psychiatric patients. Thus increased rates of arrest among psychiatric patients may not represent a basic relationship between violence and mental disorder, but rather a 'psychiatrising' of violence in ordinary life.

The third limitation of arrest-rate studies arises from their design. These studies have used general population arrest rates to compare with the study samples. However, the patients included in these studies come from hospitals and clinics which tend to serve deprived communities where rates of violence tend to be higher than average (Link & Stueve, 1995). This means that if a general population comparison group is used, it is likely to overestimate the additional risks arising from being mentally disordered.

This lack of comparative data with appropriately matched non-patient groups makes the results of the above studies speculative, and it is impossible to draw firm conclusions from them about the relationship between violence and mental disorder (Monahan, 1992). Patients in all three types of study are highly selected. For example, for studies investigating the prevalence of violence prior to hospital admission, violent behaviour is one factor which selects some mentally disordered individuals for admission from the total population of disordered people. Furthermore, many of the studies of ward-based violence have taken place in secure settings, places from which violence prone individuals are selected. Finally, the prevalence of violence after discharge may be a result of the types of patients selected for hospitalisation, the nature and duration of treatment, and the risk assessments used to determine whether an individual is eligible for discharge. To determine the true relationship between mental disorder and violence, therefore, research needs to focus on samples of mentally disordered individuals unselected for treatment status in the community.

More recently, a series of more sophisticated studies have been published which resolve many of the problems with selection bias inherent in previous research. These include birth cohort studies and prevalence studies of mental disorder incorporating arrest rate and self-reported violence using matched community controls. These will now be discussed, but more detailed findings of specific risk factors for violence will be covered in the next chapter.

2.5. Case Linkage Studies using Conviction Rates

- *We turn now to a discussion of studies which overcome some of the methodological problems already discussed*
- *Within the group of studies examining violence post discharge, two types of studies have resulted which are of a particularly high quality in determining the relationship between violence and mental disorder. These include birth cohort studies and prevalence studies of mental disorder incorporating conviction rate, arrest rate and self-reported violence using matched community controls*
- *There are a number of case linkage studies which have established a link between violence and major mental disorder, indicating two to three times the relative risk for those with psychotic disorders, and occasionally higher than this*
- *Methodological problems remain, most notably the reliance on official data*

Case linkage involves the linking of official data from different sources, in this case records on conviction and hospital admission. One type of case linkage study involves the selection of a birth cohort and compares the history of convictions of people who have become mentally disordered with those who have not. Although not without its problems, it is one of the most powerful research designs since it examines the prevalence and distribution of mental disorder and offending in an unselected birth cohort (Hodgins, Mednick, Brennan, Schulsinger, & Engberg, 1996). This makes birth cohort studies generalisable to a broader population than other designs (Link & Stueve, 1995). Three Scandinavian studies used person registers which include data on everyone born in the country over a specified time period. Case registers were used to identify all individuals admitted to psychiatric wards, and police registers were used to identify individuals with criminal convictions. Relative risk of offending was then calculated comparing those with and without a history of psychiatric admission.

Hodgins (1992) used a birth cohort of 15,117 people in Stockholm, Sweden. She found that men who had been treated for a major mental disorder (schizophrenia, major affective disorders, paranoid states and other psychoses) were 2.56 times more likely to be convicted of an offence by age 30, and 4.2 times more likely to be convicted of a violent offence than men without a history of psychiatric treatment. Among women the relative risk was 5.02 for any offence and 27.5 times for a violent offence. In a Danish study not published in English but reported by Link and Stueve (1995), Ortmann (1981) found an elevated risk of conviction for men who had undergone psychiatric treatment (43.5%) compared with men who received no treatment (34.8%).

Lindqvist & Allebeck (1990) conducted a longitudinal study in Sweden by tracing the conviction records of 644 individuals who had been admitted to hospital suffering from schizophrenia over a period of 14 years. Rates of crime in males with schizophrenia was approximately the same as the general male population, and for females with schizophrenia it was twice that for the general female population. However, the rate of violent offences were four times higher than the general population.

Wessely, Castle, & Douglas (1994) are critical of previous cohort studies (Hodgins, 1992; Lindqvist and Allebeck, 1990) as cases were only identified at hospital discharge and therefore neither of these studies is truly population-based, in that cases are highly selected. There was no account taken of the time spent at risk of offending, as many participants spent considerable time in prison or hospital where the likelihood of obtaining convictions was low. They also excluded participants who died during the study period. Wessely et al. (1994) undertook a sophisticated case linkage study in the UK which involved studying all 538 cases of schizophrenia over a 20 year period drawn from a case register and comparing them with a control group of individuals matched for age and sex, with a psychiatric diagnosis other than schizophrenia. Thus cases were not restricted to hospital discharges. The risk of conviction for any offence was increased 3.3 times for women with schizophrenia, but no differences were found for the men. However, men with schizophrenia were found to have a 3.8 times greater risk, and females with schizophrenia a 5.3 times greater risk, of conviction for assault or serious violence compared with the control group.

Hodgins et al. (1996) undertook the largest cohort study attempting to address many of the weaknesses of the previous studies. The validity of findings was increased by using an initial sample of 358,180 individuals and allowing for the examination of specific categories of mental disorder. The authors present separate data for two time periods; first, 1959–1977 when files were recorded by hand, and second, 1978–1990 when files were computerised. In both men and women, all diagnostic groups were found to be at increased risk of offending than the non-disordered group. Compared with the general population, the relative risk for committing a single violent crime for women with a major mental disorder (i.e. psychotic disorders) was 5.86 (1959–1977) and 8.66 (1978–1990); and for men was 2.42 (1959–1977) and 4.48 (1978–1990). Since the data addresses specific risk factors, these findings are discussed in detail under separate headings later. Wessely & Castle (1998) criticise the study on the basis that it does not overcome the problem of selection bias, i.e. they do not provide a matched comparison group. Link & Stueve (1995) make the further point that no birth cohort study has taken into account the temporal ordering of illness onset and conviction, and therefore cause cannot be inferred.

Belfrage (1998a) gathered data on the criminal convictions of patients discharged from psychiatric hospitals in Stockholm in 1986 over a 10 year period. The patients only included those with a diagnosis of schizophrenia, affective disorder and paranoia. Fourteen per cent of the sample received a conviction during the 10 year period and 28% had a criminal conviction at some point during their lifetime, which compares with 10% in the general population. About half these crimes were violent.

Case linkage studies have a number of biases which reduce the likelihood of positive findings. Inaccuracies or omissions in the data from either of the registers reduce the chance of a linkage. Thus greater weight should be given to positive findings. On the other hand, linkages reflect the manner in which the criminal justice system and mental health services interact. For example, the fact that distressed individuals drift to inner city areas and attract police attention may reflect their deprivation and upbringing as much as mental health problems. Thus the linkage may be falsely inflated (Mullen, 1997). A further limitation is the reliance on conviction records as the criterion for violence (this does not reflect the true incidence of violence), and therefore the possibility that people with schizophrenia are more likely to receive convictions. These studies do not, therefore, overcome the problem of the criminalisation of mental disorder mentioned earlier (Teplin, 1984).

2.6. Community Studies using Multiple Measures of Violence and Matched Controls

* *Community studies using multiple measures of violence and matched controls are considered to be the gold standard of research linking violence and mental disorder*
* *Using multiple measures of violence overcomes the problem of relying on official data, such as conviction rates. Matched control groups exclude the interference of demographic factors in the estimation of violence among the mentally disordered*
* *These studies have established two to four times the risk of violence among individuals with a major mental disorder*

In this section we continue our discussion of the issue of the prevalence of violence in the mentally disordered. A more detailed account of specific findings relating to these studies is presented later. Studies reviewed in this section have used a variety of measures of the criterion variable of violence, including arrest and conviction rates, reports by informants and self-reported violence. The incorporation of self-reported violence overcomes a major methodological weakness of arrest and conviction rate studies. While high arrest rates among psychiatric patients ('criminalisation of the mentally ill') may be the result of a greater proportion of patients coming into contact with the criminal justice system, they cannot account for self-reported violence. Furthermore, these studies also addresse the 'medicalisation of deviance' hypothesis.

Swanson, Holzer, Gunju, & Jono (1990) were the first to conduct such a study. They used data from the US National Institute of Mental Health's Epidemiological Catchment Area (ECA) study. A database of approximately 10,000 people was established by pooling representative weighted samples of adult household residents in Baltimore, Durham and Los Angeles. The Diagnostic Interview Schedule (DIS), a structured interview designed for use by trained lay people, was used to determine mental disorder according to the criteria of the Diagnostic and Statistical Manual of Mental Disorder (Third edition; DSM-III) (American Psychiatric Association, 1980). Five items on the DIS were used as indicators of the criterion variable, i.e. violence. Participants were asked about (1) hitting or injuring a spouse/partner or (2) a child, (3) getting into physical fights with others, (4) using weapons in fights, and (5) getting into fights while drinking. To be categorised as violent, the participant had to endorse one of these categories and report having engaged in it during the year prior to the interview. After controlling for demographic factors such as age and socio-economic status, the prevalence of violence was nearly four times higher in one year (odds ratio = 3.9) for those suffering from a major mental disorder according to DSM-III criteria. Findings for each diagnostic subgroup (schizophrenia, major depression, mania or bipolar disorder) were remarkably similar.

Swanson et al. (1990) note that the index of violent behaviour they used was a 'blunt measure' in that it was based upon self-report without external corroboration. Further, the questions about violence overlap, and there is no differentiation in terms of frequency or severity of violence. However, Monahan (1992) states that Swanson et al.'s (1990) findings conform to the demographic correlates of violence known from the criminological literature which increases confidence in their findings. Thus for the group as a whole, violence was seven times more prevalent among the young as the old, twice as prevalent among men than women, and three times higher among people from the lowest social class than among those from the highest.

Link, Cullen and Andrews (1992) compared arrest rates and self-reported violence (this included hitting, fighting, weapon use and 'hurting someone badly') of former psychiatric patients in an area of New York City with a control group which was comprised of a sample of approximately 400 adults from the same area who had never sought help from a mental health professional. Factors controlled for included age, gender, educational level, ethnicity, socio-economic status, family composition, and homicide rates of the census tract in which a participant lived. A Social Desirability scale was included to control for the possibility that patients may have been more willing to report a socially undesirable behaviour such as violence than the control group. The researchers used the Psychiatric Epidemiology Research Interview (PERI) to measure specific symptoms and life events. In all categories, and for both official arrest rates and self-reported violence, the patient group had higher rates of violence, sometimes two to three times the rate for the control group. For official arrest rates, they found no pattern suggestive of patients being arrested for more trivial offences. For the group as a whole, demographic factors were found to be related to violence – being male, less well educated and from a neighbourhood high in crime increased the likelihood of violence. Even after demographic and other factors (such as social desirability) were taken into account, significant differences remained between patients and community resident controls. The authors point out that although these differences were significant, the magnitude of the risk posed by the patients was modest compared to that determined by demographic factors.

Link et al.'s (1992) important finding was that by controlling for 'current symptomology' using a subscale of the PERI, differences in rates of violence between patients and controls disappeared. This is discussed in more detail below.

Steadman et al. (1998) conducted a follow-up study of patients discharged from acute psychiatric facilities and monitored their violence every 10 weeks during the first year of discharge. Participants were 1,136 men and women. The control group consisted of 519 individuals living in the same neighbourhoods in which the patients lived after discharge. In order to overcome the problem of measuring violence, Steadman et al. (1998) used multiple measures, rather than relying on a single index which characterises most previous research. The measures included patient self-reports of violence augmented with reports from collateral informants and by police and hospital records. Findings of this study indicated the importance of using multiple measures. If the index of violence was based solely on agency records (including police and hospitals), the rate of violence among discharged patients over one year was 4.5%, whereas this rose to 27.5% if three independent sources of data were used. The authors found that substance abuse was the key variable in increasing the rate of violence (to be discussed later) and that the prevalence of violence among patients who did not abuse substances was not significantly greater than the control group without symptoms of substance abuse. The authors acknowledge that individuals who refused to participate or dropped out may have compromised the representativeness of the sample. It is also possible that the intensive follow-up of patients, which included a number of contacts with the researchers, may have resulted in reducing the likelihood of violence.

Despite overcoming methodological problems of arrest-rate studies, the studies described in this section have two weaknesses. First, with the exception of the Steadman et al. (1998) study, they rely on retrospective data which does not address the issue of the temporal ordering of violence and mental disorder. Second, they rely entirely or for the most part on self-report data, and social desirability of responses may remain an issue, even though attempts were made to control for this in the Link et al. (1992) and Steadman et al. (1998) studies (Link & Stueve, 1995).

2.7. Disorder Among the Violent

- *Studies of prison populations indicate substantially raised levels of psychiatric disorder*

- *These studies are complicated by the process of selection at every level of the criminal justice system, as well as by high levels of substance abuse and personality disorder in the prison population*

- *Studies are difficult to compare because of different contexts and measures used, making rates of disorder highly variable between studies*

- *Rates of psychotic disorder in prison populations vary widely between studies, ranging from 1% to 16%. Estimations are that psychotic disorder is approximately 3 or 4 times higher than the general population*

- *Estimations of the odds of inmates having substance abuse disorder or antisocial personality disorder are 5 to 25 times greater than in the general population*

- *A recent study in the UK found 7% of sentenced men to have a psychotic illness. Between 50% and 78% of inmates received a diagnosis of personality disorder*

The second way in which to determine whether there is a relationship between violence and mental disorder is to examine the extent of mental disorder in people who have acted in a violent manner. Recall Monahan's (1992) statement of there being two ways of ascertaining this relationship, by studying people who have been institutionalised for violent behaviour (in prison), or by studying people in the open community who are violent but have not been imprisoned for it. These studies are complicated by the process of selection at every level of the criminal justice system, as well as by high levels of substance abuse and personality disorder in the prison population (Mullen, 1997). For example, Abrams & Teplin (1991) gathered data from 728 prison inmates and established that most of those meeting diagnostic criteria for major mental disorder also met criteria for substance abuse and antisocial personality disorder.

There is a large body of research estimating the prevalence of mental disorder among prison inmates. Not all inmates have been convicted of violent offences, but Monahan (1992) points out that there is no evidence that rates of disorder between inmates who are charged with violent and non-violent offences differ, and therefore data on the prevalence of mental disorder in the general prison population will reflect prevalence in violent inmates reasonably accurately.

In an early review of the prevalence of mental disorder in prison, Roth (1980) concluded that the rate of psychotic disorders was of the order of 5% or less of the total prison population, and that the rate of any disorder was in the range of 15%–20%. A more recent review of 18 studies over a period of 15 years by Teplin (1990) found that in studies which randomly sampled inmates as opposed to selecting those inmates referred for psychiatric evaluation (many studies have been conducted on this latter basis with resulting inflated rates of disorder), rates of psychotic disorder of between 5% and 16% were found. The range of prevalence from one study to another are probably due to differences in sampling and measurement techniques (Teplin, McClelland, & Abram, 1993).

Taylor & Gunn (1984) undertook a detailed examination of the psychiatric status of 1,241 men who had been remanded to HMP Brixton in London. They found that 9% of men convicted of non-fatal violent crimes and 11% of inmates convicted of fatal violence fulfilled diagnostic criteria for schizophrenia. Only nine out of 121 mentally disordered offenders did not have symptoms at the time of their offence. Steadman, Fabisiak, Dvoskin, & Holohean (1987) surveyed 3,000 prisoners in New York State and concluded that 8% had 'severe mental disability' and a further 16% had 'significant mental disabilities'. Monahan (1993a) used data from a prison study in California and found that rates of schizophrenia were approximately three times higher than in the general population. Mania and bipolar affective disorder were seven times more prevalent. Robertson, Pearson, & Gibb (1995) studied 2,721 recently arrested individuals in

London. They found that only 1.4% were actively mentally ill and 0.7% possibly mentally ill. Gunn, Maden, & Swinton (1991a) studied a sample of inmates and compared their rates of mental disorder with the general population. They found that 1.5% of men and 1.1% of women displayed symptoms of schizophrenia, compared with respective rates in the general population of 0.2% and 0.5% using the same diagnostic instrument. In a study of convicted female prisoners, Jordan, Schlenger, Fairbank, & Caddell (1996) found lifetime rates of any psychiatric disorder to be 64%, and 11% had experienced a major depressive episode in the previous six months. The odds of inmates having substance abuse disorder or antisocial personality disorder were 5 to 25 times greater than in the general population.

In an attempt to overcome problems of the lack of standardisation of measures between studies and the lack of a comparison group, Teplin (1990) used the Diagnostic Interview Schedule (DIS) and compared rates of psychiatric disorder among prison inmates with comparative data from the Epidemiologic Catchment Area (ECA) study. She found 6.4% had a severe mental disorder, of which 2.7% were suffering from schizophrenia. This is approximately three times higher than in the general population. The prevalence of major depression was three to four times higher, and the prevalence of mania or bipolar disorder was 7–14 times higher. The overall rate of mental disorder was three to four times higher in the prison populations. She did not control for demographic factors in all the samples, but in those in which race and age were controlled, differences remained robust.

Teplin, Abram, & McClelland (1996) applied a similar strategy to investigating the prevalence of psychiatric disorder among female remand prisoners in Chicago by assessing a stratified sample of 1,272 using the DIS. Over 80% met criteria for one or more psychiatric disorders in their lifetime and 70% had displayed symptoms in the previous six months. They found 15% had suffered from a severe mental disorder (schizophrenia, manic depression) within the previous six months which was two to three times the level of disorder in the general population. Substance abuse and dependence were highly prevalent, affecting over 70% of participants, 60% in the previous six months.

Teplin et al. (1993) examined the question of whether mental disorder (and substance abuse) predict violent offending among released prison inmates. They conducted psychiatric interviews with inmates and compared the criminal careers of individuals with a mental disorder and those without by examining arrest rates over a three year period. Neither severe mental disorder or substance abuse affected the likelihood of arrest for a violent crime or the number of arrests for violent offences.

Wallace et al. (1998) examined a register of all those convicted in the higher courts of Victoria, Australia during a two year period between 1993 and 1995. Their psychiatric histories were investigated by case linkage to a register which recorded contacts with psychiatric services in the area. Psychiatric contact was found in 25% of cases, although much of this was accounted for by substance abuse and personality disorder. Schizophrenia and affective disorder were associated with increased risk, particularly in conjunction with substance abuse. The findings are discussed in the next chapter.

In a case linkage study in Finland, Eronen, Tiihonen, & Hakola (1996) studied a cohort of 1423 homicide offenders to determine the extent of mental disorder. Since Finnish police have solved approximately 97% of homicides in recent decades, and almost all offenders undergo a thorough psychiatric examination, a relatively comprehensive study was undertaken. Calculations of the odds ratios indicated that the relative risk of committing a homicide was approximately 10 times greater for both men and women with schizophrenia than it was for the general population. Affective disorders, anxiety disorders, and dysthymia did not elevate the risk (Eronen, Hakola, & Tiihonen, 1996). In a Danish study, the increased risk of psychotic homicide was found to be six times higher in men and 16 times higher in women (Gottlieb, Cabrielsen, & Kramp, 1987). Eronen, Hakola & Tiihonen (1996) warns against drawing conclusions because of the retrospective nature of the study. Furthermore, these studies did not employ a control group.

The National Confidential Inquiry into Suicide and Homicide by People with Mental Illness report their findings in the recent publication *Safer Services* (Appleby et al., 1999). Over an 18 month period between April 1996 and November 1997, 718 homicides in England and Wales were reported to the inquiry. Psychiatric reports were retrieved in 500 cases. Of these, 220 (44%) had a lifetime history of 'mental disorder'. This included depression (48 cases) and personality disorder (47 cases), while 27 had delusions and/or hallucinations, indicating psychosis. Fifteen individuals were receiving intensive community care services at the time. Thus, approximately 8% of homicides are committed by individuals who have had some contact with mental health services in the year before the homicide. Fourteen per cent of homicides where there were psychiatric reports available were committed by individuals with symptoms of mental illness. These cases had particular characteristics compared to cases of homicide in which mental illness was absent. Although the majority did have a recorded history of previous violence, mentally ill patients were less likely to have had previous convictions for violence compared to the non-mentally ill; alcohol and drugs were also less likely to play a part in the offence;

and the victim was more likely to be a family member or spouse. Twenty per cent of these perpetrators had been in contact with mental health services in the year prior to the homicide.

A recent survey in the UK funded by the Department of Health was undertaken by Singleton, Meltzer, Gatward, Coid, & Deasy (1998). They interviewed 3142 male and female remand and sentenced prisoners in 131 prison establishments. They found a particularly high rate of functional psychosis. Seven per cent of sentenced men, 10% of men on remand, and 14% of women in both categories were judged to have suffered a psychotic illness in the previous year. Despite methodological difficulties which complicate comparisons with other studies, this contrasts with 0.4% of the general adult population. They reported that 20% of men and 40% of women had attempted suicide at least once. Among women, 25% had made an attempt in the previous year, and among men and women, 2% had done so in the previous week, suggesting that they were not entirely related to current circumstances. The researchers found a high prevalence of personality disorder: 78% for men on remand, 64% for male sentenced and 50% for female prisoners.

These studies have important implications in terms of highlighting the issue of the extent of violence within prison institutions and the provision of psychiatric services. However, systematic biases inherent in using identified offenders cannot address the issue of whether there is a fundamental relationship between violence and mental disorder since mentally disordered offenders may be more or less likely to be imprisoned than offenders who are not disordered (Monahan, 1992).

CHAPTER 3

FACTORS PREDICTIVE OF VIOLENCE

This chapter addresses particular risk factors associated with violence which have been investigated in empirical research. These are reviewed in the following order: base rates, demographic factors, history of previous violence, alcohol and drugs, psychiatric diagnosis, active symptoms of mental disorder, antisocial personality disorder, psychopathy, organic disorders and learning disabilities, social context, management and treatment, and biological correlates of violence

In this section we will discuss evidence for and against various factors which have been investigated as potential predictors of violence. The prediction of risk has recently been reconceptualised. Steadman et al. (1993) argue that the old paradigm of the prediction of dangerousness is shifting to one of risk assessment, based on empirical research. The main features of this are:

- shifting from a focus on the legalistic concept of dangerousness to the decision-making concept of risk
- prediction based on a continuum rather than on a simple dichotomy
- moving away from the notion of a one-off prediction to risk assessment being a day-to-day decision making process
- balancing seriousness of potential outcomes with probabilities of occurrence based on specific risk factors

3.1. Base Rates

- *We begin by discussing the notion of base rates of violence which are the most highly predictive factors of all*

- *These refer to the frequency of violence in a given population or group and do not relate to mental disorder at all*

Before discussing individual risk factors we would like to raise briefly the issue of the base rates of violence. Base rates refer to the normal frequency of occurrence of any response (in this case violence) in a population or group. This information is usually used by researchers to evaluate the effects of a specific manipulation (Reber, 1985). The principal items of information required for predicting violence are not associated with mental disorder at all, but rather relate to the base rates of violence in the population from which an individual comes (Monahan, 1981). An individual in a given area, or from a particular population, will be more or less likely to engage in acts of violence than someone in another with higher base rates of violence, whether or not they have known risk factors for violence. Thus in order to establish the predictors of violence in any population, it is important to establish the base rates of violence. Widom (1989b) argues that there is a tendency to lay too much emphasis on individual case information rather than base rates. Base rates are primary and they have important implications for policy. Monahan (1993b) stresses the regional variations in violence in the USA. In general, smaller communities have a lower prevalence of violence and, in the same city, neighbourhoods differ dramatically. Torrey (1994) provides a more dramatic example by outlining the small addition the mentally ill make to the perpetration of violent crime in the USA compared with Iceland. In Iceland 47 homicides have occurred over a period of 80 years, 13 (28%) of which have been committed by individuals with a mental disorder (Petersson & Gudjonsson, 1981). The overall base rate of violence among the mentally disordered is, in fact, extremely low. The likelihood of violent recidivism among a group of offenders is so low that it is difficult to improve on the accuracy of predicting that no-one will reoffend, even in high risk groups (Steadman, 1983).

3.2. Demographic Factors

- *Demographic factors found to contribute to violence include unemployment, young age, male gender, low socioeconomic status and poor education*

- *The average age of mentally disordered offenders is, however, higher than that for non-disordered offenders*

- *We also discuss the issues of race and ethnicity. When socioeconomic factors are controlled for, race and ethnicity do not contribute significantly to violence*

Psychological discourses have a tendency to conceptualise human experience from a solely individualistic perspective and to ignore the social contextual dimension. Smail (1993), for example, is critical of the way in which mental health professionals are inclined to consider proximal issues (eg. the quality of parenting) as important and to ignore distal issues (eg. poverty). Related, therefore, to the issue of base rates is the issue of demographic factors and their relationship with violence. Violence is in part an outcome of a complex set of economic and social conditions, as well as individual psychological factors. Some of the most significant of these factors are discussed below.

Unemployment. Following the work of Bulhan (1985), Gilligan (1996) states that in the US every one per cent increase in unemployment consistently corresponds with an increase of 2% in mortality figures, 6% in homicide and imprisonment, and 5% in infant mortality. In the US, both the arrest rate and the victimization rate for violent crime is six times higher for African-Americans than for whites (Reiss & Roth, 1993). Half of prison inmates were unemployed at the time of committing a violent offence and average income prior to arrest was approximately the federal government's official 'poverty level' (Monahan, 1993b). Singleton et al. (1998) found that only 36% of male remand prisoners, 44% of male sentenced prisoners, and 26% of female remand and 34% of female sentenced prisoners were employed prior to imprisonment.

Age. Violence is perpetrated predominantly by people in their late teens and 20s, and the risk of violence has been found to diminish with age in a variety of studies (Klassen & O'Connor, 1988a; DeJong et al., 1992). Assaultative patients tend to be younger, predominantly under 40 years of age (Barber et al., 1988; Swanson et al., 1990; Aquilina, 1991; Beck, White,

& Gage, 1991). Bjorkly (1995) makes the important point that while the risk of violence is at its height at age 18 in non-psychiatric populations, among psychiatric groups it appears to peak at the end of the 20s. Taylor (1987) also found that individuals with psychosis begin to offend later in life and Hafner & Boker (1973) established that there was an average age difference of 8 years between mentally disordered and non-disordered offenders at first offence. The prevalence of mental disorder among offenders has been found to increase with age (Taylor & Parrott, 1988).

Gender. In general, 90% of violence is perpetrated by men (Monahan, 1993b). Despite changes in gender role this figure has not altered since records began (Reiss & Roth, 1993). Men in every culture and at any time in history have never made up less than 80% of those convicted of violent crime. Most research of psychiatric populations have found men to be more likely than women to engage in violence (Hedlund, Sletten, Altman, & Evenson, 1973; Tardiff & Sweillam, 1980; Craig, 1982; Rossi et al., 1986; Buckley, Walshe, Colohan, O'Callaghan, et al., 1990). However, in Lidz et al.'s (1993) follow-up study in the community, discharged female patients were slightly more likely to be violent than male patients. In a study of violent incidents in a special hospital over a six month period, women accounted for proportionally more violent incidents than men (Larkin, Murtagh, & Jones, 1988), although other studies of inpatient violence have found no gender differences (Tardiff & Sweillam, 1982).

Socioeconomic status. Socioeconomic status and poverty are particularly important predictors of violence. In Swanson et al.'s (1990) study, for example, 16% of males in the age range 18–29 and in the lowest socio-economic group reported violence compared with the average of 2.4%. Wessely et al. (1994) found that the risk of a first conviction was increased by being male, unmarried, younger at age of illness onset, unemployed, and low social class.

Education. Monahan (1993b) states that four out of five violent offenders in prison in the US have not finished secondary school. Singleton et al. (1998) found that more than half of male remand prisoners in the UK had no educational qualifications, and that most of the others reported only basic educational attainment. Poor education is a robust predictor of both past and future arrest (Abrams & Teplin, 1990). Lack of education and low occupational status have been related to increased risk of violence in some studies (Tardiff & Sweillam, 1980; Raine, Brennan, Mednick, & Mednick, 1996; Stueve & Link, 1997), although others have found no difference (Barnard, Robbins, Newman, & Carrera, 1984; Rossi et al., 1986).

Race and Ethnicity. There is a complex link between race and ethnicity, socio-economic status, psychiatric disorder and violence. Some studies have found an increased risk of violence for non-white discharged psychiatric patients (Klassen & O'Connor, 1989; Noble & Rodger, 1989). However, further analysis reveals that this association is largely attributable to the prior relationship between socio-economic status and ethnicity. For example, in a re-analysis of the ECA data, Swanson (1994) determined that among participants with no psychiatric disorder, 2.7% of non-whites compared with 1.7% of whites were identified as having been violent. Among participants with a major mental disorder or substance abuse, where rates of violence were high, the relationship between violence and ethnicity was stronger – among participants with both mental disorder and substance abuse, 34.6% of non-whites compared with 14.1% of whites reported violence. However, Swanson (1994) points out that non-whites were more than twice as likely as whites to be in the lowest socio-economic group (33% compared with 14%). Similarly, Rossi et al. (1986) found racial differences disappeared when controlling for diagnosis and Tardiff & Sweillam (1980) found no racial differences after controlling for education. In Wessely et al.'s (1994) study, being Afro-Caribbean increased the risk of first conviction, but this was likely to be due to confounders such as poverty, school failure, family breakdown, unemployment and being more likely to be arrested by the police. As Swartz et al. (1998) state 'the living environments in which many severely mentally ill African Americans find themselves – high crime areas experienced as dangerous and threatening – explain much of the violence risk that might otherwise be statistically attributed to race per se' (p230). Much the same may be said of the UK.

Monahan (1993b) states that the problem with making sense of demographic data, and understanding whether the association is a cause or simply irrelevant, is twofold. First, as above, factors relate to one another as much as they do to violence. He names this the 'ball of wax' problem. For example, as above, if poverty is taken into account, the effect of ethnicity dramatically declines. Second, it is difficult, or near impossible, to determine which came first. This he names the 'cause and effect' problem. An important consequence of this is labelling errors. In a study of clinical estimation of risk, McNiel & Binder (1995) found that judgements which emphasised race and ethnicity were associated with more predictive errors. There were more false positives among non-white patients than white patients.

3.3. History of Previous Violence

- *History of violence and its relationship with future assaultative behaviour has been studied extensively both in inpatient and outpatient settings. Excluding demographic factors, it is the most significant clinical predictor of violence*

- *Both arrest and conviction for violence predicts future offending*

- *History of violence is a relatively crude predictor and risk assessment requires that the potentially violent need to be distinguished from a population who have been violent in the past*

- *Detailed information on the nature of an individual's violence, the type of victims, and various environmental and contextual triggers, need to be determined*

Past behaviour is one of the most stable predictors of future behaviour and a history of violence is highly predictive of future assaultative behaviour. In fact clinicians making a clinical judgement of risk tend to use history of violence as the primary predictor (McNiel & Binder, 1995). Bonta, Law, & Hanson (1998) conducted a meta-analysis comparing the prediction of risk of mentally disordered offenders and non-disordered offenders. They found that for both groups, criminal history variables were the best predictors of future offending. Mossman (1994) states that prediction based solely on a patient's previous history of violence is approximately as accurate as other forms of actuarial prediction. According to Gunn (1993) the prediction of risk based on previous history of violence correctly identifies 80% of future violence. However, its specificity is low (35%), thus two out of three individuals identified as being at risk would be unnecessarily detained.

In an early study, Cocozza & Steadman (1974) followed up the 'Baxstrom' patients, a high risk group of 967 patients released from hospitals for the 'criminally insane' to civil psychiatric hospitals. Twenty per cent of these patients engaged in assaultative behaviour over a four year period. The most robust predictors of future violence were having a juvenile criminal record, number of previous arrests, previous convictions for any offence, convictions for violent offences, the severity of the original offence and being under 50 years of age. In another study of a high risk sample, Black (cited in Gunn, 1993) conducted a five year follow-up of patients discharged from Broadmoor, and found that the best predictor of future criminal behaviour was criminal behaviour before admission.

A number of studies have established that a history of violence is a principle predictor of future violence (Swanson, 1993; Litwack, 1994; Morrison, 1994; Torrey, 1994; McNiel & Binder, 1995; Gilders, 1997), as well as among sex offenders (Grubin, 1997). Klassen & O'Connor (1988a) found that prior arrests for violent crimes predicted arrests for violent crime in the community in a sample of male patients released from a psychiatric hospital. In a follow-up study of patients after discharge, Tardiff, Marzuk, Leon, & Portera (1997) found that those who had been violent in the month prior to admission were nine times more likely to be violent in the two weeks after discharge. Cocozza, Melick, & Steadman (1978) established that a history of arrest was the best predictor of future arrest. Tiihonen & Hakola (1995) studied mentally disordered individuals who had committed homicide and found that a history of previous aggravated violent behaviour increased the risk of homicide up to 150-fold.

Studies of inpatients have yielded similar results. Janofsky, Spears, & Neubauer (1988) found that violence prior to admission was the most commonly accepted predictor of future violence, although on its own there was a large number of cases of violence which were missed (false negatives). In a retrospective study of psychiatric inpatients, Blomhoff, Seim, & Friis (1990) found that a history of previous violence was the best single predictor of violence, which correctly classified 80% of patients. Combined information concerning the patient's level of aggression rated at referral and level of anxiety rated at admission correctly classified 78% of patients who were violent. In Singleton et al.'s (1998) survey of prisoners, 80% of male inmates had a previous conviction for a criminal offence.

However, history is a crude predictor of violence. Many of the patients who have been violent are the very individuals who require an assessment of risk. Therefore the requirement is to differentiate those individuals who are likely to be violent in future from a population of individuals who have a history of violence. Furthermore, Gardner et al. (1996b) notes that information on a patient's previous history of violence is not always available. This has certainly emerged in a significant number of public inquiries (Reith, 1996).

More information is required than a simple statement of whether an individual has a history of violence in order to predict future behaviour. It is necessary to know about the nature of the violence, the type of victims and various contextual and environmental triggers. A detailed history of violent events is required in order to make an accurate assessment (Gunn, 1993). By identifying the stimulus conditions in which violence has previously taken place, it should prove more possible to accurately predict the conditions in which future violence may occur.

3.4. Alcohol and Drugs

- *Alcohol and drug abuse are principle predictors of violence, both among the mentally disordered and the non-disordered*

- *The prevalence of substance abuse is substantially higher among individuals with a mental disorder than the general population, and surveys conducted in prison indicate considerably increased rates among inmates*

- *We first consider the link between substance abuse and violence, and then discuss substance abuse, violence and severe mental disorder. There is overwhelming evidence that most violent crimes are perpetrated by individuals who are intoxicated with alcohol and/or by offenders who are alcoholics*

- *Illicit drug use has also been strongly linked to offending. Some studies indicate a stronger association with acquisitive rather than violent crime, although other research links drug abuse with violence as well*

- *Substance abuse has been shown to be an important risk factor for violence among individuals with psychotic disorders in particular, as there is a significant interactive effect between severe mental disorder and substance abuse*

- *Substance abuse has been found to double the lifetime prevalence of violence among individuals with a severe mental disorder, and increased risk is more substantial when considering risk over a shorter time period. The earlier the onset of substance abuse, the higher the risk of violence*

- *We conclude this section with a discussion of the complex link between violence, substance abuse and mental disorder and the mediating role played by a variety of cognitive, affective, social and dispositional factors*

Research on the contribution of substance abuse to criminal behaviour indicates that the use of alcohol and drugs are a principle predictor of violent offending. Estimates of the prevalence of alcohol and drug use in the UK suggest that the prevalence of alcohol dependence is 4.7% and that 29% of the general population have taken drugs (Meltzer, et al., cited in Johns, 1997). The concept of dual diagnosis has been well established in the USA and has attracted significant attention over the past decade. However, there have been few developments in the UK over this period (Smith & Hucker, 1994). For example, the Epidemiological Catchment Area Study has suggested extremely high rates of substance abuse among mentally disordered offenders (Regier, Farmer, Rae, et al., 1990). Lifetime rates among individuals with antisocial personality disorder were 84% (however, substance abuse is a diagnostic factor), 61% of those with bipolar affective disorder, and 47% of those with schizophrenia. Data suggested that a mental disorder doubled the risk of an alcohol disorder and increased by four times the risk of a drug abuse disorder. Almost one third of people with schizophrenia or schizophreniform disorder met criteria for alcohol or drug abuse or dependence (Swanson et al., 1990). There was also a high rate of alcohol and drug abuse comorbidity, alcohol abusers being seven times more likely to abuse drugs as well. Studies of incarcerated offenders indicate increased rates of substance abuse in prison. For example, Gunn, Maden, & Swinton (1991b) investigated prevalence of psychiatric disorder in sentenced prisoners in the UK between 1988 and 1990. Among men, 9% received an alcohol abuse diagnosis and 10% a drug abuse diagnosis. Among women, 24% received a drug abuse diagnosis. Teplin, et al. (1996) compared rates of psychiatric disorder in female inmates with prevalence data from the Epidemiological Catchment Area programme. Differences between inmates and the general population in substance abuse/dependence were substantial. Odds ratios ranged from 9 to 48, depending on ethnicity and age group. In the recent survey of prison inmates in the UK, Singleton et al. (1998) found that 58% of male remand prisoners, 63% of male sentenced prisoners and 36% of female prisoners reported hazardous or harmful drinking (identified using the Alcohol Use Disorders Identification Test) in the year prior to coming to prison. Less than a fifth of men and a third of women reported never having used illicit drugs. More than a half of participants in all groups reported having used illicit drugs in the year prior to prison, and drug dependence was reported by approximately 40% of male and female sentenced prisoners and about 50% of male and female remand prisoners. Among men, a third of remand prisoners and half of sentenced prisoners reported using illicit drugs during their prison term.

We begin by reviewing studies which have considered alcohol and drug abuse separately and then discuss studies which deal with substance abuse as a whole. We first consider substance abuse as a risk factor for violence in and of itself, and then go on to review studies which have considered substance abuse as a risk factor in the context of mental disorder in particular.

3.4.1. Substance Abuse and Violence

There is general agreement among studies which have investigated crime statistics which indicated overwhelmingly that the majority of violent crimes, including assault, sexual assault, family violence and murder are committed by individuals who are intoxicated with alcohol (Fitch &

Papantonio, 1983; Pihl & Peterson, 1993; Beck, 1994; Bergman & Brismar, 1994; Modestin, Berger, & Ammann, 1996). Johns (1997) reviews studies linking alcohol and violence. These indicate that alcohol is implicated in 40–60% of assaults and homicides, 30–70% of rapes and approximately 40–80% of domestic violence. Reiss & Roth (1993) estimated that approximately one third of violent offenders are alcoholics. Murdoch, Pihl, & Ross (1990) examined 26 studies involving 9,304 cases and found that 62% of violent offenders were drinking at the time of the offence. The range of alcohol-related violent crime between studies was 24%-85%, compared to a range of alcohol-related non-violent crime which was 12%-38%. Studies using measures of physical inebriation at the time of the offence have reported high levels of intoxication (Pihl & Peterson, 1993). The victims of violent crime have also tended to be intoxicated at the time (Murdoch et al., 1990), although causality is difficult to determine since intoxication may be a function of the environment in which violence occurs, and individuals who are intoxicated are more likely to be apprehended (Pihl & Peterson, 1993).

A number of people argue that illicit drugs are generally associated with acquisitive offending and trafficking (Maughan, 1993; Johns, 1997), although some studies also indicate a link with violence. Pihl & Peterson (1993) maintains that evidence for the relationship between drugs and violence is sparse because of legal restrictions on research in this area which has resulted in a dearth of experimental studies on this issue. Clinical reports suggest that cocaine, cannabis, phencyclidines, benzodiazepines and other psychotropic medications have been noted to be linked to aggression, although these reports are fraught with methodological problems (Pihl & Peterson, 1993). In the birth cohort study undertaken by Hodgins et al. (1996), compared with the general population, the relative risk for committing a single violent crime for people who had an alcohol abuse disorder among women was 6.71 to 14.87, and among men was 4.19 to 6.68. For drug abuse disorder the relative risk of a single violent crime was 10.2 to 15.08 among women and 5.94 to 8.67 among men. On the other hand, in a study of prison inmates, Abrams and Teplin (1990) found drug abuse (uncomplicated by other disorders) was inversely related to violent crime.

Wallace et al. (1998) found that substance abuse on its own resulted in a 7.1 fold increase in the rate of convictions for any offence, a 9.5 fold increase in convictions for violent offences and a 5.7 fold increase in homicides in men. In female substance abusers, convictions were increased 35.8 fold for any offence and 55.7 times for violent offences. Other studies of substance abuse in people without a severe mental disorder have found substantially increased rates of violence (Robins, 1993).

3.4.2. Substance Abuse, Mental Disorder and Violence

Substance abuse and major mental disorder comorbidity has been shown to increase the risk of violence even more than substance abuse on its own. Rice & Harris (1995a) found that in a subgroup of individuals with both mental illness and alcohol abuse, their rate of recidivism was much greater than for individuals with mental illness alone and similar results are reported elsewhere (Lindqvist & Allebeck, 1990; Swanson et al., 1990). In the ECA study, substance abuse was found to almost double the lifetime prevalence of violence among individuals suffering from a severe mental disorder. A crucial finding was that not only is substance abuse an independent risk factor for violence, but there was a significant interaction between mental disorder and substance abuse. After controlling for socio-demographic covariates, the odds ratio for violence in a year for individuals with a major mental disorder diagnosis and co–occurring substance abuse was 16.8 (Swanson et al., 1990).

In Hodgins' (1992) Swedish birth cohort study, substance abuse was present in 49% of violent mentally disordered offenders. Wessely et al. (1994) found that substance abuse increased the likelihood of a criminal record among a mentally disordered sample. One of the most impressive demonstrations of the importance of substance abuse as an associate with violence was the study reported by Steadman et al. (1998). Compared with patients with a severe mental disorder without substance abuse (17.9%), patients with a co–occurring substance abuse disorder had almost twice the rate of violence (31.1%). This was even higher for substance abusers who had an Axis II disorder (43%), i.e. a diagnosis of personality disorder. Patients were also much more likely to engage in substance abuse, suggesting a mechanism whereby mental disorder contributes to violence (31.5% of patients had symptoms of substance abuse compared with 17.5% of the control group at first follow–up). Similar results are reported by Modestin & Ammann (1995) in a Swiss study. They examined the conviction rates of mentally disordered individuals compared with carefully matched controls. Alcohol and drug abuse disorders were the most powerful discriminators between patients with and without criminal records in a multivariate analysis. Alcohol and drug abuse was highly associated with violence.

In the Finnish study by Eronen and colleagues (1996a), in which they examined a cohort of 1,423 homicide offenders, schizophrenia without the presence of an alcohol use disorder increased the risk of homicide 7.3 times for men and 5.1 times for women. Schizophrenia with a secondary diagnosis of an alcohol use disorder increased the risk for homicide 17.2 times for men and 80.9 times for women. Swanson and colleagues (1990) calculated that the prevalence of violence among people meeting criteria for alcoholism was 12 times that of people who did not receive a diagnosis, and those diagnosed as abusing drugs was 16 times higher than those without a diagnosis. When variables were combined in a regression equation, violence was most likely to occur among young lower class men, substance abusers, and those with a major mental disorder (Swanson & Holzer, 1991).

These escalated rates of violence are similar to those found by Wallace et al. (1998) who established that schizophrenia with coexisting substance abuse was associated with 12.4 times the rate of convictions for any offence, 18.8 times for violent offences and a 28.8 fold increase for homicide. Affective disorders with substance abuse were associated with 13.5 times as many convictions for any offence, a 19 fold increase in convictions for violent offences and a 17.5 fold increase in homicides. In their reanalysis of the ECA data, Swanson, Borum, Swartz, & Monahan (1996) found that individuals with threat/control-override symptoms (these are described later under section 3.6.) combined with alcohol and drug disorders were especially prone to violence, increasing their risk by eight to ten times the base rate. Swartz et al. (1998) studied a group of inpatients with severe mental disorder and found that the combination of medication non-compliance and substance abuse was significantly associated with serious violence in the community following discharge from hospital.

Swanson et al. (1990) make the point that independent of the finding that a significant proportion of the violence among people with schizophrenia is alcohol and drug related, there is a much greater chance of being assaulted by an 'alcoholic' than someone with schizophrenia. There are also many more 'alcoholics' than people with schizophrenia in the community and alcohol abusers are much less likely to receive treatment.

Fulwiler, Grossman, Forbes, & Ruthazer (1997) conducted a retrospective study of the relationship between violence and substance abuse in 64 individuals with long-term mental illness living in the community. The onset of substance abuse in late childhood or early adolescence was the single best predictor of violence. Very early onset of alcohol and drug abuse among individuals who later developed mental illness indicated the highest risk of violence in the community. These results are similar to those of Reiss & Roth (1993) who found that the likelihood of violence as an adult is increased the younger the individual is when they start drinking.

The link between substance abuse, violence and mental disorder is a complex one and intoxication is not in itself a necessary precondition for violent behaviour. Experimental studies indicate that intoxication and violence are mediated by various cognitive, social and dispositional factors (Pihl & Peterson, 1993). Smith & Hucker (1994) speculate that because of the social disadvantage associated with mental disorder, this leads many to obtain and use illicit drugs and to associate with a delinquent subculture which may increase the likelihood of violence (i.e. they move into a population with a high base rate of violence). Substance abuse may either act as a marker for an underlying propensity to be violent or may increases the possibility of violence under particular conditions. The interaction between social, psychological and biological variables in association with psychosis, substance abuse and violence is complex and obscure and requires considerable research and theory development. The extent to which the risk of violence can be attenuated by abstinence from alcohol and drugs also requires clarification.

Johns (1997) argues that risk assessment in relation to alcohol and drug use requires knowledge of the ways in which they may relate to violence. For example, this may be due to intoxication, withdrawal, acquisition, or personality change following prolonged use. In his review of the relationship between intoxication and aggression, Fagan (1990) discusses their complex relationship, substance use and violence being mediated by the type of substance and its psychoactive properties, personality factors, situational factors in the immediate situation in which use takes place, and socio-cultural factors which determine the outcome of arousal effects. Intoxication does not consistently lead to aggressive behaviour. Other models of the relationship between intoxication and aggression are presented by Pihl & Peterson (1993).

3.5. Psychiatric Diagnosis

- *The link between specific diagnostic categories and violence has been extensively studied. Previous research indicated a link between violence and schizophrenia in particular, although this was conducted mainly in inpatient settings*

- *Recent research has been more equivocal. Schizophrenia, as well as affective disorders, have been associated with increased risk of violence in some studies. Other studies have demonstrated no increased risk for individuals with schizophrenia*

- *A recent meta-analysis found psychosis to be associated with approximately a three-fold increase in the risk of violence*

Psychiatric diagnosis has been extensively used as a predictor of violence. As stated earlier, we consider this approach to be unproductive and that recent developments which have focused on the relationship between specific symptoms of mental disorder and violence represent more positive developments. Here we review some of the research on psychiatric diagnosis and violence.

In an early review of the literature, Krakowski, Volavka, & Brizer (1986) examined 13 studies investigating the issue of diagnosis and violence. They concluded that as a group, people with schizophrenia tend to be more violent than patients in other diagnostic categories. Individuals with major affective disorders, including manic-depression, were less likely than other diagnostic groups to be assaultative, although many people displaying symptoms of mania frequently behaved in a threatening manner. However, this research took place in hospital-based settings where violent individuals may be over-represented, and therefore tell us little about how people with schizophrenia behave in the community.

Recent research linking a diagnosis of schizophrenia with violence has been equivocal. Wessely et al. (1994) found that a diagnosis of schizophrenia resulted in men having a 3.8 times greater likelihood of a conviction for violence compared with other disorders. Wallace et al. (1998) found that schizophrenia without coexisting substance abuse was associated with an approximately twofold increase in the rate of convictions for violent offences and a sevenfold increase for homicide. Affective disorders without substance abuse were associated with 2.9 times the rate of convictions for violent offences and a 4.4 fold increase in homicides. Tiihonen, Isohanni, Rasanen, Koiranen, & Moring (1997) conducted a 26 year prospective study using an unselected birth cohort of 12,000 individuals born in 1966 in Northern Finland, comparing information on psychiatric hospitalisation and criminality. They found that individuals with a diagnosis of schizophrenia were seven times more likely to be convicted for violent crime, and individuals with an affective disorder were nine times more likely than those with no disorder. Swanson et al. (1990) found that people with schizophrenia were not significantly more likely to engage in violent behaviour than individuals with other severe mental disorders. Those with anxiety disorders and affective disorders had a similar prevalence of violence compared with the general population – findings similar to those of Stueve & Link (1997) who found that self-reported fighting and weapon use were higher among individuals diagnosed with psychotic or bipolar disorders, but not among individuals with non-psychotic depression, anxiety disorders or phobias in a community-based study of 2,678 young adults in Israel. The authors found this result to remain robust after controlling for substance abuse and antisocial personality disorder.

However, there are other studies which have found no relationship between psychiatric diagnosis and violence. In Modestin & Ammann's (1995) Swiss study described earlier, people with psychotic disorders were no more likely to receive convictions for violent crime than controls. In

Sweden, Belfrage (1998b) found that individuals with a diagnosis of schizophrenia had a significantly higher rate of general criminal conviction than other diagnostic groups, but there was no significant difference for violent crime specifically. Rice & Harris (1995a) argue that in samples of individuals at high risk of future violence, the evidence for the link between schizophrenia, psychotic symptoms and violence is limited. Teplin, Abram, & McClelland (1994) interviewed 728 randomly selected prison inmates in the USA and followed them up for six years after their release. They compared the arrest rate of individuals with and without a severe mental disorder. A diagnosis of schizophrenia did not increase the risk of arrest for violent crimes. Some studies have in fact found that among high risk individuals, people with schizophrenia are at lower risk of arrest (Lidz et al., 1993; Rice & Harris, 1995a).

Douglas & Hart (submitted) conducted one of the only meta-analyses of research on the association between psychosis and violence. They calculated 269 odds ratios from 105 studies which were carefully selected for quality and as representative of published research. They found psychosis to be associated with approximately a three-fold increase in the risk of violence. They found considerable dispersion of effect sizes around the central tendency which was, in part, related to methodological factors such as study design, the way in which psychosis was defined and measured, and the way in which violence was defined and measured. Therefore as a whole, psychotic disorders appear to be associated with increased risk of violence, although there are considerable discrepancies between studies about the strength of this relationship.

3.6. Active Symptoms of Mental Disorder

- Recently there has been a recognition of the limited utility of diagnosis as a risk factor and an increasing focus on active symptoms of severe mental disorder instead. We discuss psychotic symptoms under two headings: delusions (including threat/override symptoms and violent thoughts) and hallucinations

- Research on the link between delusions and violence has tended to rely on the retrospective reports of participants which weaken the validity of findings. There have also been a few prospective studies. Delusions appear to be consistently strongly implicated in the perpetrating of violence by individuals with a severe mental disorder

- *Symptoms associated with threat (the feeling that others wish to harm you) or the overriding of personal controls (the feeling that your mind is dominated by forces outside your control, or that thoughts are being inserted into your mind which are not your own) have been found by some researchers to account for violence by individuals with severe mental disorder. However, results of other studies are inconclusive about this relationship. This is an important and potentially productive area of future research*

- *Only one prospective study has examined the relationship between violent thoughts and actual violence. Patients who reported having violent thoughts during admission were more likely to be violent following their discharge*

- *Studies on the link between hallucinations and violence have examined command hallucinations which tell an individual to act. Studies have not established as strong a relationship between hallucinations and violence as between delusions and violence. Those studies which have indicated a relationship have found this to be stronger when associated with other psychotic symptoms and when the person can identify a specific person or entity and the relationship is also dependent on environmental factors*

There has been considerable interest in examining the relationship between specific symptoms of mental disorder and violence, rather than focusing solely on diagnosis. According to Monahan (2000) 'active symptoms are probably more important as a risk factor than is simply the presence of an identifiable disorder'(p315).

Studies of inpatient violence have found that violence occurs during active phases of psychosis (Planansky & Johnston, 1977; Craig, 1982). Krakowski et al. (1986) concluded that the 'frequency of violent incidents tends to reflect the course of the acute psychosis and to be positively correlated to the severity of psychotic symptoms'. Mulvey (1994) reports the results of a study of 812 psychiatric patients whose propensity to act violently was found to increase as the global severity of their symptoms measured by the Brief Symptom Inventory increased. Reviewing a series of studies, Wessely & Taylor (1991) conclude that between one and two thirds of homicidal violence committed by individuals with schizophrenia can be attributed to abnormal mental state.

3.6.1. Delusions
Following Kraupl-Taylor (1979), Taylor et al. (1994) define psychotic delusions as being 'based on an absolute conviction of the truth of a propo-

sition which is idiosyncratic, incorrigible, ego-involved and often preoccu-pying' (p163). Violence by the mentally disordered often appears to be a rational response to an irrational belief (Link & Stueve, 1994; Junginger, 1996). Junginger (1996) argues that the content of delusions and hallucina-tions frequently implies a specific course of violent action; and therefore a study of the associations between content and themes of these psychotic phenomena and violence may be informative. However, the link between delusions and action is complex and the tendency to report on delusions only when actions lead to distress on the part of patients or others biases these conclusions (Buchanan, 1993). Much of the research in this area has been retrospective and has not used comparison groups.

Green (1981) examined 58 male patients in Broadmoor who had com-mitted homicide. and estimated that in 27 cases this appeared to be a response to persecutory delusions. In a subsequent analysis of the study undertaken by Taylor & Gunn (1984) described earlier, Taylor (1985) esti-mated that 20% of actively ill psychotic individuals were directly driven to offend by psychotic symptoms, and a further 26% probably so. The moti-vation of the rest was uncertain. Taylor also noted that actions 'definitely' influenced by delusions seemed significantly more dangerous than those influenced by hallucinations. Hafner and Boker (1973) judged 38% of a group of violent patients to be directly motivated by their symptoms and a further 33% to be indirectly affected by them.

Krakowski & Czobor (1994) studied a group of 38 psychiatric patients in a secure unit. They found a significant association between paranoid symp-toms and transient ward violence. Straznickas, McNeil, & Binder (1993) found that 7 out of 24 (29%) assaults by mentally disordered individuals on their spouses were preceded by persecutory delusions. Martell & Dietz (1992) studied the mental health records of 20 individuals who were referred for psychiatric assessment after pushing strangers onto subway tracks in New York City. Only one did not have a history of psychiatric hospitalisation and was not psychotic at the time. Seven (35%) reported being influenced by delusions and 3 (15%) reported a command to carry out the offence.

Wessely et al. (1993b) conducted a retrospective study of 83 mentally disordered individuals in hospital, examining the association between delu-sions and action associated with these delusions. In each individual the researchers identified a 'principle delusion' and participants were asked whether any action (including violence) had taken place as a consequence. Additionally informants were identified who could provide information concerning the patient's behaviour prior to hospital admission. Sixty per cent of participants reported an incident of behaviour motivated by the principle delusion, 20% reporting more than one. The ratings of judges about the probability that informant-reported behaviour was related to the principle delusion suggested that 48% of patients probably or definitely acted on it in the month prior to admission. In response to any delusion, this rose to 77%. They concluded that actions linked to delusions are more common than is generally thought. Violence was not uncommon, 29% displaying minor violence and 3% serious violence. Taylor et al. (1998) studied 1,740 special hospital patients of whom 58% had a diagnosis of functional psychosis, of whom 75% were recorded as having been motivated to offend by their delusions. On the other hand, hallucinations did not have such an effect.

A few prospective studies have investigated the relationship between delusions and violence. Shore et al. (1989) followed up a group of mentally disordered individuals arrested near the White House. In cases involving no history of previous violence, there was a significant relationship between delusions of persecution and future violence. In the study by Link et al. (1992) discussed earlier, the authors examined differences between patient and community control groups on relatively recent occurrences of hitting others, fighting and weapon use when psychotic symptoms were controlled. *Recent* violent behaviour was used as the dependent variable because current psychotic symptoms were thought to relate to recent violence rather than past violence. Psychotic symptoms were tapped via questions such as 'How often have you felt that thoughts were put into your head that were not your own?'. The authors found that scores on the psychotic-symptom scale were significantly and strongly related to recent violent behaviour, even when controlling for other factors, such as alcohol and drug use. Adjusted odds-ratios for a two standard deviation difference on the psychotic-symptom scale were 2.2 for hitting others, 4.0 for fighting and 1.9 for weapon use. Therefore, almost all the differences between patients and community controls in violent behaviour were accounted for by active psychotic symptoms experienced by individuals suffering from mental disorder. Delusions and hallucinations significantly elevated their risk of violent behaviour. Incidentally, Link et al. (1992) also found that the psychotic-symptom scale predicted violence among the never-treated community control group. In Teplin et al.'s (1994) study of released prison inmates, individuals with symptoms of either hallucinations or delusions had only a slightly elevated number of arrests for violent crimes, but this was not significant.

Swanson (1994) re-examined Epidemiological Catchment Area data and identified a subgroup of individuals who suffered from a major mental disorder who were more likely to be both arrested and hospitalised. The combination of arrest and hospitalisation produced a much greater relative risk of violence. Former inpatients, free of psychopathology in the previous year, were unlikely to be violent. Swanson (1994) concludes that active symptomology, associated with mental disorder, and not merely a history of hospitalisation, is related to assaultative behaviour.

Swanson et al. (1997) combined ECA data with the Triangle Mental Health Survey data (Estroff, Zimmer, Lachicotte, & Benoit, 1994). One intriguing finding was that individuals with moderate levels of agitation and psychosis were at increased risk of violence, whereas higher levels of symptom severity were associated with a lower risk. They suggest that severe impairment accompanying severe mental disorder suppresses risk. The authors warn against reading too much into these findings due to several methodological limitations.

Threat/Control-Override Symptoms
The literature suggests that having more severe symptoms of mental disorder or having a greater number does not necessarily increase the risk of violence. Rather, the type of symptoms are a more significant determinant (Swanson et al., 1997). There has been some debate about the type of symptoms associated with violence and studies have provided conflicting results.

Building on the results of previous research which found an association between psychotic symptoms and violence, Link et al. (1992; 1994) sought to determine which kinds of symptoms explained this link. They hypothesised that mental illness was more likely to lead to violence when associated with symptoms which led to the perception of threat and/or involved the overriding of personal controls. The individuals whose psychotic experiences made them feel threatened by others were more likely to behave in a hostile manner. When they felt a weakening of self-control mechanisms (for example, through thought insertion or the feeling that outside forces dominated their minds) they were more likely to behave violently. On the other hand, other psychotic phenomena such as auditory or visual hallucinations, or having your thoughts removed, were not likely to be associated with violence.

Link & Stueve (1994) tested this hypothesis by re-analysing the data from an earlier study (Link et al., 1992). They selected three of the thirteen items in the Psychiatric Epidemiology Research Interview (PERI) psychotic symptoms scale which involved either threat (the feeling that others wished to harm you) or the overriding of personal controls (the feeling that your mind was dominated by forces outside your control or thoughts being inserted into your mind that were not your own). The other ten items were indicative of severe psychosis, but were not associated with threat/control-override. They found that the three item threat/control-override scale was strongly associated with recent self-reports of hitting, fighting and use of weapons even when the ten remaining items from the scale were controlled for. The threat/control-override scale accounted for differences in the rates of violence between patients and community controls and the ten other psychotic symptoms showed no association with violence, despite being equally severe indicators of psychosis.

Swanson et al. (1996) point out that the lack of specific diagnostic measures in Link et al.'s study limits the interpretability of their findings since while threat/control-override symptoms usually point toward major mental disorder, they may also be a feature of other disorders too, such as substance abuse, severe personality disorders and traumatic disorders. In a reanalysis of the ECA data, Swanson et al. (1996) replicated the above findings. Participants who reported threat/control-override symptoms were twice as likely as those reporting other psychotic symptoms to engage in violent behaviour and about five times as likely as those with no mental disorder.

Link & Stueve (1995) present the findings of an unpublished study which further confirmed these findings. Link et al. (Columbia University, unpublished manuscript) used data from an Israel-based study and the same findings were established. These results increase confidence that the association between violence and mental disorder is causative in that specific symptoms are associated with assaultative behaviour (Link & Stueve, 1995).

Studies relating to the threat/control-override hypothesis, however, are not conclusive and are not without their critics. Mullen (1997) raises the objection that the items, such as 'feelings of thoughts put into your head and being dominated by forces beyond your control' may be endorsed by violent offenders with personality disorders or individuals who simply lack of self control, rather than those suffering from mental illness. Estroff et al. (1994) used the same measure as Link et al. (the PERI) in the Triangle Mental Health Survey. Their sample was constituted by more severely mentally disordered individuals and threat/control-override symptoms were in fact negatively related to violence. However, violence was related to other variables which measured perceived threat more directly, such as the Perceived Hostility subscale of the PERI. This may suggest that the symptoms associated with violence are more specific.

Swanson et al. (1997) state that the above discrepancy indicates that the threat/control-override construct requires conceptual clarification and measurement development. Two potentially distinct symptom dimensions are incorporated: perceived threat and control-override. The first is related to persecutory delusions and paranoia, whereas the second does not adequately distinguish between real and imagined threats – many mentally disordered individuals live in surroundings which may be dangerous or threatening and some of the symptoms they report may reflect reality. Swanson et al. (1997) raises a number of questions about the way in which these symptoms may act together in relation to violent behaviour. The issues are clearly potentially productive, but require further clarification.

Swanson et al. (1997) combined ECA data with the Triangle Mental Health Survey data of Estroff et al. (1994) and found that the relationship between threat/control-override symptoms and violence was only significant when the independent effect of absence of treatment was controlled. This suggests, according to the authors, that openness to treatment identifies a group of individuals who are less likely to be violent when experiencing threat/control-override symptoms. A recent study by Appelbaum, Robbins & Monahan (submitted) provides the most disconfirming evidence to date for the threat/control-override hypothesis. They studied the relationship between TCO delusions and violence using data from the MacArthur Violence Risk Assessment Study. This involved the follow-up of 1136 acute psychiatric patients in the community and interviews at baseline and 10–week intervals. They found that neither delusions in general nor TCO delusions in particular were associated with increased risk of violence.

One other study is worth mentioning in this context. McNiel & Binder (1994) studied 330 patients in a locked psychiatric unit with a variety of diagnoses. Patients were rated at admission using the Brief Psychiatric Rating Scale, and violent incidents during admission were recorded. Assaultative and non-assaultative patients had different symptom patterns, and symptoms associated with violence varied according to diagnosis. There were higher levels of hostile-suspiciousness, agitation-excitement, and thinking disturbance among assaultative patients, but this was less accurate as a predictor of violence among individuals with a diagnosis of schizophrenia than those with other diagnoses.

These studies indicate that the use of symptom profiles may be a better indicator of risk than a diagnostic label. However, research in this area is at an early stage and it is difficult to draw firm conclusions for the purposes of risk assessment.

Violent Thoughts
A related field of study is the extent to which the reporting of violent thoughts in individuals suffering from a mental disorder is predictive of future violent behaviour. We are aware of only one study in this area and therefore the subject does not warrant a separate section, but is important to mention. Using data from the MacArthur Risk Assessment Study which involved the follow-up of 1136 discharged psychiatric patients, Grisso, Davis, Vesselinov, Appelbaum & Monahan (in press) examined the

prevalence of self-reported violent thoughts among hospitalised psychiatric patients and compared these with community controls. Patients were followed up after discharge and the persistence of violent thoughts was investigated. The relationship between patients' reports of violent thoughts during admission and violent actions in the 20 weeks following discharge was examined. One third of patients reported violent thoughts toward others during admission, which was more than twice that reported by controls. The reporting of violent thoughts was significantly related to being violent within 20 weeks of discharge for non-White patients, for patients without major mental disorder, but with diagnoses of substance abuse, for patients with high symptom severity during admission, and for those whose reports of violent thoughts persisted after discharge. The reporting of violent thoughts was significantly associated with psychopathy (measured by the Psychopathy Checklist – Screening Version; Hart, Hare, & Forth, 1994), anger (measured by the Novaco Anger Scale; Novaco, 1994) and impulsiveness (measured by the Barratt Impulsiveness Scale; Barratt, 1994). These findings have potential in assisting clinicians with relevant areas of inquiry in assessing risk.

3.6.2. Hallucinations

Hallucinations are perceptual experiences which have the subjective properties of a real sensory event, but without the usual physical stimulus which usually produces the impression (Reber, 1985). A command hallucination is experienced as an order to act upon the hallucination. Studies have failed to indicate conclusively that there is a relationship between assaultative behaviour and command hallucinations (McNiel, 1994). Although they may be present, evidence for whether individuals act upon them is less certain.

Some studies using quantitative clinical rating scales of psychotic individuals have tended to indicate a relationship between hallucinations and violent behaviour in the context of other positive psychotic symptoms (McNiel, 1994). Lowerstein, Binder, & McNeil (1990) studied 127 consecutive admissions to a psychiatric hospital. Patients were rated on the Brief Psychiatric Rating Scale (BPRS). Hallucinatory behaviour was significantly more pronounced in participants who were later assaultative during their hospital stay. This association between hallucination and violence took place in the context of other positive symptoms of psychosis such as thinking disturbance, hostile-suspiciousness and agitation-excitement. Studies utilising similar methods have obtained analogous findings (Yesavage, 1983; Werner, Rose, Yesavage, & Seeman, 1984; Janofsky et al., 1988). Among a sample of forensic inpatients, Rogers, Gillis, Turner, et al. (1990) found that 80% who had all recently experienced a command hallucination stated that they had complied with a command recently.

Junginger (1990) found that 20 (39%) of a sample of psychiatric inpatients and outpatients reported that they had complied with a command hallucination and 16% stated that they had complied with a dangerous command. Patients who could identify the voice as a specific person or entity were significantly more likely to state that they complied with it. Junginger (1995) found that 52 (56%) of his sample reported compliance with command hallucinations. Once again, those patients who could identify the hallucinated voice, as well as those experiencing less dangerous commands, were significantly more likely to report compliance with it, although there were also those who reported complying with more dangerous commands. The content of command hallucinations reported by those in hospital was less dangerous than those experienced out of hospital and those while in hospital were less likely to report compliance with them. Junginger (1995) concludes that the ability to identify the hallucinated voice seems to be a reliable indicator of reported compliance and that compliance appears to be related to the patient's environment.

3.7. Antisocial Personality Disorder (ASPD)

- *Antisocial personality disorder (ASPD) is a consistent pattern of ignoring and violating the rights of other individuals. It is strongly associated with substance abuse and there is also a higher prevalence among individuals with severe mental disorders*

- *There is a high prevalence of ASPD among prison inmates, approximately half of prisoners fulfilling diagnostic criteria in a recent British survey. ASPD is consistently a robust predictor of arrest and conviction for offending in general and for violence in particular*

- *Odds ratios vary from one study to another, but all indicate a substantial relative risk. Relative risk of violence tends to be higher for women than men*

- *There are problems with the construct of ASPD in that the very diagnostic criteria are features of criminality itself making the term tautological and precarious. Nevertheless, it remains a useful tool in predicting future violence*

Antisocial personality disorder (ASPD) is defined in the DSM-IV (American Psychiatric Association, 1994) as a 'a pervasive pattern of disregard for, and violation of, the rights of others which begins in childhood or early adolescence and continues into adulthood' (p.645). Robins, Tipp, &

Przybeck (1990) state that antisocial personality begins at about age eight when it is expressed by a variety of behavioural problems and is fully expressed during the twenties and early thirties. Associated problems include relationship and employment difficulties and violence. It is predominantly a male phenomenon and studies (including results of the ECA study in the USA; Robins et al., 1990) indicate a high correlation with substance abuse as well as a high rate of comorbidity with other severe mental disorders. In fact Stueve & Link (1997) attribute the elevated prevalence of violence in mentally disordered individuals to the possibility of this comorbidity.

Estimates of the prevalence of ASPD depend on the study samples, the context in which the studies are carried out and the measures used. According to Robins et al.'s (1990) ECA survey, approximately half of prison inmates could be diagnosed with ASPD, although other studies have indicated lower and higher prevalence in prison. Teplin et al. (1996) found that approximately 13% of female remand prisoners in the US received a diagnosis of ASPD. Among convicted female prisoners 28% had a diagnosis of borderline personality disorder (compared with 1.8% in the general population) and 12% ASPD (Jordan et al., 1996). Gunn et al. (1991b) investigated the prevalence of psychiatric disorder in sentenced prisoners in the UK between 1988 and 1990. They claim to have underestimated personality disorder which was 7% among men and 8% among women. In a comparison of arsonists and violent offenders, DeJong et al. (1992) found that the latter group tended to have higher rates of ASPD and lower rates of dysthymia compared with the former. The best predictor of violent recidivism among violent offenders was impulsivity in the original offence, whereas a history of suicide attempts predicted violent recidivism among arsonists. The most up-to-date survey of the prison population in the UK was undertaken by Singleton et al. (1998). They found the rate of personality disorder to be 78% among male remand inmates. The rate of antisocial personality disorder was particularly high: 63% of men on remand, 49% of sentenced men, and 31% of women in both categories.

ASPD is consistently a robust predictor of arrest and conviction for offending in general (Hodgins & Cote, 1993a and 1993b) and for violence in particular (Hodgins & Cote, 1993a; Robins, 1993; Rasmussen & Levander, 1996; Asnis, Kaplan, & Hundorfean, 1997). Hodgins et al.'s (1996) birth cohort study found that, compared to the general population, the relative risk for committing a single violent crime for people who had a diagnosis of ASPD among women was 7.86 to 12.15, and among men was 5.35 to 7.2. Eronen et al.'s (1996a) study of all homicides in Finland over an eight year period indicated that the risk of committing homicide among people with ASPD was elevated over 10 times for men and over 50 times for women compared with the general population. Wallace et al. (1998) found that among men personality disorder was associated with 12.7 times the rate of convictions for any offence, 18.7 times for violent offences and 28.7 times for homicide. In women, personality disorder resulted in 49.6 times as many convictions for violent offences.

McCann & Dyer (1996) argue that there is more potential for utilising personality disorder or personality traits to assess the risk of violence than using the more commonly studied Axis I disorders. They quote a study by Rogers, Dion, & Lynett (1992) illustrating this point. They investigated 250 adults' ratings of prototypical ASPD criteria via a factor analytic technique. An aggressive behaviour factor, including items such as violence, cruelty and fighting, accounted for a large part of the variance, rather than major mental illness.

ASPD is a useful tool in the prediction of risk, although the construct is problematic. Personality disorder, particularly ASPD, represents a medicalisation of deviance in that the very diagnostic criteria are features of criminality itself which makes the term ASPD tautological and precarious. Nevertheless, although the diagnosis should be regarded with scepticism and treated cautiously, it does have utility in the assessment of future risk, although the question of whether ASPD is a form of mental disorder is debatable.

3.8. Psychopathy

- *There is significant overlap between ASPD and psychopathy, both concepts indicating psychological disorder which is inferred from social deviance. Psychopathy is used to define an extreme personality disorder which involves ego-centred impulsive self-gratification and a callous disregard for others. Psychopathy is not used according to the Mental Health Act (1983) definition of the term*

- *Research on psychopathy has focused on the 20 item Psychopathy Checklist (PCL) and the revised version (PCL-R). Many studies have found strong correlations between PCL scores and violent recidivism among high risk samples of prison inmates and mentally disordered offenders*

- *Psychopathy has been found to be a better predictor of violence than either psychiatric diagnosis or substance abuse. Psychopathy also predicts treatment failure in that treatment has been found to increase the likelihood of violent recidivism*

> • *The construct of psychopathy has a high degree of utility in risk assessment. However, the PCL-R can result in pejorative labelling which can have negative consequences for those designated as psychopaths. It should be used with caution and sensitivity*

There is significant overlap between ASPD and psychopathy, both concepts indicating psychological disorder which is inferred from social deviance. However, we discuss these issues separately since the former refers to a diagnostic category in the DSM-IV, while psychopathy draws its definition from other sources, mainly formulations by American writers such as Cleckley (1976) who stressed ego-centred impulsive self-gratification and a callous disregard for others. According to Hare & Hart (1993) there are similarities with ASPD, but they consider psychopathy a specific form of personality disorder. The 1983 Mental Health Act defines the legal category of psychopathic disorder as 'a persistent disorder or disability of mind ...which results in abnormally aggressive or seriously irresponsible conduct on the part of the person concerned'. This description bears little relation to the North American concept, and research has indicated that the legal concept of psychopathy includes individuals who are heterogeneous in personality (Blackburn, 1998).

In recent years research on psychopathy has focused on the Psychopathy Checklist (PCL) and the revised version (PCL-R) (Hare, 1991). Other measures have been used, but the PCL represents the primary methodological advance in psychopathy research in the last decade (See Lilienfeld, 1998 for a review). The PCL served to operationalise the construct of psychopathy. There are 20 items and scores can be subdivided according to two factors, the first measuring a callous and remorseless style of interpersonal relating, and the second referring to a socially deviant lifestyle (Harpur, Hare, & Hakstian, 1989). Psychopathy has been related to ASPD as well as other personality disorders using the PCL-R (Hart, Hare, & Forth, 1994). The PCL-R has only one item which directly relates to aggression (poor behavioral controls), yet it correlates with previous and future violence (Blackburn, 1998). Hart et al. (1994) have more recently developed a screening version of the PCL-R called the PCL-SV.

The PCL-R has been extensively used in the prediction of recidivism among prison inmates. For example, Hart, Kropp, & Hare (1988) administered the PCL to 231 inmates prior to their release from prison on parole. They found that offenders with PCL scores in the top third of the distribution were approximately three times more likely to violate conditions of parole than the bottom third, and almost four times more likely to commit a violent offence. Many other studies have found strong correlations between PCL scores and violent recidivism (Harris, Rice, & Cormier, 1991; Rice & Harris, 1995a; Weiler & Widom, 1996; Harris & Rice, 1997). The PCL-R has performed well in predicting violent recidivism in high risk samples of prison inmates (Serin & Amos, 1995) and mentally disordered offenders (Harris et al., 1991; Rice & Harris, 1992). Psychopathy was found to be the best predictor of violence in the MacArthur Risk Assessment Study (Steadman, Silver, Monahan, Appelbaum, Robbins, Mulvey, Grisso, Roth & Banks; in press). Among sex offenders psychopathy scores have been significantly associated with recidivism for violent offending in general and sexual offending in particular (Rice, Harris, & Quinsey, 1990; Quinsey, Rice, & Harris, 1995; Rice & Harris, 1997). Rice & Harris (1995a) found that psychopathy had a stronger relationship to violent recidivism than either schizophrenia or alcohol abuse and Harris, Rice, & Quinsey (1993) found that PCL-R scores were the best single predictor of violence among individuals with schizophrenia and personality disorder. The comorbidity rate of schizophrenia and psychopathy was relatively low. Salekin, Roger, & Sewell (1996) conducted a meta-analysis of 18 studies which had examined the relationship between psychopathy and violence. This demonstrated a large average effect size ($d = 0.79$), indicating the predictive validity of psychopathy.

The PCL-R has also been used to investigate the relationship between psychopathy and treatment outcome. Quinsey et al. (1998) report a comparative study undertaken by Rice, Harris & Cormier (1992) examining violent recidivism rates among offenders treated in a therapeutic community, and untreated offenders. Both groups were further separated according to whether or not they met criteria for psychopathy. There were therefore four groups: treated and untreated psychopaths, and treated and untreated non-psychopaths. The treated group consisted of 176 offenders who spent two years in a therapeutic community, and the matched comparison group consisted of 146 incarcerated and untreated offenders. Those meeting the criteria for psychopathy were more likely to reoffend, but unexpectedly violent recidivism rates were particularly high among psychopathic individuals treated in the therapeutic community. The latter group were more likely to reoffend violently than untreated psychopaths as defined by the PCL-R. The opposite results were obtained for non-psychopathic offenders, the therapeutic community having a positive outcome in terms of violent recidivism for this group. These findings have important implications for the management of individuals meeting the criteria for psychopathy. Quinsey et al. (1998) hypothesise that psychopathic individuals use prosocial skills learned in the therapeutic community, such as emotional language and delayed gratification, to further exploit and manipulate others and to commit violent crime. Of course, regimes given the name of therapeutic community differ markedly from one another. Noteworthy in Quinsey et al.'s description of the programme was that patients had very little contact with staff, and little effort was expended in organised recreational programmes. Entry to and participation in the programme were not voluntary. Participants in the community were a mixture of psychotic and non-psychotic patients. A specific recommendation of the recent inquiry into the Personality Disorder Unit at Ashworth Special Hospital in the UK was that personality disordered and psychotic patients should be treated separately (Fallon, 1999). Furthermore, as the authors point out, the psychopathic group in their study had extensive histories of violent offending, and less violent psychopathic individuals may have a different treatment response.

The above research indicates the importance of the psychopathy construct and the PCL-R in the prediction of violence among mentally disordered and non-disordered populations. However, similar criticisms expressed in relation to ASPD are relevant in the context of psychopathy, perhaps more so. In a paper with the ironic title of 'Death to the Psychopath', Cavadino (1998) argues that the term 'psychopathic disorder' (referring to the use of the legalistic use of the term, but having equal relevance to the non-legalistic construct) represents moralism masquerading as medical science. Rather than assisting individuals who are diagnosed as such, the pejorative label has the effect of denying them mental health services on the basis of 'treatability'. Blackburn (1988) comments that 'Given the lack of demonstrable scientific or clinical utility of the concept, it should be discarded' (p511). However, the last decade has seen a resurgence of interest in psychopathy, and renewed optimism in its use for assessment. Lilienfeld (1998) argues that methodological innovations have led to improvements in the valid and reliable operationalisation of the construct. Undoubtedly there are many unresolved questions associated with psychopathy, and the uncritical application of the construct is potentially anti-therapeutic and damaging. Nevertheless, there is potential for psychopathy to aid the assessment of risk and this cannot be ignored.

3.9 Organic Disorders and Learning Disabilities

- *Learning disabilities have generally been associated with increased risk of violent offending, although some studies have found no relationship*

- *Studies of inpatient violence have identified that patients with neurological impairment are responsible for a significant number of violent incidents. This is particularly true of the elderly*

- *Neurological impairment tends to involve more persistent violence, whereas violence in psychiatric patients is related to one-off transient violence*

The relationship between organic disorders and learning disabilities and violence is alluded to in a small minority of studies on violence and mental disorder. Low IQ has been found to increase the likelihood of violent recidivism (Klassen & O'Connor, 1988a; DeJong et al., 1992). On the other hand, Eronen et al.'s (1996a) study of all homicides in Finland over an eight year period indicated that the risk of committing homicide among people with learning disabilities was not elevated compared with the general population. Hodgins (1992) investigated this relationship in an unselected Swedish birth cohort. She found that men with a learning disability were three times more likely to commit any offence than men with no disorder. They were five times more likely to commit a violent offence. Women with learning disabilities had five times the risk of committing any offence and were 25 times more likely to commit a violent offence. In a further Danish birth cohort study, Hodgins et al. (1996) found that, compared to the general population, the relative risk for committing a single violent crime for people with learning disabilities among women was 7.99 to 11.81 and among men was 5.89 to 7.65.

Studies of inpatient violence have identified that patients with neurological impairment are responsible for a significant number of violent incidents. Ferguson & Smith (1996) found that of 12 patients who were responsible for 68% of 834 violent incidents in a psychiatric ward for the elderly, most violent recidivists were neurologically impaired. Owen et al.'s (1998a) study of repetitively violent inpatients identified that male recidivists were significantly more likely to have organic brain syndrome. In a survey of 166 mental health facilities in the USA over a period of a year, Lehmann, McCormick & Kizer (1999) recorded over 24,000 incidents. Individuals with dementia were responsible for a significant number of incidents. The nature of this violence and the perpetrators of it are clearly different from other kinds of violence reviewed here.

Similar evidence available from birth cohort studies suggests an increased risk for organic disorders. In a Swiss study of conviction rates of mentally disordered individuals compared to matched controls, Modestin & Ammann (1995) found that men with organic disorders were more likely to be convicted for a violent crime, whereas women with organic disorders tended to be involved in more crimes against property. Hodgins et al. (1996) found that men with organic disorders were at approximately 2.5 times the relative risk for committing a single violent crime than the general population. This could not be calculated for women due to small numbers. Krakowski & Czobor (1994) differentiated between transient and persistent violence and demonstrated an association between neurological impairment and persistent violence, whereas violence in psychiatric patients was related to transient, tending to occur as a one-off event.

Evidence from these birth cohort studies is inconclusive as the measures of violence used are based upon official data. It is quite conceivable that individuals with learning disabilities or organic disorders are more likely than other members of the population to be arrested or detected by the criminal justice system.

3.10. Social Context

- *Mental disorder is an interpersonal and contextual matter and not simply a neurological or clinical one. Some recent research has focused on the social context of violence which represents a significant advance in the understanding of it*

- *The discussion of social context is linked to base rates of violence. The neighbourhood in which an individual resides is a highly significant predictor of the likelihood of violence*

- *Mentally disordered individuals are at a very high risk of violent victimisation themselves*

- *Increased size of social networks and higher concentrations of relatives in social networks have been found to increase the likelihood of violent threats by individuals with severe mental disorder*

- *The majority of violence perpetrated by individuals with a psychotic disorder is against relatives. Few strangers are the victim of violent attacks by individuals with severe mental disorder*

Earlier we discussed the importance of demographic factors in the prediction of violence, base rates being the most significant factor to take into account (Monahan, 1981). It appears that the diagnostic focus of the research on violence and mental disorder which has tended to emphasise issues such as severe mental disorder, substance abuse and personality disorder, has detracted from other important matters such as the context in which the violence occurs. Mental disorder is an interpersonal and contextual matter and not simply a neurological or clinical one (Estroff et al., 1994). We are, of course, aware that research has only recently established a link between mental disorder and violence, and therefore the examination of mediating factors such as social context is a relatively recent phenomenon. Investigation of this issue enables a different level of discourse which moves the debate from predictive factors to more complex models of violence. A few authors have addressed the social implications of mental disorder and its relation to violence (Taylor, 1987; Estroff et al., 1994; Hiday, 1995; Hiday, 1997).

Hiday (1995; 1997) argues that major mental illness is not a sufficient cause of violence. She proposes a model which posits intervening social factors, including social disorganisation and poverty, which impact upon the course of severe mental disorder and result in co-occurring substance abuse and personality disorder and a context of victimisation and violence. In our view, this represents an important challenge to the traditional focus on individual factors and is a positive attempt to move the debate from a concern with superficial indicators of violence to a deeper theoretical level which acknowledges the complexity of the relationship between violence and mental disorder.

Epidemiological surveys of violence by mentally disordered individuals which have used demographically matched control groups have typically seen the risk of violence reduced among the mentally disordered when compared to studies which have compared the mentally disordered to the general population (e.g. Swanson, et al., 1990). This is illustrated most clearly in Steadman et al.'s (1998) study, in which patients compared to individuals in the same neighbourhood were no more violent than controls. Obviously there are questions about the validity of these findings, given that much other research has produced different findings, but social context clearly contributes significantly to violence. The importance of socio-economic status is illustrated by Martell, Rosner, & Harmon (1995), who investigated the relationship between mental disorder, homelessness and violence in a group of 77 homeless and 107 domiciled mentally disordered people. Mentally disordered individuals had 40 times the rate of homelessness than the general population, and the homeless group were much more likely to be arrested and charged for violence. Drawing on data from the MacArthur Foundation Risk Assessment Study, Silver, Mulvey, & Monahan (1999) investigated the neighbourhood context of violence. Their results indicated that neighbourhood poverty was a better predictor of violence than individual characteristics among discharged psychiatric patients. The socio-economic status of individuals was not as strong a predictor of violence as concentrated poverty. They stress the importance of neighbourhood poverty and resultant low levels of social cohesion which influence an individual's propensity to resolve conflict with violence. Wessely & Taylor (1991) point out that the substantial age difference in the onset of offending behaviour between mentally disordered and non-disordered offenders (the former starting later) may indicate that the type of social deprivation which is a consequence of mental disorder, may be a mediating factor linking disorder with criminality.

Hiday (1995) argues that the direction of causality may run from violence to mental disorder, rather than vice versa. Many individuals with mental disorder experience high levels of victimisation. Once mental illness has developed, adult experiences of abuse among psychiatric patients is common (Carmen, Rieker, & Mills, 1984; Estroff & Zimmer, 1994; Estroff et al., 1994). Cascardi, Mueser, DeGiralomo, et al. (1996) studied a group of 69 individuals recently admitted to hospital and found that 63% reported physical abuse by their partners and 46% reported physical victimisation by members of their families. Goodman, Dutton, & Harris (1995) report a study of homeless women with serious mental illness. They state that the lifetime risk of violent victimisation was so high (97%) that this was a normative experience for these individuals. Adult physical abuse was reported by 84% of respondents. Hiday, Swartz, Swanson, Borum, & Wagner (1999) interviewed 331 psychiatric inpatients and found that while non-violent criminal victimisation was similar to that of the general population, criminal victimisation was two and a half times greater.

Hiday (1995) highlights the interactional aspect of violence. Mentally disordered individuals may be more vulnerable to provocation, and a history of victimisation may provoke defensive violence, active symptoms of mental illness exacerbating the likelihood of assaultative behaviour. Expressed emotion (i.e. intrafamilial hostility, criticism and over-involvement) has been investigated in families with a member who is mentally ill. Elevated levels of expressed emotion have been related to higher rates of relapse among individuals with schizophrenia (Vaughn, Snyder, Jones, & al., 1984; Falloon, 1988). Estroff & Zimmer (1994) examine the web of social networks and relationships which govern the expression of violence and are critical of the dearth of research in this area. They pose the question to be addressed by research as being 'What kinds of persons, in what situations, at what phase of their lives and illnesses, are likely to engage in dangerous behaviours' (p261). They interviewed 169 individuals with serious mental disorder and 59 of their significant others. They found that increased size of networks and higher concentrations of relatives in social networks increased the likelihood of violent threats. Respondents who threatened others described significant others as being attacking and hostile. More than half of the victims of violent behaviour were the relatives of sufferers. The most significant finding according to the authors, a finding not replicated elsewhere, was that the most frequent targets of violence were mothers of respondents (Estroff & Zimmer, 1994; Estroff et al., 1994).

Many family caregivers routinely experience threats and violence from family members with mental disorder causing stress and a decline in physical and emotional well-being, which also exacerbates the patient's disability (Hyde, 1997). Straznickas et al. (1993) surveyed psychiatric patients admitted to hospital who had physically attacked someone in the two weeks before admission. In 56% of cases a family member had been a victim of the assault. Similarly, Tardiff (1984) found family members to be the victim of assaults in 65% of cases. Binder & McNeil (1986) found that 54% of violent patients assaulted a family member, and that most of these individuals planned to return home following their hospitalisation. Steadman et al. (1998) found that 86% of violent acts by former patients took place within the context of family and friendship networks. In fact, the control group in their study were significantly more likely to target patients than the patient group! Vaddadi, Soosai, Gilleard, & Adlard (1997) found that 32% of relatives of patients admitted to an acute psychiatric unit had been physically assaulted by them. More than 50% reported verbal abuse and threats. Almost 80% of relatives reported significant emotional symptomology as a result of the burden of care. Taylor and Gunn (1999) studied changes in Home Office figures of homicide by people with mental illness convicted of manslaughter on the grounds of diminished responsibility in England and Wales over a 38 year period. Attacks on strangers were the exception and there has been little change over the period, the highest proportion occurring in 1995 (13.8%).

3.11. Management and Treatment

- *Little research has been conducted on management and treatment in relation to the amelioration of the risk of violence, although it is claimed that the ability to accept and use treatment is likely to reduce the risk of violence*

- *Medication non-compliance has been shown to increase the likelihood of rehospitalisation and violence, although there have been no prospective studies to date linking medication (or therapy) non-compliance with violence*

- *Strategies to improve compliance include psycho-educational interventions encouraging simple daily rituals, the involvement of patients in decision making processes and cognitive-behavioural interventions*

- *Individuals who have mental health professionals in their social networks have been found to be at reduced risk of violence*

One difficulty in determining the impact of treatment in reducing violence is that it is frequently hostile behaviour that brings people into treatment in the first place. As research on inpatient violence has indicated, violent individuals are often over-represented in treatment settings (Swanson et al., 1997). Little research has been conducted on management and treatment in relation to the amelioration of the risk of violence, although it is claimed that the ability to accept and use treatment is likely to reduce the risk of violence (Webster, Douglas, Eaves, & Hart, 1997). According to Torrey (1994), medication non-compliance is an important predictor of dangerousness in those with a psychotic disorder. Medication non-compliance has been shown to increase the likelihood of rehospitalisation and violence (Bartels et al., 1991), but there have been no prospective studies to date linking medication (or therapy) non-compliance with violence. Kemp, Hayward, & David (1997) quote a global compliance rate of approximately 50% of patients with schizophrenia and cite rates of poor compliance of between 10% and 80% among patients with psychotic disorders. A recent review estimates that 70% of psychiatric patients discharged from hospital are likely to stop taking medication within a period of two years (Howlett, 1998). A variety of strategies have been developed to improve compliance. These include psycho-educational interventions to encouraging simple daily rituals, the involvement of patients in decision making processes (Howlett, 1998) and more formal cognitive-behavioural interventions (Kemp, et al., 1997).

Howlett (1998) studied the role of non-compliance with treatment in inquiry reports into homicides by individuals suffering from mental illness. Out of 35 independent inquiry reports examined, 20 (57%) indicated that medication non-compliance was a major contributory factor in the breakdown of care prior to the homicide. Factors influencing non-compliance were side-effects of old-style medication, poor aftercare and supervision, lack of insight, substance abuse, poor communication with family and/or patient and non-attendance by the patient at outpatient appointments.

Estroff et al. (1994) found that individuals with psychotic disorders who included mental health professionals in their social network had a lower probability of committing violence, possibly a result of professionals being able to identify early warning signs of violence prior to its occurrence. Swanson et al. (1997) combined ECA data with the Triangle Mental Health Survey data. They found that violence was associated with absence of recent contact with community mental health services, although the relationship between lack of treatment and increased risk of violence was not as evident among participants with substance abuse comorbidity. Furthermore, disengagement from treatment appeared to compound the risk of violence among individuals who had low levels of psychoticism and agitation, whereas treatment had little impact in terms of ameliorating the risk of violence at higher levels of symptom severity. The authors attribute this to risk already being reduced by the impairment associated with severe symptoms.

3.12. Biological Correlates

- *Many biological factors from the genetic to biochemical have been suggested as being linked to violence, yet there is a general lack of evidence for these*

- *There is some evidence to support a biosocial model of violence*

The review is not intended to cover the complex and extensive literature concerned with the genetic, neuroanatomical and biochemical basis for mental disorder and violence. As is evident from previous chapters, mental disorder includes an enormous array of categories, each of which has a significant body of literature. For example, schizophrenia has been extensively researched from a genetic (Gottesman & Shields, 1982; McGuffin, 1988; Marshall, 1990), neuroanatomical (Jernigan, 1992; David & Cutting, 1999) and biochemical (Bowers, 1974; Jackson, 1990; Warner, 1994) perspective. It is evident that no simple explanatory organic cause has been identified in spite of over fifty years of research, although over time there have been a number of particular variables which have been identified as causal only later to be disconfirmed by subsequent research (Lavender, 1999). The most widely accepted view of schizophrenia is that a multi-causal model is required and a number of stress vulnerability models have been proposed (see Turpin & Clements, 1992; Warner, 1994 for reviews). These models propose that a number of environmental and biological factors lead to individuals being vulnerable to psychosis, but that particular environmental stressors are required to precipitate the onset of psychosis. Some of the environmental stressors that have been identified include particular events (e.g. the break up of relationships, losing job) or periods of transition (e.g. late adolescence to adulthood).

For other disorders where there has been less research such as anti-social personality disorders, the evidence, even when reviewed by strong proponents of biological explanations, is rather inconclusive (Frith & Blair, 1998). These researchers remain optimistic about that the new methodologies (i.e. Magnetic Resonance Imaging (MRI) and Positron Emission Tomography (PET)) now available to investigate neuroanatomical variables will reveal significantly dysfunctional areas within the brain (Frith & Blair, 1998). Frith & Blair (1998) suggest the likely importance of the orbital frontal cortex and amygdala for psychopathy, although similar areas have been implicated in schizophrenia (Gray, Feldon, Rawlins, Hemsley and Smith, 1979; Reynolds, 1983; 1987). It is, however, likely that these complex disorders will require complex explanations which draw on biological, social and psychological variables.

A similar picture emerges from reviews of the biological correlates of violence and indeed most authors who consider biological factors as important do so in the context of proposing biopsychosocial models (Eysenck, 1977; Mednick, 1977, Moffitt, 1993). In reviewing the evidence for biological factors, Monahan (1993a) concludes that, although many biological factors from the genetic to biochemical (e.g. hormones such as testosterone, neurotransmitters such as serotonin, and blood abnormalities such as hypoglycaemia) to the neurological (e.g. frontal lobe deficits) have been suggested as being linked to violence, the evidence is less than convincing. For example, while the serotonin-aggression link is frequently cited as providing the brain-behaviour link with violence, in their review, Berman, Tracy & Coccaro (1997) conclude that the evidence is considerably less compelling than is usually assumed. Monahan (1993a) states that the National Academy of Sciences review of hundreds of studies on the relationship between biology and violence concluded that 'No patterns precise enough to be considered reliable biological markers for violent behaviour have yet been identified' (Reiss, 1993).

This view is not, however, shared by all researchers and there is a body of evidence for biological models which propose that aggressive behaviour is caused by a combination of biological, psychological and contextual factors. This model is intuitively appealing (Baron & Richardson, 1994), but finding evidence for multi-determined, and therefore highly complex explanations, is extremely problematic. This is in part because much research approaches the problem of violence from a single domain and studies investigating the complex interplay of multiple variables are rare (Berman, 1997). Thus, Brennan & Raine's (1997) review of biosocial models provides a rich theoretical account, but very few studies providing convincing evidence.

Among the strongest support for such biosocial models comes the work of Raine, Brennan & Medrick (1994). The study tested the biosocial inter-action hypotheses that delivery complications combined with maternal rejection of the child predispose to violent crime. The study included 4269 males in a Danish birth cohort, from between September 1959 and December 1961. Delivery complications (e.g. pre-eclampsia, breech delivery, hypoxia) were taken as indications of neurological damage at birth. An individual was considered to be violent if they had been arrested for one or more violent crimes and was considered to have experienced childhood maternal rejection, for example, if there had been an attempt to abort the foetus or a period of institutional care as a child. The study found a combination of birth complications and maternal rejection led to an exponential increase in violence. This study can be criticised in terms of the extent to which delivery complications indicated neurological damage. It also appeared that it was maternal rejection that was the particularly potent factor in predicting violence in individuals with a high level of delivery complications. Thus, although according to Brennan & Raine (1997) this provides good evidence for a biosocial explanation, the study is open to alternative interpretations and, as the authors acknowledge, biosocial models in general have not generated very specific testable hypotheses.

In a thoroughly researched and accessible book, Paris (1996) argues for a biopsychosocial model of personality disorder. While there is currently no evidence for biological factors in the development of various categories of personality disorder, there are reliable indications that personality traits are heritable. Rutter (1987) has argued that both temperament and social learning influence the development of traits. Observational studies of human infants indicate the importance of temperament and the variations in levels of activity, sociability and emotionality found among infants and young children. Paris (1996) quotes an interesting series of studies in the relatively new discipline of behavioural genetics which utilizes various types of twin studies to examine heritability. The most common method of determining the heritability of personality traits is to compare monozygotic and dizygotic twins. This research indicates that personality traits have rates of heritability in the range of 40–50 per cent (Plomin, DeFries & McClearn, 1990; Livesley, Jang, Schroeder & Jackson, 1993), suggesting that up to half of the variance in personality traits can be attributed to genetic factors. Paris (1996) argues that temperamentally difficult children are more likely to come into conflict with their parents, and problems may be exacerbated by a poor fit between parents and their children. These children may be more likely to suffer negative events in childhood. Rutter & Quinton (1984) have shown that temperamentally difficult children are more likely to receive worse treatment by their parents. The conclusion, therefore, is that biological factors are likely to have a role in the genesis of violence in combination with those psychosocial and developmental factors which are the focus of the next chapter.

CHAPTER 4

CLINICAL, PSYCHOLOGICAL AND DEVELOPMENTAL ASPECTS OF RISK

> *This chapter is concerned with the underlying dynamics of mental disorder and violence. We propose that advances in the field of violence and mental disorder require a focus on complex pathways to particular outcomes, which will advance knowledge from the relatively unsophisticated level of particular factors and their association with violence to a more complex theoretical understanding of the dynamics of psychopathology and violence. A variety of issues are discussed in this chapter: clinical aspects of risk assessment, early environment, conduct disorder, attention deficit disorder, peer relations and social functioning, and attachment*

We turn now to a discussion of issues which have not traditionally been the focus of research and literature on risk assessment. Efforts have been concentrated on various factors and their relationship with the outcome variable of violence. In our view, violence and mental disorder research has much to learn from the field of developmental psychopathology, which examines 'the evolution of psychological disturbance in the context of development' (Cole & Putman, 1992). It does so by investigating complex pathways to particular outcomes and, in doing so, has advanced knowledge from the relatively unsophisticated level of surface phenomena to the more complex theoretical understanding of the dynamics of psychopathology and violence. We consider this a necessary development in the field of risk assessment, which requires a move from the purely descriptive to the explanatory. The issues in this chapter are concerned with attempting to understand the underlying dynamics of mental disorder and violence. We believe that increasing attention will need to be paid to these matters in view of, for example, the current debate over the detention of individuals who are deemed untreatable and whose psychopathology is not understandable within traditional medical discourse.

4.1. Clinical Aspects of Risk Assessment and Management

- *The dichotomising of actuarial and clinical approaches to risk assessment, in which the clinical approach has been equated with subjective judgement, has been unhelpful. A thorough assessment of each actuarial risk factor requires expert clinical judgement. Insights gained using clinical impressions provide important additional information which is useful in planning the management of risk*

- *There has been a general lack of attention to the internal world of the offender, which includes the individual's background, disrupted familial bonds, violence experienced during childhood, as well as the meaning of the violence to the perpetrator. Such factors may not in themselves cause violent actions, but may structure potential violence and determine triggers to later assaultative behaviour. This information is essential for a thorough risk assessment*

- *We discuss a possible framework for understanding violence based on Glasser's work which differentiates self-preservative and sadistic violence. The former relates to the elimination of a threat, whereas the latter has the function of deriving gratification from violence. Assessment and management are very different for these two core types of violence*

- *The personal reactions of the assessor which are formalised in the notions of transference and countertransference are discussed*

While acknowledging the value of empirical research, some individuals have commented on the risk of discounting information which is difficult to quantify by using purely actuarial information for the assessment of risk (Gardner et al., 1996b; Glasser, 1996a). In our view, there has been a rather unhelpful and synthetic split between actuarial and clinical approaches to risk assessment, in which the clinical approach has been equated with subjective judgement. Yet a thorough assessment of each risk factor requires expert clinical judgement. For example, psychopathy, substance abuse or mental disorder all require careful assessment to determine their level and nature. We are not advocating using subjective judgement in the assessment of risk, but insights gained using clinical impressions provide important additional information which is useful in planning the management of risk.

Glasser (1996a) is critical of the lack of attention to the offender's inner world in current discourses on risk assessment; by which he means an individual's background, disrupted familial bonds, and violence experienced during childhood. Such factors may not in themselves cause violent actions, but may structure potential violence and determine triggers to later assaultative behaviour. 'It is not psychological malfunctioning *per se* which causes a schizophrenic to carry out his homicidal act' (p273). In other words, even when the behaviour of a psychotic individual may seem to lack coherence, a violent act appearing to be a random phenomenon, detailed examination reveals a meaning which frequently relates to early experiences. Violence is understood as expressing difficulties in thinking capacity (Perelberg, 1999). 'As part of a fundamental difficulty in thinking, there is a tendency for body and mind to become confused, so that violent acts on one's own or another's body are used to get rid of intolerable states of mind' (p6). Perelberg (1999) cites Meninger (1968) who suggests that all incidents of violence have a meaning: they represent an attempt to avoid something worse. For example, an individual may kill another in order to preserve their sanity.

Glasser (1996a) discusses a possible framework for making sense of violence in order to aid risk assessment. He proposes two fundamental types of violence. The first is biologically motivated and is an autonomic response aimed at eliminating danger or threat. It may be characterised as 'self-preservative'. The second, according to Glasser's typology, has the aim of inflicting physical and/or emotional pain on the victim and may be characterised as 'sadistic'. Glasser (1996b) has previously illustrated how these two types of violence are interrelated in that sadistic violence arises from the self-preservative instinct: 'the anxious intention to destroy is converted into the gratifying intention to hurt' (p276). From this perspective, violence exists on a continuum. At one end lies ordinary teasing, shading into sadomasochistic relationships in which individuals play destructive games with one another; then perversions, sexual crimes, rape, bodily harm, and at the extreme end of the continuum, homicide. In order to determine an individual's potential dangerousness, both the meaning of the act to the perpetrator and the quality of the violence are essential pieces of information.

The nature of psychotic violence is most frequently of the self-preservative kind, whereas malicious acts are generally perpetrated by relatively more psychologically integrated individuals. The consequence of this scheme is that decisions about risk, treatability and management are fundamentally different. The self-preservative types are generally safe as long as they remain out of contact with the trigger of their violence and the 'stimulus conditions' in which the violence occurs. Glasser (1996a) proposes that a primary task of risk assessment in this context is a microscopically detailed discernment of the trigger. Treatment should aim to diminish vulnerability associated with it, and management should assist the perpetrator in avoiding contact with the trigger until it no longer has the power to act as such. On the other hand, the maliciously motivated (sadistic) offender presents more difficult and complex problems. Glasser (1996a) recommends the careful building of a relationship in which the offender feels able to trust, and this may extend to a psychotherapeutic relationship, where the basis for the violence can be identified and corrected.

A major issue in the malicious (sadistic) group is 'simulation', which may be a pitfall in assessing risk, treatability and management (Glasser, 1996a). 'Simulation' is distinguished from 'deception' in that the former is entirely unconscious. The individual may appear to comply with demands and to relate with genuineness, although this is false and has the function of protecting true individual identity which remains concealed by the outward compliance. Thus the individual's true self is always defined negatively, i.e. by refusing to do or be what is expected of them. This sheds light on why antisocial behaviour is so important – it both expresses and affirms the individual's sense of self, albeit negatively. A major aspect of these individuals' psychopathology is also explained in that they tend to describe having no real sense of identity and complain of chronic feelings of emptiness. Simulation presents major pitfalls in treatment and management in that the clinician is always in a double bind since attempts to assist the individual in altering their ways of relating are sabotaged under the guise of (false) compliance.

Recent research indicates that clinical judgements are more accurate in predicting violence than previously thought (Lidz et al., 1993). The feelings and responses of patient and professional are formalised in the notions of transference and countertransference. These issues are of particular importance in a forensic setting and assist in understanding the complex and highly disturbed aspects of the internal world of offenders which is acted out in offending behaviour.

The recognition that past relational patterns are replicated in the context of the relationship with the therapist has a long history (Freud, 1914). Indeed, in both psychoanalytic, and some systemic theory, access to these repeating patterns which are re-enacted in the 'here and now', rather than remembered, provides the therapist with the opportunity to facilitate the development of insight and cognitive, emotional and behavioural change. A patient's early relationships are therefore brought to life in the context of the therapeutic relationship. Transference and countertransference have recently been applied to cognitive therapy in the treatment of personality disorder (eg. Layden, Newman, Freeman & Morse, 1993) and it is generally recognised that these aspects of the therapeutic relationship offer vital information for the assessment and treatment of severe personality disorder. Transference is not confined to the therapeutic relationship and is a feature of all human relationships: it involves the repetition in the present of past ways of relating to

important figures from early life. It is essential for all mental health professionals to be aware of these aspects of the therapeutic relationship and to recognise
and understand them, even though it may be inappropriate to take these up
with the patient. This understanding helps to prevent the professional from
re-enacting destructive patterns of behaviour with the patient, which are
derived from the past (Temple, 1996).

Every patient leaves a unique imprint on those involved with his or her
care. By behaving in a child-like manner, for example, some may evoke a
parental response. Others may evoke lack of interest, hostility, or outright
contempt. Both the patient's behaviour, and the team's reaction to it, are
essential pieces of data about the patient's internal world and these are
useful for risk assessment.

A central problem in undertaking work with mentally disordered
offenders is the powerful thoughts and feelings it evokes. There is a
complex communication between the clinician and the patient which
takes place at both a conscious and an unconscious level. The consequence
for the clinician is the experience of complex countertransference feelings
which properly belong to the patient. For example, the fear and threat one
feels with a violent patient may at least in part be due to a weak, vulnerable part of themselves which they are unable to accept.

Temple (1996) delineates the particularly sado-masochistic character of
the therapeutic relationship in working with forensic patients. The clinician may experience him or herself as feeling sadistic, representing the
cruel internal figure of the patient. This might be a manifestation of the
patient's own harsh internal conscience which may be inclined toward
cruelty in judgement, rather than fairness. This in turn may provide clues
about the childhood experiences of the patient, such as his or her experience of being a victim.

Psychological change is an important aspect of attempting to ameliorate
violence. However, with the proliferation of various treatment programmes in secure hospitals and prisons, it would be wise to heed Cox's
(1982) caution that the development of insight does not imply reduced risk
of recidivism.

4.2. Early Environment

*The relationship between early environment and violence is discussed under two
headings: childhood abuse and neglect; and childhood experiences, mental disorder and violence*

4.2.1. Childhood Abuse and Neglect

- *In this section we consider studies which have confirmed the 'violence begets violence' hypothesis, whether or not a formal diagnosis of mental disorder is present. Abused or neglected children are much more likely to engage in violence*

- *Factors linked to later violence include: lack of parental supervision, parental rejection, lack of parental involvement, parental discord and criminality in parents, parental alcoholism and parental personality disorder, harsh parental attitude and discipline, corporal punishment, low income, separations from parents and institutional care, high ratings for daring and low IQ*

- *Violent boys have been found to be more likely to have experienced, or to have witnessed, extreme physical abuse or mothers being beaten by fathers. Abused children, however, do not necessarily grow up to perpetrate violence*

- *Specific forms of child abuse are associated with specific patterns of violent offending. Individuals who were physically abused are more likely to offend with physical violence and those who were sexually abused are more likely to offend sexually*

- *Research has also demonstrated that a combination of biological and psychosocial factors is particularly important in predicting later violence. Birth complications in combination with early childhood rejection are associated with violent crime in early adulthood*

There has been a widespread belief for some time that childhood victims of violence become perpetrators later in life; yet it is only in the last 10 years that the 'cycle of violence' hypothesis has been firmly established empirically. In a review of the literature in 1989, Widom (1989c) concluded that despite the generally held view of the intergenerational transmission of violence, there was a surprising dearth of empirical literature to support it. Existing studies at the time of her review suffered from methodological weaknesses due to reliance on self-report, retrospective data and small-scale clinical reports. Nevertheless, findings suggested that there was a higher likelihood of parents abusing their children if they themselves were abused and of violence being perpetrated by childhood victims of abuse. Loeber & Stouthamer-Loeber (1986) reviewed studies investigating familial factors, conduct disorder and delinquency. They identified lack of parental supervision, parental rejection and low parental involvement as the principal predictors of delinquency. Secondary predictors included parental discord and criminality in parents. In one study, for example, 10% of children who were not delinquent were poorly supervised by their parents, compared with 75% of repeat offenders.

In a review of studies concerning sexual victimisation, Ryan (1989) suggests that as many as 70%–80% of adult sexual offenders have suffered sexual abuse as children. A number of studies have investigated the reports of childhood factors by men who batter their wives. Compared to non-violent men, men who batter their wives tend to report having witnessed their mothers being beaten by their fathers and to have been disciplined with corporal punishment themselves (Fitch & Papantonio, 1983; Kalmuss, 1984; Briere, 1987; Caesar, 1988; Johnston, 1988). According to Robins (1991), poor parental disciplinary practices are one of the strongest correlates of conduct disorder. In a comparison of violent and non-violent offenders, McCord (1979) found that they were similar in having poor parental supervision, but that parental conflict and aggressiveness in the parents were better at predicting violence. Maternal affection and paternal criminality were better predictors of property offences. Farrington (1978) found that the most important early forerunner of violence and aggression in boys was a harsh attitude and discipline on the part of parents towards them at age 8. Additionally, other important factors measured between age 8 and 10 included low income, criminality in the parents, poor parental supervision, separations from parents, high ratings for daring and low IQ. Violent boys have been found to be more likely to have experienced or witnessed extreme physical abuse (Lewis et al., 1980; Fitch & Papantonio, 1983). Abused children are also more likely to abuse alcohol (Fitch & Papantonio, 1983).

Widom (1989b) conducted a landmark study which sought to overcome the methodological weaknesses of earlier research. This included unambiguous definition of violence, a prospective design, separation of abused and neglected children and a demographically matched control group. She found that abused and neglected children had a significantly greater chance of arrest for delinquency, adult criminality and violent behaviour, these being significantly higher in the physically abused group, although none of these variables were as powerful as gender, age and ethnicity at predicting violence. An important caveat to this research is that while over one quarter of victims of abuse went on to offend, a significant number did not, raising important questions about resilience and other contributory factors. However, it is important to remember that Widom used the relatively blunt instrument of arrest which underestimates actual violence and criminality. The use of official arrest records has been shown to have limitations in recent community studies of violence and mental disorder (op. cit.).

Widom (1989b) stresses the need to distinguish between different forms of abuse and neglect. She suggests that some research indicates that neglected children appear to be more dysfunctional than abused children. According to Oliver (1993) 'A hated, despised, or emotionally broken child is more likely to become a dangerous parent than a beaten one' (p1316). Furthermore, the observation of violence has in some studies been demonstrated to have as many harmful effects on the child as actual physical abuse. Bandura, Ross, & Ross (1963) showed how children acquired aggressive behaviour by modelling themselves on their parents. Children who observed a violent adult, either on film or in vivo, were more likely to behave aggressively. Importantly, being the victim of abuse has been shown to be independent of the child's temperament (Dodge, Bates, & Pettit, 1990a; Weiss, Dodge, Bates, & Pettit, 1992).

Since then many studies have confirmed that childhood abuse leads to adult offending (Lewis, Mallouh, & Webb, 1989; Widom, 1989a; Rivera & Widom, 1990; Fergusson & Lynskey, 1997; Haapasalo & Kankkonen, 1997; Herrenkohl, Egolf, & Herrenkohl, 1997), for both men and women offenders (Lake, 1995). Lake (1993) found that early physical abuse was associated with earlier entry into crime and more diverse criminal activity in female inmates. In an examination of the cycle of violence hypothesis, Dutton & Hart (1992) conducted a case note study of 604 prison inmates. Men who were abused as children were three times more likely to engage in violence as adults compared with non-abused men. Additionally, specific forms of child abuse were associated with specific patterns of violent offending. Individuals who were physically abused were more likely to offend with physical violence and those who were sexually abused were more likely to offend sexually. This finding of the specificity of victimisation and perpetration of offending has been established elsewhere (Prentky, Knight, Sims Knight, & Straus, 1989; McCormack, Rokous, Hazelwood, & Burgess, 1992). Prentky et al. (1989) interviewed 82 sex offenders and collected case note information. They found that sexual and non-sexual violence were related to distinct developmental histories. Caregiver inconsistency and sexual deviation in family of origin was associated with severity of sexual violence, whereas institutional care and physical abuse and neglect in childhood was associated with severity of non-sexual violence. Tingle, Barnard, Robbins & Newman (1986) interviewed 64 sex offenders in prison and compared childhood antecedents of rapists and paedophiles. Rapists were more likely to come from disrupted families and to report physical abuse in their family of origin, whereas paedophiles were more likely to report close attachments to their mothers.

Reiss & Roth (1993) found that among people who have grown up in foster care, the likelihood of arrest for violence was correlated with the number of foster placements they experienced during childhood. Similarly, Muetzell (1995) investigated the development of 345 teenagers who were taken into care by social services in Stockholm, Sweden and compared them with a matched control group. Those in care were more likely to abuse alcohol and drugs, to have psychosocial problems and to be violent in their behaviour. Singleton et al. (1998) found that a quarter to a third of prison inmates in the UK reported being in local authority care as a child.

Parental alcoholism (particularly in the father) has been associated with violent offending (Moffitt, 1987; Rydelius, 1994) and recidivism among violent offenders (DeJong et al., 1992). A diagnosis of personality disorder in fathers was found to predict criminal involvement in sons, but not parental psychosis (Moffitt, 1987). Bergman & Brismar (1994) compared violent and non-violent alcoholics. Those who were assaultative reported more violence in childhood and fathers who had alcohol problems; and they had started drinking at a younger age. Weiler & Widom (1996) investigated the relationship between childhood victimisation, psychopathy and violence among 652 individuals who reported abuse and neglect as children, and compared them to a matched control group. Controlling for demographic factors as well as criminal history, those reporting abuse and neglect had significantly higher Psychopathy Checklist – Revised (PCL-R) scores and were more likely to be violent.

In an interesting series of studies Raine and colleagues (Raine, Brennan, & Mednick, 1994; Raine et al., 1996; Raine, Brennan, & Mednick, 1997) challenge the long-standing view among criminologists that biological factors play only a peripheral role in predisposing individuals to crime and that social factors are the principal determinant by proposing and testing a biosocial approach. Raine et al. (1994) studied a sample of 4,269 male participants. They recorded birth complications, and demographic, family, and psychosocial variables were collected through interviews during pregnancy and then when participants were one year old. They determined that birth complications in combination with early childhood rejection were associated with violent crime in early adulthood. This multidimensional model is consistent with research in developmental psychopathology, which has established that *single* risk factors in childhood rarely result in mental disorder in adulthood (Rutter, 1987; Rutter & Rutter, 1993).

Raine et al. (1996) studied a group of 397 individuals from birth and identified three groups of individuals: a group with obstetric risk factors only, a group with poverty risk factors only, and a biosocial group who had both early neuromotor deficits and unstable family environments. The last group were found to have more than twice the rate of crime (they accounted for 70% of all crimes committed by the whole sample), including both adult violence and theft, and had significantly more behavioural and academic difficulties in adolescence. Thus it is the clustering of biological and psychosocial factors which were reported as leading to offending.

Raine et al. (1997) identified several limitations in the 1994 study, namely that offending was previously measured at age 18. They extended the follow-up period to 34 years of age, thus trebling the sample of violent offenders and permitting a more detailed analysis of onset and type of violence, the form of maternal rejection and the effects of maternal mental disorder. The interaction between biological and psychosocial factors previously observed persisted for violent, but not for non-violent crime, suggesting very early risk factors unique to violent offending. The interaction also held for severe forms of violence, such as rape, robbery and murder, but not for less serious threats of violence, such as verbal threats. The biosocial interaction held for arrests for violent crime before age 18, but did not hold for individuals arrested for violence after age 18. According to the authors, this lends support to the notion of a relatively small group of individuals whose early onset of offending corresponds with lifelong antisocial personality problems. The authors were able to specify components of early maternal rejection which interact with birth complications. These consist principally of institutionalisation of the infant in the first year and an attempt to abort the foetus during pregnancy, rather than, for example, simply stating that they did not want the pregnancy. Maternal mental ill health had no effect.

Finally we turn to the intergenerational transmission of child abuse. A number of studies have confirmed that abused children are at significantly increased risk of abusing their children (Carroll, 1980; Milner, Robertson, & Rogers, 1990; Hemenway, Solnick, & Carter, 1994). The younger an individual is when they are abused, the higher is their potential to become an abuser (Milner et al., 1990). In a review of the literature, Oliver (1993) estimated that roughly one third of victims of child abuse grow up to repeat a pattern of seriously inept, neglectful or abusive parenting, a third do not, and the other third remain vulnerable to social stress which increases the likelihood of their engaging in abusive parenting practices.

4.2.2. Childhood Experiences, Mental Disorder and Violence

- *In this section we consider the specific relationship between mental disorder, childhood experiences and violence*

- *Studies of individuals with mental disorder have indicated that they have more frequently been the victims of childhood abuse and victimisation within families*

- *This area of research has particular methodological problems, including lack of adequate control groups. There is a dearth of prospective studies*

- *Nevertheless, studies of criminal and non-criminal individuals with severe mental disorder indicate similar background factors which increase the risk of adult violence compared to non-mentally disordered individuals*

Studies of individuals with mental disorder have indicated that they are more frequently the victims of childhood abuse and victimisation within families (Herman, Perry, & Van der Kolk, 1989; Gross & Keller, 1992; Convoy, Weiss, & Zverina, 1995; Kessler & Magee, 1994; Goodman et al., 1995) and that they are also more likely to be the victims of abuse as adults (Gilbert, El Bassel, Schilling, & Friedman, 1997). Surveys enquiring about the experience of being the victim of the range of different types of abuse among individuals with mental disorder report rates of up to 81% (Hiday et al., 1999). An important finding of research in developmental psychopathology is that, on the whole, a single negative event does not result in future mental disorder (Rutter & Rutter, 1993). Research on violence and mental disorder has tended to ignore childhood factors, and investigations into the childhood origins of the perpetration of violence have generally tended to ignore mental illness. However, studies on predictive factors of violence in those suffering from severe mental disorder have failed to explain why some individuals with constellations of symptoms which place them at high risk fail to act violently; and some attention has turned to studying childhood experiences in the mentally ill in particular. This area of study is fraught with methodological problems in that mental illness is strongly associated with poor premorbid functioning in a wide range of areas. Poor premorbid functioning may easily be confused with factors related to the development of delinquency (Heads, Taylor, & Leese, 1997).

Widom (1989b) refers to a few early studies which have examined the link between violence and neglect in psychiatric patients. Although findings have generally supported the association between early neglect and abuse and later violence, conclusions are hampered by methodological problems, in particular the universal lack of matched control groups providing baseline data. In one prospective study of 170 hospitalised children with psychiatric problems at age 12 or less, criminality in a parent and assaultative behaviour in the child predicted adult imprisonment at follow-up (Lundy, Pfohl, & Kuperman, 1993).

Several retrospective comparative studies have been conducted. Addad, Benezech, Bourgeios, & Yesavage (1981) compared criminal and non-criminal groups of people with schizophrenia. The former were more likely to have reported a negative relationship with their mothers, parental discord, a lack of affection from their parents and alcoholic fathers. In another comparative study, Hafner and Boker (1973) identified significantly higher rates of suicide, crime and alcoholism in the families of people with schizophrenia who had committed homicide or attempted murder. They also had increased premorbid levels of antisocial personality traits compared to a non-violent patient group. Yesavage et al. (1983) studied male inpatients with schizophrenia and found a positive correlation between severity of parental discipline, particularly from the father, family conflict and inpatient assaults. In the Klassen & O'Connor (1988a) study discussed earlier, those participants who had suffered injury at the hands of an adult prior to age 15 and whose parents had engaged in physical violence with others were at significantly greater risk of perpetrating violence when they were followed up.

Blomhoff, Seim, & Friis (1990) conducted a study of psychiatric inpatients and compared two groups on the basis of whether or not they were violent after admission. An increased level of violence in the family of origin was the only demographic variable which distinguished between the groups. Heads et al. (1997) conducted a case note study of the childhood experiences of 102 Special Hospital patients with schizophrenia and a history of violence. They identified four subgroups: individuals with early conduct disorder but unremarkable environmental disadvantage (primary delinquents), individuals with multiple early environmental disadvantage related to conduct problems (secondary delinquents), individuals with childhood neurotic problems without obvious environmental disadvantage, and finally individuals whose psychotic illness arose following an unremarkable childhood ('pure' schizophrenia). Participants in the primary and secondary delinquent groups had a significantly increased tendency to be frequently violent. There was no relationship between group membership and the seriousness of the violence, although those with 'pure' schizophrenia tended to be violent in response to psychotic symptoms. Glasser's (1996a) scheme seems particularly relevant in this context, since this research appears to indicate a continuum between different types of violence.

4.3. Conduct Disorder

- *Conduct disorder is defined as a repetitive and persistent pattern of behaviour involving the violation of major age-appropriate societal norms or rules and the basic rights of other individuals*

- *It is most frequently observed in boys with low IQ, poor co-ordination and motor skills and developmental delays. Socioeconomic status is an important correlate, and family characteristics include parental alcoholism, parental discord, severe punishment, abuse, neglect and personality disorder*

- *Two groups have been identified: an early onset and a late onset group. Research indicates that general behaviour patterns are remarkably unchanging, and that the later onset group tends to have a more benign course than early onset conduct disorder*

- *Conduct disorder has been strongly associated with later offending, both violent and non-violent. The relationship between conduct disorder and criminality may be mediated by substance abuse. The number of symptoms of conduct disorder in childhood has been found to predict the severity of later difficulties and violence*

DSM-IV defines conduct disorder as a repetitive and persistent pattern of behaviour involving the violation of major age-appropriate societal norms or rules and the basic rights of other individuals. This behaviour causes clinically significant impairment of social, academic and occupational functioning, and is present in a variety of settings, including home, school or community (American Psychiatric Association, 1994).

Based on a number of epidemiological surveys, Robins (1991) estimates the prevalence of conduct disorder in the general population to be between 3.2% and 6.9%, although the cultural relativity of the diagnosis is attested to by DSM-IV indicating rates of 6% to 16% for boys, and 2% to 9% for girls. There is considerable overlap in diagnosis between conduct disorder and attention deficit disorder (ADHD). Diagnostic systems (DSM-IV) recognise that conduct disorder is part of a developmental continuum with antisocial personality disorder (ASPD) in that both diagnoses cannot be made simultaneously (Robins, 1991). Conduct disorder is most frequently observed in boys with low IQ, poor co-ordination and motor skills, and developmental delays (Robins, 1991). Socio-economic status is an important correlate, and family characteristics include those described in the previous section including parental alcoholism, parental discord, severe punishment, abuse, neglect and personality disorder.

Childhood aggressive behaviour is a stable and detectable early personality characteristic (Loeber, 1982; Roff, 1992). Research indicates that for individuals identified early these general behaviour patterns are remarkably unchanging, whereas a later onset group appears to have a more benign course than early onset conduct disorder (Robins, 1991). Patterson & Yoerger (1993) define *early starters* as children arrested prior to age 14 and *late starters*, after 14. Studies of early starters indicate that they are more likely to reoffend and to have multiple arrests later, while late starters are less at risk of adult offending (Loeber, 1982; Patterson & Yoerger, 1993). Stattin & Magnusson (1989) illustrated these points in a prospective study of the relationship between aggressive behaviour in childhood and later delinquency in a sample of 1,027 boys and girls. Aggressiveness, measured by teacher ratings at ages 10 and 13, was highly predictive of adult criminality for males. Early aggressiveness was the strongest predictor. Particularly high ratings of aggression were associated with males who later committed violent offences and those who displayed criminal versatility. For females, ratings of aggressiveness were not associated with later offending until they reached the age of 13. This relationship was found to be independent of intelligence and family education.

Using the Epidemiologic Catchment Area survey data, Robins (1993) found a strong relationship between conduct disorder and both adult antisocial behaviour and substance abuse. There was a weaker, but nonetheless highly significant, relationship between conduct disorder and mental disorder. Robins also examined the hypothesis that the relationship between mental disorder and crime was simply a consequence of both of these factors being linked to conduct disorder. When conduct problems were controlled for, the strength of the relationship diminished, but remained significant. However, Robins found that if substance abuse was controlled for, the significance of the relationship was greatly reduced, suggesting that substance abuse is an important mediating factor for the relationship between conduct disorder and adult psychopathology. These findings were confirmed by Hodgins & Cote (1993b), who found a strong relationship between adult antisocial personality disorder and previous childhood conduct problems. Robins (1993) examined different elements of conduct problems to determine whether any were better predictors of later antisocial behaviour. Truancy, running away, vandalism and fighting were found to be significant, but lying and stealing were not. An important caveat to these findings is that many children with conduct disorder do not progress on to ASPD. One quarter with three symptoms of conduct disorder prior to age 15 went on to develop ASPD. Seventy one per cent of individuals with 8 or more symptoms before age 6 developed ASPD (Robins, 1991). Thus it appears that the number of childhood symptoms of conduct disorder, rather than a particular pattern of difficulties, predict adult problems (Maughan, 1993). The ECA study also established a link between conduct disorder and substance abuse disorders, schizophrenia, mania and obsessive-compulsive disorder (Robins, 1991).

Conduct disorder is an important predictor of adult offending. In fact, Robins (1993) found that conduct disorder predicted offending independent of mental disorder, antisocial behaviour and substance abuse. Findings from the Cambridge Study in Delinquent Development indicate that aggressiveness at age 8 rated by teachers predicted self reported violence at age 18 (Farrington, 1978). Farrington (1991) extended the follow-up period to age 32 and found that those who were aggressive in childhood and adolescence were also deviant as adults, more in conflict with their partners (including violence towards them), more likely to be unemployed, consumed more alcohol and illicit drugs, and committed more offences including violence.

Farrington (1991) raises the issue of the specialisation in violence of some offenders, arguing that this is in fact a relatively rare occurrence. He argues that many studies have established that the majority of offences committed by violent offenders are non-violent. Farrington (1978) found that violent offenders tend to commit many more crimes than non-violent offenders, which has also been established elsewhere (Guttridge, Gabrielli, Mednick, & Van Dusen, 1983; Piper, 1985). The findings that chronicity of offending tends to be associated with violent offenders suggests, according to Farrington (1991), that the difference between violent and non-violent offenders may be quantitative rather than qualitative, in turn suggesting a general syndrome of antisocial behaviour which arises in childhood and persists into adulthood.

Conduct disorder has also been associated with a wide range of poor prognostic outcomes such as marital break-ups and poor employment histories (Farrington, Gallegher, Morely, St Ledger, & West, 1988), higher mortality rate (Rydelius, 1988), higher school failure independent of IQ, financial dependency, and poor parenting of children (Robins, 1991). In their meta-analysis Loeber & Stouthamer-Loeber (1986) found that variables related to parenting – lack of involvement, rejection and lack of supervision – were better at predicting later conduct disorder and delinquency than parental criminality.

4.4. Attention Deficit Hyperactivity Disorder (ADHD)

- *Attention Deficit Hyperactivity Disorder (ADHD) is defined as a persistent pattern of inattention and/or hyperactivity-impulsivity which is more frequent and severe compared with the behaviour observed in other individuals at a similar level of development*

- *Pervasive hyperactivity/attention deficit is strongly associated with childhood aggression and has been shown to lead to later conduct problems*

- *Research has found that children with hyperactivity and conduct disorder have consistently been shown to be at increased risk of arrest and conviction in adulthood*

- *ADHD and conduct disorder have been related to different early background factors, the former having more cognitive handicaps, the latter having poor parenting and disrupted family functioning. Individuals with ADHD tend to have convictions at a young age, whereas conduct disorder is associated with self-reported delinquency, adult convictions and recidivism*

DSM-IV defines ADHD as a persistent pattern of inattention and/or hyperactivity-impulsivity which is more frequent and severe compared with the behaviour observed in other individuals at a similar level of development. It should be present for a number of years and interferes with social, academic or occupational functioning appropriate to the particular developmental stage (American Psychiatric Association, 1994).

Prevalence of ADHD is estimated at 3% to 5% (Cantwell, 1996). Pervasive hyperactivity/attention deficit is strongly associated with childhood aggression and has been shown to be related to later conduct problems. There is a high degree of comorbidity between ADHD and conduct disorder (Maughan, 1993). Research suggests that this comorbidity relates to individuals with early onset conduct disorder (Moffit & Silva, 1988; Farrington, Loeber, & Van Kammen, 1990). On the other hand, individuals with hyperactivity but with few conduct problems have been found to be less at risk of adult criminality (Mannuzza, Klein, & Bonagura, 1988).

Farrington et al. (1990) review literature on the long-term criminal outcome of ADHD, which indicates that children with hyperactivity and conduct disorder have consistently been shown to be at increased risk of arrest and conviction in adulthood (Satterfield, Hoppe, & Schell, 1982). In a longitudinal study, Weiss & Hechtman (1986) followed up 104 children with ADHD and compared them with a matched control group. At age 25 23% of participants who had ADHD as children had an antisocial personality disorder diagnosis, compared with 2% of participants in the control group. Dalteg & Levander (1998) studied the background of 75 juvenile delinquents with conduct disorder, 68% of whom were rated as previously suffering from ADHD. An estimated average of 1,000 offences were committed by each individual. Individuals with ADHD tended to have better psychosocial backgrounds, but more problems at school, elevated levels of criminality and worse social outcomes. While ADHD was related to the volume of crime and versatility, there were no differences in the number of violent offences committed by individuals previously identified with ADHD. Farrington et al. (1990) conducted a longitudinal survey of 411 boys. They found ADHD and conduct disorder to have independent effects on individuals having juvenile convictions, as well as chronic offending. ADHD and conduct disorder were related to different early background factors, the former with cognitive handicap, the latter with poor parenting and disrupted family functioning. Individuals with ADHD tended to have convictions at a young age, whereas conduct disorder was associated with self-reported delinquency, adult convictions and recidivism. ADHD and conduct disorder also had an interactive effect. Cantwell (1996) estimates that about 30% of individuals diagnosed as ADHD in childhood are developmentally delayed, but their symptoms remit in early adulthood. Approximately 40% continue to have functionally impairing symptoms later in life, accompanied by a variety of social and emotional difficulties. The other 30% of individuals continue to display symptoms of ADHD in adulthood, as well as developing more serious psychopathology, including substance abuse and personality disorder.

4.5. Peer Relations and Social Functioning

- *This area of research is associated with the field of developmental psychopathology which moves from a purely descriptive level to an explanatory one. Studies in this area have identified mediating factors between abuse and later offending*

- *Maltreated children have been found to respond with anger and aggression both to friendly gestures from other children and to signs of distress from peers. They have been found to have more difficulties in understanding negative affect, are deficient in social competence and display immaturity in their thinking, independent of IQ*

- *Abused children tend to be less attentive to relevant social cues in interpersonal situations and are inclined to attribute hostile intent to others. Researchers in this field posit overlapping pathways to violence and mental disorder*

Much of the research on peer relations and social functioning has taken place within the framework of developmental psychopathology. This field introduces a greater degree of complexity into the discussion of the link between particular factors in childhood and the outcome of violence or mental disorder by examining combinations of variables and risk factors in the context of the mediating role played by other elements. In doing so it moves from a purely descriptive level to an explanatory one. A detailed exposition of this literature is beyond the scope of this review, but a brief introduction to some of the main findings is given below.

Maltreated children have been found to be both aggressive and socially withdrawn (e.g. George & Main, 1979; Weiss et al., 1992). Weiss et al. (1992) conducted a prospective study with two cohorts of children at kindergarten. Harsh parental discipline was found to be associated with later aggressive and 'internalising' behaviour in children. This relationship was unaffected by confounders such as socio-economic status, child temperament and marital violence. Rogosch & Cicchetti (1994) identified a subgroup of children who had been maltreated, who were aggressive, withdrawn and exceedingly low in social competence. Maltreated children have been found to respond with anger and aggression both to friendly gestures from other children and to signs of distress from peers (Howes & Espinosa, 1985; Main & George, 1985; Klimes-Dougan & Kistner, 1990). Maltreated children have also been observed to respond to distress in peers by exhibiting fear and vacillating between comforting and attacking behaviour (Main & George, 1985).

Rogosch, Cicchetti, & Aber (1995) studied the links between child mal-treatment, early deviations in cognitive and affective processing and later difficulties in peer relations by comparing two groups of low-income indi-viduals who had or had not been maltreated as children. The maltreated group showed significantly more difficulties in understanding negative affect and displayed immaturity in their thinking. In their relationships with peers, maltreated children were deficient in terms of their social com-petence in relationships with children of the same age, which was shown to be independent of IQ. They were more likely to be avoided in social situations, isolated and rejected by their peers and displayed more aggres-sive behaviour.

Related to the literature on peer relations are investigations into the social cognitions of children with problematic peer relationships. Dodge and colleagues (1990a) investigated the relationship between childhood abuse, social-cognitive processes and aggressive behaviour in a prospective study of a representative sample of 309 children. Abused children were found to be less attentive to relevant social cues in interpersonal situations and tended to attribute hostile intent to others. These cognitive processes were shown to mediate the relationship between abuse and aggression. Physical abuse resulted in a three fold increase in the risk of chronic aggres-sive behaviour patterns in children when other demographic and child biological variables were held constant. Weiss et al. (1992) attributes the link between harsh discipline and aggression in their study to problematic social-cognitive processing. In another observational study of 774 six and eight year old boys Dodge, Price, Coie, & Christopoulos (1990b) showed that aggressive and antisocial behaviour usually takes place in dyadic peer relationships. Boys who were socially rejected by their peers were more likely to develop dyadic relationships in which mutual aggression took place.

Researchers in this field posit overlapping pathways to violence and mental disorder. For example, Kuperschmidt, Coie, & Dodge (1990) found that children who are rejected or neglected by peers are at risk of a number of later difficulties, including juvenile and adult offending, as well as psychopathology in adulthood.

4.6. Attachment

- *Attachment research overlaps with developmental psychopathology. From an attachment perspective, primary attachments lead to the internalisation of working models which represent complex interactions between the infant and its caregiver*

- *Early disruption of attachment results in later psychopathology and offending behaviour*

- *Observation of infant attachment behaviour has been linked to later patterns of attachment representation in adulthood. These representations have in turn been related to particular patterns of psychopathology and offending behaviour*

- *Research in this area is at an early stage. It potentially offers major insights into psychopathology and violent offending by shedding light on the mechanisms whereby abuse and neglect lead to later violence*

An overlapping area of study with the above is that of attachment research. This area of research is important because it has the potential to illuminate why some individuals with constellations of symptoms which place them at high risk, fail to act violently. It can also shed light on the nature of mediating processes involved in early disruptive experiences and later deviancy. The examination of human violence and trauma is shedding new light on the importance of human attachment (De Zulueta, 1993). From an attachment perspective, primary attachments lead to the internalisation of working models which represent complex interactions between the infant and its caregiver. These are replayed in all subsequent relationships and in attachment to others in later life. Thus early trauma results in predictably disturbed forms of later personal and interpersonal behaviour.

Bowlby (1944) recognised the potential of attachment theory to shed light on criminality and took a keen interest in the 'affectionless character' of those involved in early delinquency, and later psychopathy and offending behaviour. Yet it is only relatively recently that the growing area of lifespan research, and the increasing focus on the developmental nature of psychopathology, has returned to focus on the link between early trauma involving the disruption of early patterns of attachment and later offending behaviour. Some of this impetus has come from the development of the Adult Attachment Interview (AAI), an instrument which determines the way in which individuals linguistically represent their early attachment experiences. The AAI has successfully operationalised Bowlby's theoretical formulations and in so doing, is enlightening our understanding of psychological mechanisms underlying psychopathology in a clinically meaningful way.

4.6.1. The 'Strange Situation'

Mary Ainsworth and others developed Bowlby's ideas about the predisposition of humans and other animals to form attachments to their caregivers by studying infants in the 'Strange Situation' (Ainsworth, Blehar, Waters, & Wall, 1978). This involved exposing a young child to an unfamiliar place and person, parental separation and the experience of being alone with the stranger, and subsequent observation of the quality of the behaviour upon reunion with the parent. They identified secure and insecure attachment patterns as follows:

- Securely attached infants protested upon separation and responded positively to reunion, returning quickly to exploration and play.
- Insecure *avoidant* infants explored or played with little reference to the attachment figure and appeared to ignore the attachment figure upon reunion.
- Insecure *ambivalent* infants were highly distressed upon separation and found it difficult to stop protesting and settle upon reunion.
- A *disorganised* category was developed later to distinguish a group of insecurely attached infants who did not appear to have a coherent attachment strategy and demonstrated extremely disturbed and disorganised behaviour in relation to the attachment figure (Crittenden, 1988).

Securely attached one year-old infants were observed to be self-confident and to have the capacity to form satisfactory relationships and to treat other people with empathy. On the other hand, insecurely attached infants who had been emotionally deprived or abused tended to have little self-confidence, had difficulty relating to other people and related with hostility. Troy & Stroufe (1987) observed 19 pairs of children aged 4 and 5 who had previously been observed in the Strange Situation. Where one or both partners in play had previously been categorized as insecurely attached, victimisation between children took place. In these pairs the abuser was typically avoidantly attached and the victim was insecurely attached. Securely attached children were neither victims or abusers.

4.6.2. The Adult Attachment Interview

Main, Kaplan, & Cassidy (1985) shifted the focus of the study of attachment from the level of observation of parent-child interaction to the level of the representation of the parent-child relationship in the adult's mind. They developed the Adult Attachment Interview (AAI), which asks adult participants questions about their early experiences and categorises adults according to the attachment categories observed in the Strange Situation, though with different names (Secure, Dismissing, Preoccupied and Unresolved) (Main, 1991). The interview has been described as one of 'surprising the unconscious' (George, Kaplan, & Main, 1996). The basis of the interview is that primary attachments which lead to the internalisation of working models representing the complex interactions between the infant and its caregiver are replayed in all subsequent relationships and in attachment to others in later life.

There is a growing body of literature which has focused on non-offender populations. Much of this research has studied the predictive power of the AAI to determine infant Strange Situation behaviour from the response of the parent to the AAI, typically involving the mother. Van Ijzendoorn (1995) conducted a meta-analysis of 18 studies involving a total of 854 participants, and found a correspondence of 75% between adult representation and their infant's behaviour when categories were collapsed into a two-way classification of secure and insecure attachment patterns.

4.6.3. Attachment, Mental Disorder and Offending Behaviour

Van Ijzendoorn et al. (1997) investigated the relationship between attachment representation and personality disorder in 40 men in a Dutch forensic psychiatric hospital who had committed serious offences. They hypothesised that therapeutic progress was linked to attachment representation, in that the problems of therapeutic compliance in a forensic setting represent the repetition of parent-child attachment behaviour. They also predicted a relationship between certain types of personality disorder and patterns of attachment representation. For example, lack of parental affection may be found in schizoid individuals, and rejection and hostility on the part of the parent may characterise the early experiences of individuals who are paranoid, avoidant or anti-social. The authors used the AAI in combination with the Structured Interview for Disorders of Personality-Revised (SIDP-R) and the Dutch Forensic Staff-Patient Interaction Inventory (DFSI), the latter measure to assess the quality of the patients' interaction with staff. Van Ijzendoorn et al. (1997) found secure attachment patterns to be almost non-existent in the sample. The more insecurely attached participants were, the greater the number of personality disorder symptoms were identified. Dismissive and preoccupied attachment representation tended to be associated with different clusters of personality disorder, the preoccupied group tending to be more disturbed. Attachment insecurity was associated with patients rated by staff as 'angry dominant' and engaging in 'abuse of contact'.

In a related study, Holtzworth-Munroe, Stuart, & Hutchinson (1997) found that perpetrators of violence tended to be insecurely attached. They studied the attachment history of maritally violent and non-violent men. Most violent men were insecure in their attachment histories.

Fonagy, Target, Steele, & Steele (1997) discuss an almost completed study comparing prison hospital patients with matched psychiatric controls (Levinson & Fonagy, submitted). Inmates were either on remand or sentenced for a wide variety of offences including burglary, theft, handling stolen goods, damage to property, obtaining property and services by deception, gross indecency, possession of and intent to supply heroin, importation of drugs, grievous bodily harm, malicious wounding, multiple armed robbery, kidnapping, rape and murder (N=22). They were individually matched with non-psychotic inpatients. They report some striking similarities between attachment representation in a subgroup of the criminal group and borderline patients in the hospital sample, both groups receiving 'entangled' classifications (preoccupied), and extreme deprivation and abuse in childhood. The offender group could be subdivided on the basis of AAI classification into a dismissing, preoccupied subgroup and a more disturbed subgroup who were more likely to receive an unresolved or cannot classify categorisation. The offence characteristics of the first group were predominantly crimes against property, whereas those of the latter group were likely to be more serious offences, such as violence, rape and murder.

Two further studies have investigated the link between AAI responses and personality disorder. Fonagy et al. (1996) compared attachment representation in non-psychotic psychiatric patients with a matched control group. Psychiatric patients were more likely to be classified as preoccupied and unresolved. Borderline Personality Disorder (BPD) was associated with severe trauma and lack of resolution of the trauma. Patients with BPD were significantly lower on a scale measuring awareness of mental states. Patrick, Hobson, Castle, Howard, Maughan (1994) compared patients with BPD with a group diagnosed with dysthymia. BPD was associated with enmeshed and unresolved patterns of responding to the AAI. Stalker & Davies (1995) found female victims of sexual abuse to be insecure, having unresolved/disorganised attachment status.

Increasing attention is being paid to the disorganised category of insecurely attached infants. Carlson, Cichetti, Barnett, & Braunwald (1989) found maltreated infants to be frequently disorganised in their responses to primary caregivers. In the presence of attachment figures, maltreated infants displayed interrupted movements and expressions, dazing, freezing and stilling behaviours, and apprehension. Their caregivers have been observed to display inconsistent behaviour toward their infants and to be both frightened and frightening towards them (Main & Hesse, 1990).

4.6.4. Theoretical Issues

A number of theoretical issues arise from this framework. Raine et al. (1997) hypothesise that disruption of the mother-infant attachment process in the early stages of development can result in unempathic, affectionless, psychopathic interpersonal behaviour in the child which increases the likelihood of violence. From an attachment perspective, Bowlby (1944) identified the psychological state of protest associated with the disruption of early attachment, followed by despair which involves preoccupation, withdrawal and hopelessness. In addition to protest and despair, a third state, that of detachment, is regarded as particularly important in the study of mental disorder and criminality (Fonagy et al., 1997). Recovery from protest and despair are only apparent, and normal attachment behaviour is not resumed, the infant remaining self absorbed and detached. According to Bowlby (1944), psychopathy, violence and crime are primarily related to disorders of attachment and represent distorted attempts at interpersonal emotional exchanges. Fonagy et al. (1997) argue that disrupted attachment leads to an incapacity to represent the mental states of others (meta-cognitive reflective functioning) and the disavowal of other individuals leads to the lack of inhibition of violent impulses. Thus crime derives, in part, from lack of empathy which itself is a consequence of an inability to identify with other individuals because of disrupted early attachments.

Fonagy & Target (1999) offer a model of how physical or emotional abuse in childhood leads to later violence. First, the child's psychological self is damaged by the mother or primary caregiver's inability to treat the child as an intentional being whose behaviour is motivated by its own thoughts, feelings and desires. Second, as a result of this, the child uses aggression to defend their psychological self from an assumed hostile other. Third, because self expression and aggression are so regularly associated, they become pathologically fused. Finally, the inability to mentalise, to consider the other as having a mental life of their own, diminishes inhibition, because the victim is seen devoid of humanness.

Human nature requires that pain and violence be given meaning. In the face of disaster and helplessness the individual needs to feel guilty to regain a sense of control and from this arises the belief that they are in some way to blame for what has transpired (De Zulueta, 1996). Identification with the aggressor frees the individual from experiencing a sense of weakness and endows a sense of power, the passive experience being turned into an active one. Stoller (1975) views perversion as an effort at reversal of the trauma of childhood humiliation by triumphing over the humiliator. This is particularly true for the male victim. Female victims seem to internalise their control-seeking behaviour, whereas male victims are more likely to turn these outward with aggressive and antisocial behaviour (Summit, 1983).

A final point involves the transfer of aggression from the situation of the family, particularly the father, to wider society. Limentani (1991) states that 'the externalisation of aggression can find a suitable target in those persons who symbolise the superego, such as school authorities, political parties, the police, prison officers, nurses in psychiatric hospitals, social workers and so on' (p211). Fonagy et al. (1997) make a similar point. Bonds between children and parents get transferred to social institutions and adult figures representing them. When internal working models of attachment are distorted by adverse early experiences, various constellations of problematic behaviour ensue in a recreation of disrupted early attachment behaviour in the present.

4.7. The Institutional Response to Violence

- *We conclude this chapter with a discussion of the psychological dynamics of violence and the nature of communication between the violent offender and society. This aspect of the review is purely theoretical, rather than based on empirical research*

- *Being the victim of humiliation and shame is central to the early experiences of violent offenders. Violence leads to harsh treatment, which leads to more violence, in an endless vicious cycle of violence*

- *Based on Gilligan's work, we argue that prison serves a useful function by simultaneously fulfilling the wish for punishment and also the wish to be taken care of. The manner in which offenders are cared for in prison is brutal, which is reminiscent of the care (or lack of it) they received in the past. Being in prison conceals the wish to be cared for and the whole political establishment with all its institutions unwittingly colludes with this*

We conclude this chapter with a discussion of the nature of communication between the violent offender, the institutions they become part of, and society, and the resulting psychological dynamics arising between these individuals and institutions. This is a purely theoretical discussion and is not based on empirical research.

Aggression is transferred from the adult figures of childhood to social institutions, heralding a conflictual exchange between the offender and society. The perpetrator of violence becomes the victim of a cruel and per-secuting system, paradoxically recreating the circumstances of their experience of being on the receiving end of punishment. Thus, one of the basic assumptions of current thinking about crime and criminal justice policy – that the problem can be solved by teaching the perpetrator the dif-ference between right and wrong through punishment – is fundamentally flawed. Statements by politicians that 'prison works', that 'it is time to understand less and condemn more', and the requirement to be 'tough on crime' through the creation of an ever more hostile and punitive penal environment may therefore collude with the very pathology that leads criminals to arrive at their destinations in the first place. Harsh penal con-ditions have been found not to affect recidivism rates (MacKenzie, 1991).

Gilligan (1996) argues that the external conditions of incarceration per-petuate the notion in the minds of offenders that it is something external that needs to change and draws attention away from their own internal state of violence. If the environment were more humane it could assist these men in recognising that the source of their intolerable distress is rooted in the internal world of their memories and fantasy. Being the victim of humiliation and shame is central to the early experiences of violent offenders. Punishment leads to greater shame. The more violent people are, the more harshly they are treated, and the more harshly they are treated, the more violent they become in an endless vicious cycle of violence (Gilligan, 1996). Glasser's notion of sadistic violence illustrates that the aim of the perpetrator is not simply to triumph over the abuser from their own past, but also to gratify a perverse desire for punishment. The act of violence and its punishment therefore fulfil the circle of the sado-masochistic wish, the perpetrator occupying both the position of per-petrator and victim. The two positions are therefore entirely interchangeable.

The issue of dependence is central to the perpetration of violence. Not far beneath the surface, these individuals want desperately to be taken care of. However, acknowledging this wish is completely unacceptable, for revealing vulnerability is deeply humiliating and to be avoided at all costs. Prison serves a very useful function for these men because it simultaneously fulfils the wish for punishment and also the wish to be taken care of. The manner in which care is provided in prison is often brutal, which is remi-niscent of the care (or lack of it) experienced in the past. Being in prison conceals the wish to be cared for very well, and the political establishment, with all its institutions, unwittingly colludes with this. To quote Gilligan (1996), 'violent behaviour accomplishes the return of the repressed wishes to be loved and taken care of by others, but in a way that is face-saving, so that a man who feels ashamed can tolerate letting those wishes be gratified;

and it is face-saving because violent behaviour is the mirror-image, the exact reversal, of those wishes' (p119). Violence as a symptom therefore both expresses and conceals that wish. It is a compromise formation, having both an expressive and defensive function. Difficulties with engagement with violent men relate to problematic attachments and their denial of feelings of vulnerability and dependence. When issues of attachment arise, they are felt to be unbearable.

In the context of the earlier discussion of attachment, insecure attachment patterns which persist into adulthood are played out between the offender and the institution. The multi-disciplinary team in the context of secure hospitals, or prison officers in the prison context, advertently or inadvertently, replace the caregivers/abusers from the past. The strength with which disturbed attachments from the past are recreated invites the carers/incarcerators to partake in a repetition of that abuse, potentially gratifying conscious and unconscious wishes in *all parties*, which can lead to organisational ill-health. Considerable competence is required if professional carers are to create conditions which allow development and growth rather than the repetition of earlier damaging cycles.

CHAPTER 5

PREDICTION INSTRUMENTS

> *In this chapter we describe three actuarial schemes used to identify factors associated with the risk of future violence. These include the HCR-20, the Violence Risk Appraisal Guide, and the MacArthur Risk Assessment Study*

As knowledge about the prediction of risk has improved, there has been a growing interest in the development of risk scales which have the potential for increasing the accuracy of risk assessment. The purpose of these scales is to structure and standardise the process of risk assessment and thereby offer a more systematic approach to the prediction of violence. However, there have been few attempts to adopt risk assessment instruments in routine clinical practice (Belfrage, 1998b). They remain primarily research instruments which are largely ignored by clinicians (Steadman, et al., in press). In this section we briefly review three schemes for the prediction of risk.

5.1. HCR-20

> - *This is a checklist of 20 items which is divided into historical, clinical and risk management domains*
>
> - *The checklist has not been evaluated prospectively, but preliminary research shows promise*

The HCR-20 is probably the best known risk assessment instrument. It was first published in 1995 (Webster, Eaves, Douglas, & Wintrup, 1995) and was revised in 1997 (Webster et al., 1997). It is the outcome of a project funded by the British Columbia Forensic Psychiatric Services

Commission in Canada and represents the outcome of an up-to-date amalgamation of current research and thinking on violence and mental disorder. The HCR-20 is continually being updated and the most recent revision represents work in progress. The authors are attempting to improve the administration and coding procedure and are in the process of evaluating the inter-rater reliability and predictive validity of the instrument.

The HCR-20 is a checklist of 20 items which are considered risk factors for violent behaviour. These are divided between 10 past ('Historical') factors, 5 present ('Clinical') factors, and 5 future ('Risk Management') factors. According to Webster et al. (1997), an important aspect of the HCR-20 approach is the inclusion of past, present and future considerations, static historical factors being weighted equally with present clinical and future risk management variables. Figure 1 reproduces Webster et al.'s (1997) scheme for the revised version.

The Psychopathy Checklist – Revised (PCL-R) is included as an item in the HCR-20 (H7). As discussed previously, the PCL-R is in itself a highly valid predictor of violence (see section 3.8). A screening version of the PCL-R is also in use which is quick and easy to administer and has been found to be valid and reliable (PCL-SV). It requires relatively little time and effort, and training in administration and scoring (see Hart, Hare & Forth; 1994).The HCR-20 also follows the format of the PCL-R, items being scored 0 (No), 1 (Maybe) and 2 (Yes).

The validity of the HCR-20 has not yet been evaluated thoroughly in prospective studies, but preliminary findings of research indicate positive results. The measure has been found to have good inter-rater reliability (Pearson correlations of between 0.80 and 0.82) (Belfrage, 1998b; Douglas, Ogloff, Nicholls & Grant, 1998). Douglas & Webster (1999) report an unpublished study by Wintrup (1996) in which 80 forensic psychiatric patients were coded on the HCR-20 and the PCL-R. Correlations between both these measures and violence averaged just below $r=.30$. The HCR was more strongly linked to readmission to forensic hospital ($r=.38$) and to psychiatric hospitalisation ($r=.45$) than to violence at follow-up. The PCL-R was not as strongly related to these indices as the HCR. Douglas & Webster report the results of another unpublished study in which Douglas, et al. (1998) followed up 279 discharged psychiatric patients over two years. They found the HCR to be highly predictive of violence after discharge. Strand, Belfrage, Fansson & Levander (1999) conducted a retrospective study of 40 mentally disordered offenders, one group having reoffended and the other not. Results showed a high overall predictive validity of the HCR-20, although contrary to expectations, historical data had none, or low validity, while clinical and risk management data had

Historical (Past)	Clinical (Present)	Risk Management (Future)
H1. Previous violence	**C1.** Lack of insight	**R1.** Plans lack feasibility
H2. Young age at first violent incident	**C2.** Negative attitudes	**R2.** Exposure to destabilisers
H3. Relationship instability	**C3.** Active symptoms of major mental illness	**R3.** Lack of personal support
H4. Employment problems	**C4.** Impulsivity	**R4.** Non-compliance with remediation attempts
H5. Substance use problems	**C5.** Unresponsive to Treatment	**R5.** Stress
H6. Major mental illness		
H7. Psychopathy		
H8. Early maladjustment		
H9. Personality disorder		
H10. Prior supervision failure		

FIGURE 1: HCR-20 ITEMS FROM Webster et al. (1997)
Copyright © 1997 by the Mental Health, Law, and Policy Institute, Simon Fraser University, Burnaby, British Columbia, Canada, V5A 1S6. All rights reserved. Reproduced by permission.

high validity. However, this is probably due to the highly selected sample of participants (forensic patients) most of whom had a high score on historical variables. In the only study of released prison inmates, Douglas & Webster (1999) retrospectively investigated the relationship between the HCR-20, the VRAG (see below), the PCL-R and past violence in 75 prison inmates who were identified as requiring mental health care while in custody. The HCR was more strongly predictive of past violence than the other two measures. Scores above the median on the HCR resulted in a four fold increase in the odds of past violence and antisocial behaviour. According to Webster et al. (1997), there are a number of large-scale prospective studies currently underway in general and forensic settings. The authors caution that at present it is a research instrument and an *aide mémoire* rather than a scale that should be routinely used in clinical practice.

5.2. Violence Risk Appraisal Guide (VRAG)

> • *The VRAG is a list of 12 predictor variables which have indicated predictive potential on the basis of longitudinal research*
>
> • *The advantage of the VRAG is that variables are weighted according to their importance in predicting violence. An individual score is placed in one of nine categories of risk each of which is associated with a per centage chance of violent offending within seven and ten years*

Following a series of studies investigating the link between a variety of variables and violent recidivism, Harris et al. (1993) combined samples and common variables in the construction of a statistical prediction instrument, originally named the Risk Assessment Guide (RAG) and later the VRAG (Rice & Harris, 1995b). They report the results of this, based on a seven year follow-up of 618 men who had been treated or assessed in a maximum security forensic hospital following the commission of serious criminal offences.

The researchers compiled a list of 12 predictor variables in their instrument. A high score on the Psychopathy Checklist (PCL), separation from parents before age 16, never having been married, lack of adjustment at primary school, failure on prior conditional release, a history of property offences, being relatively young at index offence, a history of alcohol abuse and diagnosis of personality disorder all significantly predicted violent recidivism. Victim injury in index offence, diagnosis of schizophrenia, and female victim in index offence were negatively predictive. The accuracy with which they were able to classify participants was 75%.

Quinsey et al. (1998) describe the clinical application of the VRAG. They provide an appendix for scoring individuals according to the 12 predictor variables. Scores then enable the rater to assign an individual to one of nine categories according to their level of risk. Each of these categories is associated with a per centage chance of violent recidivism within seven and ten years. The VRAG has also proved valid for the prediction of violent recidivism among sex offenders (Rice & Harris, 1997). Quinsey et al. (1998) report the compiling of a prediction instrument for sexual offending, the Sex Offender Risk Appraisal Guide (SORAG).

Rice & Harris (1995b) recommended anchoring clinical judgement with the use of actuarial data and combining this with dynamic (i.e. changeable) variables such as treatment progress, change in cognitive distortions associated with offending and level of supervision included in the release plans in order to adjust the actuarial prediction. However, Quinsey et al. (1998) have recently altered their position and now recommend that these 'clinical' variables be eliminated and risk appraisal should be based solely on actuarial data.

5.3. MacArthur Risk Assessment Study

- *A range of variables thought to be predictive of future violence have been considered under four headings: dispositional, historical, contextual and clinical factors*

- *Recent developments based on the study involve the classification tree approach which shows promise*

The ongoing MacArthur Risk Assessment Study is assessing a large sample of psychiatric patients on a wide range of variables which have shown promise as predictors of violence. These risk factors fall into four generic 'domains' as follows: *dispositional, historical, contextual and clinical* factors (Steadman et al., 1994). A list of factors within each of these domains is presented in Figure 2. The study is investigating the relationship between the variables in each of the domains and the criterion variable of violence in the community. The advantage of this scheme is that it incorporates both risk assessment and management goals of the research, all domains being concerned with risk assessment. However, only contextual and clinical domains are the concern of risk management, since dispositional and historical factors are given and cannot be managed.

Steadman, et al. (in press) argue that there are two reasons for actuarially based risk assessment tools not being routinely adopted in clinical practice. First, most assessment procedures are based on the principle that a single solution fits all cases in which an individual's risk of violence is being evaluated, but clinicians do not believe this to be valid. Second, while assessment tools do improve upon chance, the magnitude of this improvement is not viewed as clinically significant. Based on their work in the MacArthur Risk Assessment Study, Steadman, et al. (in press) propose a model of risk assessment based on the *classification tree* approach which addresses these two problems. This approach is characterised by an interactive and contingent model of violence in which different combinations of risk factors can classify an individual as high or low risk. The approach involves questions being asked during the clinical assessment which depend on the answers given to previous questions. The classification tree establishes a sequence in which all individuals are asked an initial question. Further questions are contingent on the individual's answer to the previous question. Then a second question is asked, and so on, until each subject is classified according to their risk. This is fundamentally different from the traditional *linear* approach, in which all individuals are asked a common set of questions, and answers are given fixed weights to produce a score indicating the level of risk posed by an individual. The authors illustrate this approach empirically using data from the MacArthur Risk Assessment Study. They regard the approach as being closer to the practical situation of clinical risk assessment. They have developed a version of the tool which uses factors routinely collected in clinical practice, or are generally easily obtained from hospital records (Monahan, Steadman, Appelbaum, Robbins, Mulvey, Silver, Roth & Grisso; in press). The objective of this method is to provide a dichotomous assessment of risk, indicating individuals as being either high or low risk. The process of risk assessment according to the classification tree approach involves working through more than one tree and classifying each individual as being low or high risk on several of these. Some individuals may not be classified on the first tree. For example, Monahan, et al. (in press) use three trees. Those not classified on the first were classified in the second, and those not classifiable in the second, were classified in the third. For a detailed exposition of this approach, see Monahan, et al. (in press) and Steadman, et al. (in press), both due for publication in 2000.

Much research on prediction instruments remains to be undertaken. Additional research is required to determine whether the validity of actuarial prediction generalises to other populations (Monahan, 2000). In particular, the classification tree approach, named by the authors as the Iterative Classification Tree (ICT) is in the early stages of development. The goal would presumably be a sophisticated range of variables for different populations and settings, including community-based and forensic patients, and short and long term prediction of risk.

1. Dispositional Factors

    Demographic
       Age
       Gender
       Race
       Social Class

    Personality
       Personality Style
       Anger
       Impulsiveness
       Psychopathy

    Cognitive
       IQ
       Neurological Impairment

2. Historical Factors

    Social History
       Family History
          Child rearing
          Child abuse
          Family deviance
       Work History
          Employment
          Job perceptions
       Educational History

    Mental Hospitalisation History
       Prior Hospitalisations
       Treatment Compliance

History of Crime and Violence
    Arrests
    Incarcerations
    Self-reported violence
    Violence toward self

3. Contextual Factors

    Perceived stress

    Social support
       Living arrangements
       Activities of daily living
       Perceived support
       Social networks

    Means for violence (i.e. guns)

4. Clinical Factors

    Axis I diagnosis

    Symptoms
       Delusions
       Hallucinations
       Symptom severity
       Violent fantasies

    Axis II diagnosis

    Functioning

    Substance Abuse
       Alcohol
       Other Drugs

FIGURE 2: DOMAINS IN THE MACARTHUR RISK ASSESSMENT STUDY (Steadman et al., 1994)
Reproduced by permission.

CHAPTER 6

EVALUATION

Research on violence and mental disorder has made significant advances recently and is increasingly influencing clinical practice. Nevertheless, a number of notable limitations remain which we discuss in this chapter

The field of violence and mental disorder has undergone significant advances in recent years and research undertaken in this area has made many important contributions to clinical practice. Nevertheless, there are a number of notable limitations which will now be discussed.

6.1. Diagnosis versus Active Symptoms

- *The focus on diagnostic categories as predictors of future violence has been narrow and restrictive*

- *Recent research which examines constellations of symptoms and their relationship with risk is more productive*

Recent research confirms our view that the focus on diagnosis has been unhelpful. According to Mulvey (1994), it is the presence of active symptomology rather than mental disorder per se which is a risk factor for violence. The relationship between violence and mental disorder is best considered as a dynamic process which places certain people at elevated risk at different times, possibly as a result of a particular constellation of symptoms and beliefs. Future research is likely to focus on the relationship between symptom patterns and violence rather than diagnostic categories

(Monahan, 2000). In our opinion this will provide much more useful information and points toward a more productive paradigm, rather than the narrow and restrictive focus on diagnosis alone. The move away from the medical model is welcomed.

6.2. Relevance to Clinical Practice

- *The problem of actuarial research on risk having a limited effect on clinical practice remains. Considerable work needs to be undertaken to make empirical research relevant to clinical practice and thereby persuade clinicians to adopt these methods*

- *There is an inherent limitation to empirical approaches which predict the behaviour of an individual on the basis of generalisations about a population*

Despite the accuracy of actuarial methods, clinicians tend to avoid their use (Gardner, Lidz, Mulvey, & Shaw, 1996b), as they question the relevance of statistical findings of academic researchers (Webster & Cox, 1997). 'The challenge in what remains of the 1990s' argue Webster & Cox, 'is to integrate the almost separate worlds of research on the prediction of violence and the clinical practice of assessment. At present the two worlds scarcely intersect' (p1).

The epidemiological nature of the research on violence and mental disorder tends to lack an individual focus and explains little about the dynamic interaction between processes both within an individual and in their interactions with others. The empirical approach which identifies the presence or absence of violence risk factors tends to seem to clinicians to be removed from the clinical context. Realistic concerns are frequently raised about a particular individual's risk who does not fulfil actuarial criteria indicating potential for violence. Glasser (1996a) points out the inherent limitation of an actuarial approach which is based upon generalisations about a population, but which clinicians wish to use to predict the behaviour of a specific individual who is a member of that population. Hinshelwood (1999) describes the retreat into a 'scientific attitude' when faced with difficult patients. The complex difficulties of the patient are dealt with by adopting an objective, scientific approach which blinds the clinician from the subjective experiences of the patient.

Webster & Cox (1997) make a number of recommendations to assist in drawing together actuarial research and clinical practice. They suggest that nomothetic and idiographic material should be balanced and that a single method should not be solely relied upon. Summary results should be presented in a simple visual way to assist interpretation. Case studies could be used to illustrate actuarial points raised. The logic of risk assessment should be explicated and a balanced scientist-practitioner model should be presented.

6.3. Theoretical Limitations

- *The lack of theory in the highly empirical field of violence and mental disorder is posited as a possible reason for the lack of intersection between research and clinical practice*

- *A relevant theory needs to address biological, socio-economic and conscious and unconscious psychological factors*

One possible reason for the lack of intersection between the worlds of research and clinical practice is that the field of violence and mental disorder is highly empirical, but lacking in theoretical formulations at a psychological level which link these empirical observations. There have been some attempts at theoretical formulation, such as the models offered by Novaco (1994) and Hiday (1995), but in our view these remain fairly superficial and do not explain the dynamic interaction between severe mental disorder, developmental factors and violence. For example, Hiday emphasises the social context of poverty and disorganisation, but does not address the issue of individual differences within the same social context in the expression of violence. Lacunae in this model are background factors, including developmental issues and early childhood experiences. Childhood factors are known to be important in the aetiology of personality disorder (e.g. Fonagy, et al., 1996) and there is an elevated comorbidity of personality disorder among the mentally ill. A comprehensive theory would therefore need to address biological, psychological, developmental and socio-economic factors in the aetiology of violence and mental disorder as outcomes in themselves, as well as in combination with one another. There is a need to address both conscious and unconscious processes associated with the expression of violence. The stress vulnerability models which have been developed with schizophrenia (Nuechterlein & Dawson, 1984; Clements & Turpin, 1992; Warner, 1994) may provide one such overarching theoretical framework within which these factors could be linked.

All fields require that the scope of study be limited, and therefore the boundaries of an area of study are defined by those who are involved in it. However, this process of outlining the perimeter of a field of study is not undertaken in a vacuum, but is highly dependent on the context of the dominant paradigm in the field. This issue is therefore related to the earlier discussion of the formulation of diagnostic categories. The dominant paradigm in this field is undoubtedly an empirical one and its concern is for observable phenomena rather than for underlying psychological processes. While this focus serves the useful purpose of managing vast amounts of information, in our view one impediment to psychological theoretical development in this area is that violence tends to be investigated in isolation from other outcomes (for example, suicide). This necessary limitation of scope may be valid at the level of observable phenomena, but categories imposed by researchers in this field may not reflect underlying processes which are important from a theoretical point of view.

These limitations may require both new theoretical developments, and the use of alternative research methodology (Denzin & Lincoln, 1994; Richardson, 1996). Thus, recent theoretical developments in the area of metacognition, derived from the work of Flavell (1979), holds some promise in terms of developing more sophisticated psychological formulations[1] linking violence and mental health problems, as well as suggesting particular psychological interventions (Teasdale, 1993; Padesky, 1994; Pretzer, 1994; 1996; Ryle, 1997; Nelson, Stuart, Howard & Crowley, 1999). With regard to alternative research methodologies, a good example utilising the idiographic method of case studies, rather than using large scale empirical research, is that of Perelberg (1999) who arrives at a rather different conceptualisation, examining violence and suicide as arising from a similar source[2].

The issue of theoretical limitations is not simply conceptual, but is also empirical. While some association between mental disorder and violence has been established, there is no firm evidence for causality. Monahan (2000) notes that data is absent on the causal pathways which result in the association between violence and mental disorder. Magnusson & Bergman (1990) point out that one central characteristic of developmental research is that it is *variable oriented*. In other words, it is particular variables which are the object of interest. Although undoubtedly important, serious problems are raised from a theoretical and empirical point of view, in that variable-oriented research does not address the interaction between various components. Little research has been undertaken which examines longitudinally why some individuals with severe mental disorder are violent, whereas the vast majority are not. Out of a large population of individuals

---

[1] A psychological formulation involves an analysis, based on theory and research, of information collected about an individual. This analysis should provide an understanding of the nature of the current problem(s), and its historical, developmental, social and cultural context.
[2] For a full discussion of the nature of the theoretical link between violence and suicide, see Perelberg (1999).

who experience persecutory delusions, only a small proportion act upon these. Important questions concerning developmental issues in the mentally disordered, and theoretical links with others who are violent, but are not labelled as suffering from a mental disorder remain unanswered. Raine et al.'s (1997) biosocial interaction findings, which apply to a distinct category of violence, raise questions as to whether different types of violence have unique aetiological pathways. Indeed, it is entirely possible that research investigating people with particular patterns of violence regardless of whether they are also diagnosed with a mental health disorder may prove more fruitful.

According to Robert Oppenheimer, 'It is a profound and necessary truth that the deep things in science are not found because they are useful; they are found because it was possible to find them' (cited in Marshall, Laws, & Barbaree, 1990, p5). Clearly, such a degree of sophistication requires expensive research which may prove difficult to undertake.

6.4. Cultural Context of Research

- *Most research has been undertaken in the USA, Canada and in Scandinavian countries where base rates of violence are different from those of the UK. Consequently, the contribution of violence by the mentally disordered to the overall level of violence in the society is different from the UK*

- *The clinical application of knowledge based on research to risk assessment in any particular society should be cautiously applied*

- *Context specific research should be undertaken in order to support risk assessment in that context*

Studies from different parts of the world are consistent in their findings of the link between violence and mental disorder. However, the strength of association depends on the social context and the results of a particular investigation represents the average association found in that particular context. Research may therefore say more about where the studies have been undertaken than about the actual link (Link & Stueve, 1995).

Most research has been undertaken in the USA, Canada and some in Scandinavian countries, but only a handful of high quality studies have been carried out in the UK. The contribution of violence by the mentally disordered varies according to the overall level of violence within that community. The USA has a much greater prevalence of violence than in the UK, and studies carried out in the USA have utilised highly selected populations (Prins, 1990). On the other hand, the quality of official records in Scandinavian countries is thought to be unequalled in the world, strengthening the validity and reliability of these findings. However, these are distinctive societies with relatively homogenous populations, low crime rates and uniform prosperity. Their criminal justice systems and health and social services are different in character, and attitudes concerning the disposal of the violent and the mentally disordered are also different (Marzuk, 1996).

The prediction of risk is exceedingly complex. Different individuals with the same diagnosis may behave differently under particular social conditions, age, gender, cultural background, etc. Therefore the clinical application of knowledge based on research to risk assessment in any particular society should be cautiously generalised to other contexts. Context specific research should be undertaken in order to support risk assessment in a particular context.

In a more general sense, Mulvey & Lidz (1995) are critical of the context-free approach to prediction of risk and the use of risk assessment algorithms which function as if particular factors are consistent across contexts. The clinician is not a 'consistent, cue–utilising, rational problem solver'. They suggest a 'conditional model' which proposes that the prediction of the risk of violence be based on assessing what particular type of violence the individual will engage in and under what circumstances.

6.5. Ethical Issues

- *Risk assessment has profound ethical implications because of the conflict between protecting the community from violence on the one hand, and the curtailment of liberty on the other*

- *Risk assessment takes place within a socio-political context which determines the way in which the assessment is conducted, as well as the consequences of it*

- *Risk assessment has significant implications for patients and their families in terms of the consequences of being labelled. These issues highlight the need for practitioners to have an up-to-date knowledge of the literature, in order that risk assessment may be undertaken to the highest level of accuracy possible*

Risk assessment raises some of the most important ethical issues in mental health, and the duty to avoid harm being done to patients and others frequently comes into conflict with individual liberties and freedom. It is not so much the prediction of violence which is the issue, but rather the consequences of such an assessment which is critical, because of the curtailment of liberty. These issues are particularly pertinent at a time when preventative detention is being considered for individuals who are not necessarily treatable but are detained purely to protect the public. According to Eastman (1999), this legislation will be framed within a health order so that article 5 of the European Convention on Human Rights can be satisfied. This specifies that the only condition of preventatively detaining unconvicted people is that they are judged to be of 'unsound mind'. This will necessitate that specialist secure services are legally defined as 'hospitals', despite their regimes being concerned with management and containment rather than treatment.

Risk assessment does not take place in a vacuum, but is conducted within a socio-political context, which has practical implications both for the outcome of the assessment itself and for the consequences of that assessment in terms of how individuals deemed potentially dangerous are managed. Recent high profile cases of homicide and consequent inquiry reports may encourage the over-prediction of dangerousness, and in some cases resultant detention. A related issue is that individuals deemed at risk should be allocated the necessary resources to ameliorate symptoms which place that individual at risk.

Attaching a label of dangerousness is dangerous in itself (Shaw, 1973). Risk assessment may have substantial social, psychological and economic costs for patients and their families. A label of being at high risk of violence is easy to attach and difficult to remove, and contributes to its own perpetuation (Scott, 1977). According to Bingley (1997), there are bound to be a certain proportion of individuals assessed as being potentially dangerous who are not (false positives), and others who are thought not to be at risk who are (false negatives), 'How many false positives is society prepared to accept in pursuit of a social goal?' (p28). All sex offenders serving a sentence could be detained for the rest of their lives which would prevent a significant number of future offences, but the societal costs in terms of liberty of such preventative detention would be significant, particularly in a political climate which encourages overcautious risk assessment.

The statistical prediction of risk, which involves the identification of violence potential by group membership, raises the important issue of how to treat actuarial information and how significant a part of the role of risk assessment this is given (Bingley, 1997). Demographic factors are known to be better predictors of violence than mental disorder itself. If it is known that most violent crime is committed by young, economically deprived men, does this imply that individuals with these characteristics should be imprisoned? This is particularly important when considering the strong association between socio-economic status and race and ethnicity.

Actuarial prediction of dangerousness is a relatively new field, and it is by no means an exact science. Recall Gunn's (1993) point that while prediction may correctly identify the vast majority of individuals who later commit a violent act, its specificity is low. In other words, two out of three patients are unnecessarily detained, which raises important civil liberties issues. Even if they are not detained, a label of dangerousness has potentially disastrous consequences for an individual. Labelling is a particular concern within the actuarial framework, since the most significant aspect of prediction is based upon historical variables (for example, a history of institutional care) which are fixed and invariable and consequently may damn some people for life. Blackburn (1998) is critical of the notions of antisocial personality disorder and psychopathy, since these reflect the 'nothing works' view of offender rehabilitation, and may be regarded in some quarters as more of a moral judgment than a clinical concept.

The sharing of information between agencies raises the issue of breaking confidentiality if clinicians acquire information which relates to risk. Clearly it is important to protect individuals from significant harm. However, in an increasingly litigious environment with little toleration for risk, there is a danger of patient consent and confidentiality being undermined. The Tarasoff decision and its aftermath in the USA (see section 1.6.) is becoming increasingly the norm in the UK.

These issues highlight the need for practitioners to have an up-to-date knowledge of the literature in order that risk assessment may be undertaken to the highest level of accuracy possible (Milner & Campbell, 1995). The consequence of risk assessment and the potential costs make it imperative that prediction becomes a more exact science through more research and attention to the interface between academic investigation and clinical practice.

6.6. Compression of Morbidity

- *The period of time in which mentally disordered individuals are at increased risk of committing violence may be significantly less than for the rest of the population*

- *Findings of the increased risk of violence posed by the mentally disordered may therefore be underestimated*

According to Mackenbach, Kunst, Lautenbach, Bijlsma, & Oei (1995), the methodology of cause–elimination life tables, which chart life expectancy and death by a variety of different causes, makes the assumption that various causes of death are statistically unrelated to one another, so that the mortality rates of individuals who are saved from a particular outcome which is eliminated equals the risk of dying from other causes observed in the general population. Robertson (1987) conducted a 23 year follow up of deaths among mentally disordered offenders. A quarter of these deaths were unnatural, involving either suicide or accidental death. Men in most age groups were two to three times more likely to commit suicide than the general population. Since the population of individuals who are violent shares characteristics with those more likely to die relatively early in life (and are therefore taken out of circulation), odds ratios may not reflect the true extent of increased risk since violent people are different in many respects from the general population they are being compared with, even when socio–economic status and other variables are controlled for. Violent people are also more likely to spend periods in hospital and prison, therefore further reducing the time at risk of violence. Violence and mental disorder are studied in isolation from other outcomes, yet the factors studied are the same as in the study of many other outcomes. The time at risk of offending for mentally disordered individuals may therefore be significantly less than that of the rest of the population and findings of the increased risk of violence posed by the mentally disordered may be underestimates.

CHAPTER 7

CONCLUSIONS: IMPLICATIONS FOR POLICY PRACTICE AND FUTURE RESEARCH

This chapter considers the implications of research on public policy and clinical practice. Directions for future research in the field are discussed

Studies using very different designs with varying degrees of strengths and weaknesses have, with few exceptions, established a link between violence and mental disorder. While the reliance on self-report and retrospective data raises questions about the reliability of community-based epidemiological studies, the prospective arrest-rate studies based on official records, although flawed, present similar findings overall. Specific arguments about the weaknesses of one particular study or type of investigation founder when the full range of research is considered (Link & Stueve, 1995). Despite methodological weaknesses of many of the studies, those which are more methodologically sound yield similar results. Taken together research indicates that a history of previous violence, the constellation of demographic variables such as age, gender and low socio-economic status, in combination with specific symptoms of mental disorder, personality disorder, substance abuse and specific social contexts are particularly strong in their association with violence. Research indicates that when measures of violence are used which do not over-represent violence in the mentally disordered or under-represent violence in the non-disordered, and when the mentally disordered are compared to a control group matched for demographic and socio-economic factors, the rate of violence by the mentally disordered is, on balance, marginally more than the general population.

Despite the increase in knowledge about the link between violence and mental disorder in recent years, the impact on policy and practice has been variable. We conclude with a consideration of the implications of the research on clinical practice and the public sphere, and finally some remarks on directions for future research in the field.

7.1. Clinical Practice

- *Risk containment describes the process of risk assessment and management, as well as wider service strategies*

- *Risk assessment requires clinical judgements about the presence and nature of actuarial predictors of violence. A nine step procedure for assessment is described*

- *Following on from assessment is the management of risk. This entails the provision of security, supervision and support to ameliorate problems identified in the assessment*

- *There is a requirement for better services to address alcohol and substance abuse, and personality disorder in the UK, as well as services targeting families and carers*

- *Every aspect of clinical practice needs to remain under constant review. Training in assessment and management strategies is a further important issue*

The term *risk containment* describes the entire process which begins with risk assessment, proceeds to risk management, and then to wider service strategies, such as having a satisfactory information base, proper documentation, policies and guidelines related to risk and a system of response for dealing with crises (Monahan, 1993c). We consider implications of the literature on violence and mental disorder for clinical practice within this framework.

Risk assessment involves making clinical judgements about the presence and nature of known actuarial predictors of violence. There has been a tendency to rely less on empirical research in making predictions about future violence. We have sought to emphasise the full range of variables which may play a role in risk assessment, including individual historical, clinical and contextual factors. Gunn (1993) recommends a seven step procedure for the assessment of risk which we have found useful:-

Step 1   a detailed history from birth using every available informant and agency for validation

Step 2	special attention to substance abuse especially alcohol, with information about dosage taken, reasons for taking it, and its effects
Step 3	special attention to sexual interests, attitudes and ideas
Step 4	a detailed account of any criminal and/or antisocial behaviour; police records should be sought whenever possible, remembering that an uncorroborated account from the patient is insufficient. The account should be discussed with the patient in terms of his thoughts, fears, feelings at the time. The account should, if possible, give a description of the build-up to the antisocial behaviour and the situation in which it occurred
Step 5	a psychological assessment, including an assessment of intelligence, an assessment of personality and, if relevant from step 3, a detailed assessment of sexual feelings and sexual responses
Step 6	a mental state assessment, not just a mental state assessment at the time of one interview, but a description, if possible, of thoughts, moods, fears over the period of time covering any antisocial behaviour; an attempt should be made to relate any abnormalities to the antisocial behaviour. Particular emphasis should be given to feelings of anger and temper control
Step 7	a description of behaviour, attitudes and responses to any treatment

Quoted verbatim from Gunn (1993).

We would, however, wish to add the following two steps to this guidance.

Step 8	an assessment of the social contexts of the individuals. This should include where and how they have spent their time and the cultural norms which operate in those contexts. Particular attention needs to be paid to the specific context and circumstances in which the violence occurred because the chances of repeated violence will increase if the same contexts are replicated in the future. For example, sending an individual to the same home circumstances where they have previously been violent to a family member, without change in their response either to treatment or to those circumstances, is likely to increase the chances of a repetition of violence

Step 9   that of using this information to provide a psychological formulation. A formulation should provide an analysis, based on theory and research, of information collected during assessment which provides a psychological understanding of the history and development of the individual's difficulties (including the meaning of the violent act), and which takes account of their social and cultural context

Further work is needed to deepen both the understanding of violent acts and to make such understanding more widely used in services. Glasser (1996a) proposes the need for a typology of violence according to the motives of the perpetrator. His notion of self-preservative versus sadistic violence offers pointers in this direction. A typology could involve a retrospective examination of individuals convicted of homicide or other violent offences which could illuminate the psychic mechanisms underlying various offences. Glasser's (1996a) notion of simulation is particularly useful in assisting in the management of personality disordered individuals.

Some of the risk factors reviewed are changeable, whereas others are not. Mental disorder itself is not fixed over time. Kraemer et al. (1997) regard mental disorder as a *variable risk factor* because it is mutable. Risk assessment therefore involves identifying which risk factors are variable, and suggesting ways in which these can be altered through treatment and management.

Assessment of risk involves determining whether an individual is dangerous, in what circumstances they are likely to pose a risk, which factors can be altered and how this can be undertaken (Gunn, 1993). Following on from this is the management of risk which entails the provision of security, supervision and support to ameliorate problems identified in the assessment. Snowden (1997) recommends the use of the term risk management to refer specifically to decision making processes and planning related to individual patients. Therefore the process may be defined as the systematic identification of methods to reduce the severity and frequency of clinical risks for individual patients, including medical, psychological and social strategies.

The National Confidential Inquiry (Appleby et al., 1999) found that in 8% of cases of homicide, perpetrators had been in contact with mental health services in the year prior to the offence. They found that in a third of cases in which the perpetrator had contact with two hospitals, there were no written details passed from one hospital to another. Previous convictions for violence were often not documented in the notes of mental health services. A number of these individuals were not compliant with treatment or were out of contact with mental health services at the time of the homicide. A postal survey of Trusts in England found that only a minority had written policies on how to respond to non-compliance and non-attendance, or the communication of risk assessment. The inquiry team make 31 recommendations for the improvement of services. These include recommendations about training in the assessment and management of risk, documentation (including introducing 'patient passports'), use of modern drugs and psychological treatments, maintaining contact with patients who are disengaged from services, improved drug and alcohol services, and changes in the Mental Health Act to allow compulsory community treatment.

While acknowledging the value of the National Confidential Inquiry report in providing a cross section of the characteristics of homicides and suicides, Geddes (1999) warns against the wholesale implementation of these recommendations. Homicide is a rare event. Out of a population of individuals identified as being high risk, few will commit violence, particularly homicide, and therefore the focus of mental health resources on the issue of risk may be counterproductive in that other pressing priorities may be ignored. Appleby et al.'s conclusions relating to homicide are nevertheless useful. Indeed, many of the recommendations reiterate the findings and recommendations from the independent inquiries into individual cases of homicide (Sheppard, 1996). Some of the areas highlighted, as they apply to clinical practice, are discussed below.

Training. There are significant training issues in facilitating the spread of knowledge on risk assessment and management in clinical teams. Risk assessment is not the sole province of forensic mental health services, but also requires expertise in community mental health teams. Reed (1997) recommends training in three areas: risk assessment, the effective use of the Mental Health Act (1983) and the appropriate use of security according to the problems an individual presents. The National Confidential Inquiry found that only half of the mental health trusts in England and Wales provide training on the assessment of risk. They recommend training in recognition, assessment and management of risk and this should be focused upon indicators of risk, periods of risk, managing non-compliance and loss of contact with particular patients, communication, and mental health legislation (Appleby et al., 1999).

Documentation. Communication between mental health professionals is a key aspect of ameliorating risk. The National Confidential Inquiry makes a number of recommendations in this area, suggesting a simplified and universal system of documentation (patient passports) which would have the purpose of recording indicators of risk, CPA allocation on the basis of risk and easy transfer of information between services. Case notes for all disciplines should be unified and risk-related information on previous convictions should be readily available (Appleby et al., 1999).

Treatment. In his review of medication and non-compliance, Howlett (1998) concludes that conventional drugs which have disabling side-effects still continue to be prescribed, despite the availability of new medication for the treatment of schizophrenia. He attributes this to cost and ignorance. Appleby et al. (1999) make specific recommendations about the need to offer patients modern drug treatments, such as the 'atypical' anti-psychotic medication which has fewer side-effects. Family and psychological interventions should be more widely available and disengagement from treatment should be addressed by a comprehensive psycho-social package of care.

Comorbidity. Alcohol and drug abuse far outweigh mental disorder as a risk factor for violence, and therefore service provision necessarily involves a discussion of these issues. The provision of services to people with substance abuse problems and personality disorder is problematic in the UK; and individuals with mental illness, substance abuse and personality disorder co-occurrence have been identified as presenting the most important challenge to mental health services (Taylor & Gunn, 1999). There has been some debate over whether mental health and substance abuse services should be separated. Swanson et al. (1997) identifies this as a major problem in service provision and Smith & Hucker (1994) argue for integration rather than specialisation. This is currently a principal area for service development in the UK. The National Confidential Inquiry make specific recommendations highlighting the importance of service provision in this area.

Families and Carers. Prior to recent research, one unfortunate consequence of the belief among mental health professionals that there was no relationship between violence and mental disorder was that caregivers' experiences of fear tended to be trivialised or denied (Mullen, 1997). This threatens the patient's tenuous system of social support and fails to make use of a significant sign of relapse, since threatening, irritable behaviour is an important prodromal symptom. Estroff's (1994) research identified more relatives in the social networks of violent individuals with mental disorder and found that mothers were most often the victims of violence by mentally disordered children. Risk management requires the targeting of services to families and carers.

Audit. Risk containment requires that each aspect of clinical practice needs to remain under constant review. This may involve clinical audit which identifies various levels of untoward incidents according to their seriousness. Clinicians should take the lead in developing audit procedures which target those areas of clinical practice which involve the management of risk (Snowden, 1997).

7.2. The Service & Policy Context

- *The mentally ill make a small contribution to the overall level of violence in society. The true magnitude and nature of the risks posed by the mentally ill need to be realistically considered*

- *We discuss the adoption of the Care Programme Approach (CPA) in the UK. While this may have benefits, there are also significant problems with it*

- *It has been stated that local homicide inquiries foster a 'culture of blame' and should be abandoned. The view has also been expressed that inquiries are methodologically inadequate in that they are retrospective and encourage the simplistic notion that homicide and suicide are preventable*

- *Proposals for detaining individuals with personality disorder raise significant civil liberty issues. Personality disorder is a significant health issue, and improvements in services are required for its management and treatment*

- *Scientific findings are often only peripherally related to societal views, and are often ignored in the development of policy and legislation. This is important because public perceptions tend to drive policy in the direction of control and containment*

- *A consequence of the focus on violence and mental disorder is that the provision of mental health services becomes dependent on the potential of violence, and violent behaviour becomes one of the only means of achieving longer-term inpatient care*

- *If we are to make progress in addressing the problem of violence in society, a criminal justice system which reinforces a state of ignorance in those who are incarcerated requires re-evaluation. As a society we require new types of criminal justice institutions which facilitate rather than inhibit the process of thinking in those who are violent*

Research indicates that the link between violence and mental disorder is modest when compared to other known causes and correlates of violence such as gender, age and socio-economic status (Link & Stueve, 1995). Monahan (1992) makes the point that 90% of ECA study participants who had a mental illness were not violent, and Wessely (1993a) calculated the attributable risk of violence by the mentally disordered using the ECA data. He found that only 3% of violent incidents were due to mental illness. According to Monahan (1992), mental disorder (by which he means DSM-IV Axis I disorders) makes a very small contribution to the overall level of violence in society. Nevertheless, although modest in per centage terms, this does represent a substantial amount of violence and consequent human tragedy which, where preventable, is important to address. This point was recognised by Shaw, et al. (1999) in commenting on the small number of individuals with a mental illness who committed homicide in the UK identified by the National Confidential Inquiry. Thus it is necessary that public policy address the issues of violence and mental disorder, while simultaneously recognising the inherent limitations of 'solving' the problem of violence by focusing on the contribution of mental disorder.

Despite the small contribution to levels of violence made by the men-tally ill, the subject is debated widely in a way that other socio-demographic correlates of violence are not. Young men are not stig-matised, yet youth and gender are more potent predictors of violence than mental disorder. Mental health legislation has allowed the detention of mentally disordered individuals (partly because of the risk of harm to others) a long time before the link was established by empirical research. Taylor & Gunn (1999) have recently shown that there has been little change in the contribution of mentally ill people, convicted of manslaugh-ter on the grounds of diminished responsibility, to the number of homicides in England and Wales over a period of 38 years, despite changes in policy over the same period. While there is a small proportion of indi-viduals at high risk, it is important to understand the true magnitude and nature of the risks involved (Reed, 1997; Taylor & Gunn, 1999).

These points raise many issues about how such individuals might be helped by services. A brief overview of the service context in the UK is therefore important in considering the implications of this review. Broadly, there are three organisational systems which are likely to become involved with people with a history of mental disorder and violence, including the National Health Service, Social Services and the criminal justice system. These systems need to work together in a coherent way, which is perhaps made more difficult by the significant levels of organisational change that they have been required to manage over the last two decades (Timmins,

1996). In the remainder of this section, the discussion moves from considering the implications for mental health services provided mainly by the NHS and Social Services, to implications for the criminal justice system.

Within mental health services, the most significant development has been the attempts to shift the focus of care from one based in large institutions to a more community orientated approach (Lavender & Holloway, 1988; Rogers & Pilgrim, 1996; Peck & Parker, 1998). In spite of the many successes of this change in the focus of care (Mueser, Bond, Drake & Resnick, 1996; Shepherd, 1998), the inability of these services to manage people who have both been mentally disordered and have committed violent acts has led to ministerial pronouncements that community care has failed (Department of Health, 1998b; Burns & Priebe, 1998). This is not to say there are not problems with these developments, because it has meant that building on the successes has become more difficult and may encourage institutions and practices which are more concerned with containment and control. Such developments are likely to have a detrimental effect on service users, the vast majority of whom are not violent.

Services in the USA have stressed the importance of a comprehensive range of community support services and intensive case management as being key to both good quality care (Bachrach, 1980) and the reduction of the risk of violence among individuals with severe mental disorder (Dvoskin & Steadman, 1994). Case management involves 24–hour availability of case managers, small caseloads and strong links between the criminal justice system and agencies providing mental health, social services, and substance abuse treatment. Individuals with a history of violence and severe mental disorder require continuous, rather than episodic care. Several of these programmes have been evaluated in Canada and the USA. Some positive results have been reported in terms of reducing substance abuse, violence and arrest (Dvoskin & Steadman, 1994; Ventura, Cassel, Jacoby, & Huang, 1998), although Solomon, Draine, & Meyerson (1994) found no difference between individuals receiving intensive case management, with and without a special treatment team, among homeless mentally disordered people who have left prison.

The need to develop comprehensive community based services, as advocated in the USA, has become enshrined in British government policy (Department of Health, 1995; Department of Health, 1996). While housing and work schemes are vital alongside good quality acute psychiatric services in the treatment, care and support of people with severe mental disorders, it is the community mental health teams (CMHTs) which should provide the essential 'continuity' of care offered by mental health services. The Care Programme Approach (Department of Health, 1990), described below, provides a system for ensuring this continuity.

CMHTs have been subject to considerable criticism (Galvin & McCarthy, 1994; Onyett & Ford, 1996) about their failure to operate effectively, although laudable attempts have been made to provide guidance about how this might be changed (Onyett, Heppleston & Muijen, 1995). It is clear that if CMHTs are to work effectively for people with severe mental health disorder, teams must give priority to this group and currently there is considerable variability in whether this explicitly forms a core part of their work (Onyett, 1999a). Such a purpose needs to be clear in the operational policies of CMHTs and to be valued by the wider organisations (primarily NHS trusts and social service departments) and by the team members.

Onyett (1999b) has argued that crucial to the work of these teams is the development and maintenance of 'effective relationships' between users and staff. However, this review has examined some of the difficulties which may be encountered in developing such relationships, particularly when there is a tendency for a re-enactment or repetition of an earlier 'parental' relationship. Effective relationships may require members of teams to develop a level of understanding of service users which is currently perhaps less available in services than it is either 'desirable' or 'safe'. The consequences of not improving the quality of these relationships, and the team's ability to manage these, is that the difficulties become mirrored in the fragmented functioning of teams and services (Heginbottom, 1999).

There are a number of policies which have been introduced which should provide the basic structure for the delivery of effective community care. Among these is the Care Programme Approach (CPA) instituted by the Department of Health, which aims to address the issues of planning discharge of psychiatric inpatients, and developing and reviewing community care plans (Department of Health, 1990). This work involves the assessment of need (including risk), the development of a package of care and the nomination of a key-worker, to both carry out aspects of the care package and organise the regular review and monitoring of the care plan. Such overview and co-ordination was lacking in some cases in which individuals with severe mental health problems committed acts of homicide (Sheppard, 1996; Reith, 1998), although the benefits of hindsight were clearly not available at the time. Members of CMHTs are vital as key workers in this process, i.e. they should be around to provide the continuity of care across inpatient and community based residential settings as well as liase with other community based services (e.g. day care, education, etc.). If, however, these individual key workers are to develop the effective relationship which Onyett (1999b) has argued is so important in providing high quality care, this is likely to require the development of competence in understanding the complex nature of their relationships with users

(Chadwick, 1993; Hingley, 1997a & 1997b; Svanberg, 1998). While important, the current trends stressing the importance of having practitioners who are competent to deliver particular psychological or psychosocial intervention (Lam, 1991; Kuipers, Garety, Fowler, Dunn, Bebbington, Freeman & Hadley, 1997; Tarrier, Yusupoff, Kinney, McCarthy, Gledhill, Haddock & Morris, 1998), they may not necessarily be able to create effective relationships alone which need to be developed and sustained over long periods. This will be particularly important if assertive outreach teams are to be able to address the problems of non-compliance and disengagement as hoped for (Department of Health, 1998b), and in a way that is viewed positively by users. There are, however, significant problems with CPA. No longitudinal research has been undertaken on the effectiveness of CPA and increases in administration have not been accompanied by demonstrable benefits. There is also no mechanism of appeal for individuals placed on CPA (Brooke, personal communication).

Within mental health services, a number of the National Confidential Inquiry's recommendations apply specifically to local policy issues. They stress the need for mental health trusts to have written policies on non-compliance and disengagement. The Inquiry recommends that individual local homicide inquiries should be discontinued because they foster a 'culture of blame'. We are in agreement with this and also have some sympathy with Geddes (1999), who views inquiries as methodologically inadequate for making general recommendations about mental health provision. They are also retrospective and encourage the simplistic notion that homicide and suicide are preventable. Nevertheless, they do have useful qualitative information to contribute to policy considerations and should be examined along with other data sources.

It is important to restate the need for good community care services, particularly targeting high risk individuals. Successive inquiries following homicides by mentally disordered individuals have highlighted, among other issues, serious shortcomings in service provision. In considering the findings of Singleton et al. (1998), Fryers, Brugha, Grounds, & Meltzer (1998) point out that six years after the Reed report recommended the diversion of mentally disordered offenders into psychiatric care (Department of Health and Home Office, 1992), and an initial expansion of court diversion schemes, the number of mentally disordered individuals within the prison system remains substantial. This is despite a Health of the Nation strategy five years ago that made mental health a key area and specifically highlighted the needs of mentally disordered offenders (Performance Management Directorate, 1993). The survey suggests that figures in the region of 4,500 men and 400 women are currently in prison with a psychotic illness. A further related resource issue is that of the preventative detention of personality disordered individuals. There is a danger that the prioritising of containment will lead to poorly resourced services with inadequate treatment options, which will exacerbate hopelessness in detainees (Eastman, 1999).

Proposals in the UK to allow the preventative detention of individuals who are considered dangerous (without their necessarily having a conviction) have the clear public policy objective of public protection (Eastman, 1999), but raise significant civil liberty issues. In addition, there are far more effective ways of having an impact on the overall level of violence in society. Scientific findings are often only peripherally related to societal views, and are often ignored in the development of policy and legislation. While this may be a rather obvious point to make, it is important in this field because public perceptions tend to drive policy in the direction of control and containment rather than necessary improvements in services. In the context of a climate which encourages a great deal of caution among clinicians, Holloway (1998) makes the point that good practice requires the balancing of risks and benefits and the taking of a level of risk in decision making about patient care. Harm frequently arises from unnecessarily conservative risk policies and the delaying of decisions about discharge.

One consequence of the focus on violence and mental disorder is that the provision of mental health services becomes dependent on the potential of violence, and violent behaviour becomes one of the only means of achieving longer-term inpatient care. Resources therefore need to be targeted at specific lower risk groups in order to prevent them from becoming higher risk.

The current review of the Mental Health Act (1983) by the government involves, in part, a consideration of the introduction of community treatment orders (MACA, 1999). It is also one of the recommendations of the National Confidential Inquiry (Appleby et al., 1999). Geddes (1999) argues that since homicide (and violence) is a rare event, any increase in restriction would affect many individuals who would not go on to perpetrate violence. In fact the National Confidential Inquiry report states that improving compliance by introducing a community treatment order may prevent two homicides per year, and that financial and humanitarian costs would be substantial. Nevertheless, a recent poll conducted by the National Schizophrenia Fellowship (1999) found that 58% of service users thought that compulsory treatment in the community should be provided for a limited number of individuals.

One of the recommendations of the National Confidential Inquiry is the dissemination by the Department of Health of clear policies on the clinical management of personality disorder (Appleby et al., 1999). People with personality disorder were the largest diagnostic group in cases of homicide, and were further found to have high rates of previous convictions for violence, high levels of disruption of care, particularly treatment non-compliance and loss of contact with services. Findings relating to homicide are corroborated by the findings of this review, that personality disorder contributes substantially to violence in general. Mental health services are currently unable to respond to the treatment needs of this group. Neither CPA nor mental health legislation are geared to responding to the challenges presented by individuals with personality disorder who tend to fall between health services and the criminal justice system. Appleby et al. (1999) argue that bringing people with personality disorder more firmly within mental health services would be unacceptable to many staff, patients and families, and that a better solution (both in terms of acceptability to the individuals involved as well as the broader benefit of reducing criminal recidivism) would be for them to be dealt with by a more therapeutically orientated criminal justice system.

The issue of personality disorder brings into sharp focus the psychological dynamics of offending. However, in keeping with our position stated in the opening chapter, we would like to emphasise that personality disorder should not be viewed as a category. We focus instead on the importance of considering personality and disorders of personality as central to our thinking on violence. The current debate about personality disorder affords the opportunity of considering the psychological life of offenders, the nature of the internal world, and the meaning of the offence. Personality governs everyone's behaviour, and not just those with a personality disorder. In section 4.7. we described the complex relationship between violent offenders and prison establishments, the conditions of incarceration partly reflecting the psychological dynamics which gave rise to the violence. Human nature involves, in part, the denial of painful truths in order to maintain a state of psychological equilibrium. Violence partially reflects the need to maintain a position of ignorance about the source and nature of psychological distress. We described the way in which society and its institutions collude with this defensive position, prison serving the useful function of concealing psychological need, and thereby maintaining the psychological state of affairs which gave rise to the offending in the first place. If we are to make progress in addressing the problem of violence in society, a criminal justice system which reinforces a state of ignorance in those who are incarcerated requires re-evaluation, and other options other than imprisonment need to be considered.

While it is a requirement that those who cannot restrain themselves from violence need to be physically checked, to engage in punitive treatment in the hope of achieving retribution fails to address the problem of violence and colludes with the very pathology of the violent individual.

Punishment encourages the suspension of thinking. As a society we require new types of criminal justice institutions which facilitate the process of thought in those who are violent. These establishments should encourage education and learning, the development of skills, and various therapeutic interventions with high levels of expertise which address the early experiences of victimhood, and the perpetration of violence on self and others.

There are pockets of enlightened practice within the prison system, such as prisons run as therapeutic communities (TC), such as HMP Grendon Underwood. TCs are based on the principle of a democratic style of staff-patient interaction, and residents actively participate in their own treatment and take responsibility for the day-to-day running of the establishment. A review of the literature on the treatment of antisocial personality disorder by Dolan & Coid (1993) found that there were fewer serious incidents among violent offenders in prisons run as TCs than in the normal prison system, and symptoms of psychological distress have been found to be ameliorated in these groups. HMP Grendon has had only one hostage incident, one escape and no major disturbances in its long history. Uncharacteristically for a prison, it has a waiting list of 200 individuals who have volunteered to go there (Wilson & Ashton, 1998). Long-term outcome remains uncertain, and results are conflicting. Rice, Harris & Cormier (1992) found that violent recidivism increased among psychopaths who underwent compulsory treatment in a therapeutic community. On the other hand, Marshall (1997) studied 700 prisoners admitted to Grendon between 1984 and 1987. They were found to be less likely to be reconvicted than prisoners who were on a waiting list but who never had a chance to go there. Furthermore, the longer individuals stayed at Grendon, the lower were their rates of reconviction.

7.3. Future Research

- *The gold standard of research on violence and mental disorder has been set by recent studies which have used community controls and multiple measures of violence*

- *Such a study would be useful in the UK, in order to overcome the problem of applying findings from the other countries to risk assessment in Britain*

- *We describe an approach to research which specifies seven characteristics of studies on the prediction of violence*

- *The focus on symptoms rather than diagnosis is to be welcomed. Substance abuse is one of the most robust predictors of violence, and future research could include a more precise investigation of which symptom patterns combine with this to cause violence*

- *More complex longitudinal research is required to identify developmental pathways to the outcome of violence and mental disorder*

- *Further research is required on treatment non-compliance and the social context of violence*

There is now a substantial body of research on violence and mental disorder with a high degree of certainty in some of its conclusions. This is beginning to have a significant impact upon clinical practice as mental health professionals recognise the value of empirical research in guiding the assessment of risk. Risk assessment is likely to continue to develop in the direction of actuarial approaches (Monahan, 2000). Directions for future research are now considered.

A central issue is that most research has been conducted in the USA, Canada and Scandanavian countries and this has limited applicability in the UK. The methodologically sophisticated MacArthur Risk Assessment Study has been highly influential and has increased confidence in findings. There have been a few high quality studies in this country, but conclusions have been hampered by singular measures of violence and lack of adequate control groups. A large scale epidemiological survey in the UK using multiple measures of violence would be an important contribution to the literature.

Despite the fact that conclusions concerning the link between violence and mental disorder are based on a substantial body of research, Link & Stueve (1995) argue that confidence in the results would be improved by

studies using better measures and designs. They recommend the epidemiological cohort design which specifies the mental disorders of interest, uses
representative samples of individuals with no history of mental disorder as
community controls, and compares the groups' subsequent involvement in
violence. Multiple measures of violence should be used including self
report, informant report and official records. Adequate controls for confounders should be used by including a comprehensive set of background
variables.

Monahan & Steadman (1994) put this more formally. Research on the
prediction of violence should have seven characteristics:

1. Dangerousness must be disaggregated into its component parts – the
   variables used to predict violence (risk factors), the amount and type
   of violence being predicted (harm), and the likelihood that harm will
   occur (risk)
2. A rich array of theoretically-chosen risk factors in multiple domains
   must be chosen
3. Harm must be scaled in terms of seriousness and assessed with multiple measures
4. Risk must be treated as a probability estimate that changes over time
   and context
5. Priority must be given to actuarial research that establishes a relationship between risk factors and harm
6. Large and broadly representative samples of patients at multiple, co-
   ordinated sites must participate in the research
7. Managing risk as well as assessing risk must be a goal of the research

Monahan (1996) adds a further item to this list:

8. Risk communication as an essential adjunct to risk assessment

We support efforts to shift the focus of research from diagnosis to phenomenological aspects of presentation. Substance abuse is one of the most
robust predictors of violence, and future research could include a more
precise investigation of which symptom patterns combine with this to
cause violence (Monahan, 2000). Marzuk (1996) makes the similar point
that instead of studying categorical disorders (such as schizophrenia), the
outcome of research suggests that it may be more productive to investigate
temperaments, psychological traits such as impulsivity, and active symptomology. Further research needs to be undertaken into the link between
violent thoughts and future assaultative behaviour. There is also a requirement for a typology of violence which differentiates between, for example,

a one-off impulsive act and more enduring violence. In addition, there would appear to be a place for investigating, using qualitative methodologies, the process of 'recovery from violence' to illuminate the factors which facilitate and inhibit this process.

The main body of research on violence and mental disorder is concerned with current or recent adulthood variables. We require more detailed research on aspects of early childhood and their relationship with violence. Precise epidemiological information is required about subtle differences in childhood and their relationship with violent outcome. This could also shed light on the issue of resilience, i.e. given childhood adversity (for example, abuse) which accounts for a more positive outcome among some individuals. A further question to be addressed in the context of childhood factors is why some individuals with severe mental disorder are violent, whereas others are not. The relationship between background history, severe mental disorder and violence requires longitudinal research which utilises both qualitative and quantitative methodologies.

There has been a reasonable amount of research on mental disorder in the prison population in the UK. However, results of Teplin et al.'s (1996) study of female remand prisoners in the US indicates a need for similar prevalence data in the UK, combined with a thorough needs assessment. If male prisoners are regarded low on the list of priorities for mental health services, females are even worse off.

More research is required on the social context of violence. This includes the impact of support systems, families and carers. Some studies have evaluated the impact of intensive case management on individuals with severe mental disorder. To date, however, there has been no prospective research on the link between treatment non-compliance and future violence. Since the social context of violence is highly variable cross culturally, there is a particular need to undertake these investigations in the UK.

7.4. Concluding Remarks

The development of risk assessment has progressed apace in the past two decades. However, significant lacunae remain. This review has highlighted a number of problems for the application of knowledge. These include difficulties in relating empirical research to clinical practice, actuarial data appearing to lack relevance to clinicians. One reason for the lack of clinical relevance of research findings is the absence of a broad theoretical approach which explains these findings and links them with practice. Research requires a clinically meaningful context. A further problem is the cultural context of research. Most studies have been undertaken in the USA,

Canada, and Scandanavian countries, and findings should be cautiously applied in the UK.

The mentally ill make a very small contribution to violence in society. The true magnitude of violence perpetrated by the mentally ill should be placed in perspective. Focusing on the mentally disordered tends to obscure other important causes of violence.

Several high profile cases have highlighted the necessity for good quality community care in preventing harm to the public. These developments have inevitably emphasised the need for better risk assessment and management, and consequently there has been a growing interest in these issues. This will be an area of considerable development over the next decades as community care, public scrutiny, the removal of individuals' liberty and the balancing of this with the protection of peoples' rights become important issues.

We conclude by sounding a caution regarding the link between mental disorder and violence. Actuarial data provides information on populations, whereas clinical practice requires a focus on the individual. In the current social climate which lays such emphasis on risk assessment and the management of violence, there is a danger that important aspects of an individual's care are forsaken as carers and professionals become preoccupied with the risk of violence. The only aspect of clinical opinion which becomes important is potential dangerousness, while other aspects of formulating management and care are disregarded. The overall risk of violence posed by individuals with mental disorder is low, while their needs are substantial.

GLOSSARY OF TERMS

Actuarial prediction	Refers to prediction based on empirical research which identifies the risk of a particular event based on the membership of an individual to a group
Attributable risk	A measure of the impact a particular variable makes on a population. Thus attributable risk indicates the proportion of violence in the total population which is attributable to mental disorder
Base rates	Refers to the normal frequency of occurrence of any response (in this case violence) in a population or group. This information is used by researchers to evaluate whether a specific manipulation results in an increase or decrease in the frequency of the response
Birth cohort	A group of individuals having the common characteristic of being born at around the same period. These individuals are then followed up and their outcomes compared
Case linkage	Refers to studies which link official data from differentsources. In the case of research on violence and mental disorder, this involves linking case records on conviction and hospital admission

Covariate	Refers to changes in one variable being accompanied by concurrent changes in another
Criterion variable	Refers to the particular outcome that is being investigated, in this case violence
Developmental	Examines 'the evolution of psychological disturbance in the psychopathology context of development' (Cole & Putman, 1992)
ECA data	Data from the Epidemiological Catchment Area study
Expressed emotion	A measure of the quality of social interaction between a patient and their carer, rated on the basis of verbal information. This involves monitoring critical comments and positive remarks. Global ratings of hostility, warmth and emotional over-involvement are also made (Bebbington & Kuipers, 1994)
False negatives	The failure to predict violence in individuals who were violent later
False positives	Predicting violence in individuals when they were not violent later
Index offence	The most recent offence or the offence for which the individual is incarcerated
Odds ratio	This indicates the increased relative risk of a particular outcome, in this case violence associated with a particular variable which is the risk factor. An odds ratio of 1 represents no association, and the more it increases above 1, the greater the positive association or increased risk. A negative association indicates decreased risk
Predictor variables	Factors which are used to predict the criterion variable (in this case violence). These include, for example, history of violence, substance abuse and personality disorder

Relative risk	A measure of the strength of association. The number represents the number of times greater the risk is above the base rate
Selection bias	Bias resulting from the way in which a research sample is selected
Severe mental disorder	Those 'major' disorders of affect and thought which form a subgroup of Axis I disorders in the Diagnostic and Statistical Manual of Mental Disorder (4th Edition; DSM-IV)
Special Hospital	These secure hospitals provide psychiatric care to individuals requiring the highest level of security in the UK. There are three special hospitals in England: Broadmoor, Rampton and Ashworth; and one in Scotland, the State Hospital at Carstairs
Stratified sample	The population is divided into strata, such as men and women, black and white, and random samples are drawn from each strata
Therapeutic Community	Therapeutic communities (TCs) are based on the principle of a democratic style of staff-patient interaction. Patients actively participate in their own treatment and take responsibility for the day-to-day running of the establishment. The social interaction of participants is examined within the context of the interpersonal relationships of members of the community
Threat/control-override symptoms	Psychotic symptoms which lead to the perception of threat (the feeling that others wished to harm you) and/or involve the overriding of personal controls (the feeling that your mind is dominated by forces outside your control or that thoughts are being inserted into your mind that are not your own). See section 3.6. for full explanation

Transference/
Countertransference

The process whereby a patient displaces thoughts and feelings related to past figures onto the person of the therapist. Countertransference refers to the therapist's transferences to the patient. By extension, the therapist's emotional attitude to the patient, which includes reactions to specific items of the patient's behaviour (Rycroft, 1968)

Validation sample

The study group

REFERENCES

Abrams, K. M., & Teplin, L. A. (1990). *Drug disorder, mental illness, and violence*. Chicago, IL, US: Northwestern U Medical School, Psycho-legal Studies Program.

Abrams, K. M., & Teplin, L. A. (1991). Co-occurring disorders among jail detainees: implications for public policy. *American Psychologist, 46,* 1036–1045.

Addad, M., Benezech, M., Bourgeios, M., & Yesavage, J. (1981). Criminal acts among schizophrenics in French mental hospitals. *Journal of Nervous and Mental Disease, 169,* 289–93.

Ainsworth, M. D. S., Blehar, M. C., Waters, E., & Wall, S. (1978). *Patterns of Attachment: A Psychological Study of the Strange Situation.* Hillsdale, N.J.: Lawrence Erlbaum Associates.

American Psychiatric Association. (1980). *Diagnostic and Statistical Manual of Mental Disorders (3rd Ed.).* Washington, DC: Author.

American Psychiatric Association. (1994). *Diagnostic and Statistical Manual of Mental Disorders (4th Ed.).* Washington, DC: Author.

Appelbaum, P.S., Robbins, P.C. & Monahan, J. (submitted). Violence and delusions: Data from the MacArthur Violence Risk Assessment Study.

Appleby, L., Shaw, J., Amos, T. & McDonnell, R. (1999). *Safer Services: National Confidential Inquiry into Suicide and Homicide by People with Mental Illness.* London: Department of Health.

Aquilina, C. (1991). Violence by psychiatric inpatients. *Medicine, Science and the Law, 22,* 203–12.

Asnis, G. M., Kaplan, M. L., & Hundorfean, G. S. W. (1997). Violence and homicidal behaviors in psychiatric disorders. *Psychiatric Clinics of North America., 20,* 405–425.

Association of Chief Officers of Probation. (1994). *Guidance on Management of Risk and Public Protection.* London: ACOP.

Bachrach, L. L. (1980). Overview: Model programmes for chronic mental patients. *American Journal of Psychiatry, 137*, 1023–1031.

Bandura, A., Ross, D., & Ross, S. A. (1963). Imitation of film mediated aggressive models. *Journal of Abnormal and Social Psychology, 66*, 3–11.

Barber, J. W., Hundley, P. L., Kellogg, E., Glick, J. L., et al. (1988). Clinical and demographic characteristics of 15 patients with repetitively assaultive behaviour. *Psychiatric Quarterly, 59*, 213–224.

Barnard, G., Robbins, W. L., Newman, G., & Carrera, F. (1984). A study of violence within a forensic treatment facility. *Bulletin of the American Academy of Psychiatry and the Law, 12*, 339–48.

Baron, R. A. & Richardson, D. R. (1994). Human Aggression. (2nd Ed). New York: Plenum Press.

Barratt, E. (1994). Impulsiveness and aggression. In J. Monahan & H. Steadman (Eds.), *Violence and Mental Disorder: Developments in risk assessment* (61–79). Chicago, IL, US: University of Chicago Press.

Bartels, J., Drake, R. E., Wallach, M. A., & Freeman, D. H. (1991). Characteristic hostility in schizophrenic outpatients. *Schizophrenia Bulletin, 17*, 163–171.

Bass, C., & Murphy, M. (1995). Somatoform and personality disorder: Syndromal comorbidity and overlapping developmental pathways. *Journal of Psychosomatic Research, 39*, 403–427.

Bebbington, P. & Kuipers, L. (1994). The predictive utility of expressed emotion in schizophrenia: An aggregate analysis. *Psychological Medicine, 24*, 707–718.

Beck, J. C. (1994). Epidemiology of mental disorder and violence: Beliefs and research findings. *Harvard Review of Psychiatry, 2*, 1–6.

Beck, J. C., White, K. A., & Gage, B. (1991). Emergency psychiatric assessment of violence. *American Journal of Psychiatry, 148*, 1562–5.

Belfrage, H. (1998a). A ten-year follow-up of criminality in Stockholm mental patients: New evidence for a relationship between mental disorder and crime. *British Journal of Criminology, 38*, 145.

Belfrage, H. (1998b). Implementing the HCR-20 scheme for risk assessment in a forensic psychiatric hospital: Integrating research and clinical practice. *Journal of Forensic Psychiatry, 9*, 328–338.

Bentall, R. P. (1990) Reconstructing Schizophrenia. London: Routledge.

Bentall, R.P., Jackson, H.F. & Pilgrim, D. (1988). Abandoning the concept of 'Schizophrenia': Some implications of validity arguments for psychological research into psychotic phenomena.' *British Journal of Clinical Psychology, 27*, 303–324.

Bergman, B., & Brismar, B. (1994). Characteristics of violent alcoholics. *Alcohol and Alcoholism, 29*, 451–457.

Berman, M. E. (1997). Biopsychological approaches to understanding human aggression: The first 30 years. *Clinical Psychology Review*, 17(6), 585–588.

Berman, M. E., Tracy, J.I. & Coccaro, E.F. (1997). The serotonin hypothesis of aggression revisited. *Clinical Psychology Review*, 17, 651–665.

Binder, R., & McNeil, D. (1986). Victims and families of violent psychiatric patients. *Bulletin of the American Academy of Psychiatry and the Law*, 14, 131–139.

Binder, R., & McNeil, D. (1988). Effects of diagnosis and context on dangerousness. *American Journal of Psychiatry*, 145, 728–732.

Bingley, W. (1997). Assessing dangerousness: Protecting the interests of patients. *British Journal of Psychiatry*, 170 (Suppl 32), 28–29.

Bjorkly, S. (1995). Prediction of aggression in psychiatric patients: A review of prospective prediction studies. *Clinical Psychology Review*, 15, 475–502.

Blackburn, R. (1988). On moral judgements and personality disorders: The myth of psychopathic personality revisited. *British Journal of Psychiatry*, 153, 505–512.

Blackburn, R. (1998). Psychopathy and the contribution of personality to violence. In T. Millon, E. Simonsen & M. Birket-Smith (Eds.), *Psychopathy: Antisocial, Violent and Criminal Behaviour* (pp50–68). New York: Guildford Press.

Blom-Cooper, L., Hally, H. & Murphy, E. (1995). *The Falling Shadow – One Patient's Mental Health Care 1978–1993. Report of the Committee of Inquiry into the events leading up to and surrounding the fatal incident at Edith Morgan Centre, Torbay on 1 September 1993* (Chair, Louis Blom-Cooper). London: Duckworth.

Blomhoff, S., Seim, S., & Friis, S. (1990). Can prediction of violence among psychiatric inpatients be improved? *Hospital and Community Psychiatry*, 41, 771–775.

Bonta, J., Law, M., & Hanson, K. (1998). The prediction of criminal and violent recidivism among mentally disordered offenders: A meta-analysis. *Psychological Bulletin*, 123, 123–142.

Bowers, M. B. (1974). Central dopamine turnover in schizophrenic syndromes. *Archives of General Psychiatry*, 31, 50–54.

Bowlby, J. (1944). Forty-four juvenile thieves: Their character and home life. *International Journal of Psycho-Analysis*, 25, 19–52;107–127.

Boyd, W. (1996). *Report of the Confidential Inquiry into Homicides and Suicides by Mentally Ill People* (Director, Dr William Boyd). London: Royal College of Psychiatrists.

Boyle, M. (1990). *Schizophrenia: A Scientific Delusion?* London: Routledge.

Brennan, P. A., Mednick, S. A., & Jacobsen, B. (1996). Assessing the role of genetics in crime using adoption cohorts. *Ciba Found Symp, 194,* 115–23.

Brennan, P. A. & Raine, A. (1997). Biosocial bases of anti-social behaviour: Psychophysiological, neurological and cognitive factors. *Clinical Psychology Review, 17,* 589–604.

Briere, J. (1987). Predicting self-reported likelihood of battering: Attitudes and childhood experiences. *Journal of Research in Personality, 21,* 61–69.

Brown, A., Harrop, H., Cronin, H. & Harman, J. (1996). *Report to Northumberland Health Authority of the Independent Inquiry Team into the Care and Treatment of Richard Stoker* (Chair, A.G. Brown). Northumberland: Northumberland Health Authority.

Buchanan, A. (1993). Acting on delusions: A review. *Psychological Medicine, 23,* 123–134.

Buchanan, A. (1998). Criminal conviction after discharge from special (high security) hospital. *British Journal of Psychiatry, 172,* 472–6.

Buckley, P., Walshe, D., Colohan, H. A., O'Callaghan, E., et al. (1990). Violence and schizophrenia: A study of the occurrence and clinical correlates of violence among schizophrenic patients. *Irish Journal of Psychological Medicine, 7,* 102–108.

Bulhan, H. A. (1985). *Fantz Fanon and the Psychology of Oppression.* New York, NY: Plenum Press.

Burns, J. & Priebe (1999). Mental health care failure in England: Myth and reality. *British Journal of Psychiatry, 174,* 191–192.

Caesar, P. L. (1988). Exposure to violence in the families-of-origin among wife-abusers and maritally nonviolent men. *Violence and Victims, 3,* 49–63.

Campbell, J., Stefan, S., & Loder, A. (1994). Taking issue: putting violence in context (Editorial). *Hospital and Community Psychiatry, 45,* 663.

Cantwell, D.P. (1996). Attention deficit disorder: A review of the past 10 years. *Journal of the American Academy of Child and Adolescent Psychiatry, 35,* 978–987.

Carlson, V., Cichetti, D., Barnett, D., & Braunwald, K. (1989). Disorganised/disoriented attachment relationships in maltreated infants. *Developmental Psychology, 25,* 525–531.

Carmen, E., Rieker, P., & Mills, T. (1984). Victims of violence and psychaitric illness. *American Journal of Psychiatry, 141,* 378–383.

Carroll, J. C. (1980). The intergenerational transmission of family violence: The long-term effects of aggressive behaviour. *Advances in Family Psychiatry, 2,* 171–181.

Cascardi, M., Mueser, K. T., DeGiralomo, J., et al. (1996). Physical aggression against psychiatric inpatients by family members and partners.

Psychiatric Services, 47, 531–533.

Cavadino, M. (1998). Death to the psychopath. *Journal of Forensic Psychiatry, 9,* 5–8.

Chadwick, P. K. (1993). The stepladder to the impossible: A first hand phenomenological account of a schizo-affective psychotic crisis. *Journal of Mental Health, 2,* 239–250.

Ciompi, L. (1980). The natural history of schizophrenia in the long term. *British Journal of Psychiatry, 136,* 413–420.

Ciompi, L. (1984). Is there really a schizophrenia? The long term course of psychotic phenomena. *British Journal of Psychiatry, 145,* 636–640.

Cleckley, H. R. (1976). *The Mask of Sanity.* Saint-Louis: Mosby.

Clements & Turpin (1992). Vulnerability models in schizophrenia. In M. Birchwood & N. Tarrier (Eds.), *Innovations in the Psychological Management of Schizophrenia.* Chichester, John Wiley & Sons.

Cocozza, J. J., Melick, M. E., & Steadman, H. J. (1978). Trends in violent crime among ex-mental patients. *Criminology: An Interdisciplinary Journal, Vol 16,* 317–334.

Cocozza, J. J., & Steadman, H. J. (1974). Some refinements in the measurement and prediction of dangerous behaviour. *American Journal of Psychiatry, 131,* 1012–1014.

Cocozza, J. J., & Steadman, H. J. (1978). Prediction in psychiatry: an example of misplaced confidence in experts. *Social Problems, 25,* 265–276.

Cole, P. M., & Putman, F. W. (1992). Effect of incest on self and social functioning: A developmental psychopathology perspective. *Journal of Consulting and Clinical Psychology, 60,* 174–184.

Convoy, H., Weiss, P., & Zverina, J. (1995). Sexual abuse experiences of psychiatric patients. *Medicine and Law, 14,* 283–292.

Cox, M. (1982). The psychotherapist as assessor of dangerousness. In J. Hamilton & H. Freeman (Eds.), *Dangerousness: Psychiatric Assessment and Management* (81–87). London: Gaskell.

Craig, W. (1982). An epidemiologic study of problems associated with violence among psychiatric inpatients. *American Journal of Psychiatry, 139,* 1262–66.

Crittenden, P. M. (1988). Relationships at risk. In J. Belsky & T. Nezworski (Eds.), *Clinical Implications of Attachment* (136–174). Hillsdale, NJ: Lawrence Erlbaum Associates.

Dalteg, A., & Levander, S. (1998). Twelve thousand crimes by 75 boys: A 20–year follow-up study of childhood hyperactivity. *Journal of Forensic Psychiatry, 9,* 39–57.

David, A. S. & Cutting, J. C. (1999). *The Neuropsychology of Schizophrenia.* Hove: Lawrence Erlbaum.

Davis, S. (1991). Violence by psychiatric inpatients: a review. *Hospital and Community Psychiatry, 42*, 585–590.

De Zulueta, F. (1993). *From pain to violence: The traumatic roots of destructiveness*. London, UK: Whurr Publishers.

De Zulueta, F. (1996). Theories of aggression and violence. In C. Cordess & M. Cox (Eds.), *Forensic Psychotherapy: Crime, Psychodynamics and the Offender Patient* . London: Jessica Kingsley Publishers.

DeJong, J., Virkkunen, M., & Linnoila, M. (1992). Factors associated with recidivism in a criminal population. *Journal of Nervous and Mental Disease, 180*, 543–550.

Department of Health. (1990). *The Care Programme Approach for People with a Mental Illness Referred to the Specialist Psychiatrist Service. HC(90)23/LASSL(90)II*. London: Author.

Department of Health (1994a). *Introduction of the supervision register for mentally ill people from April 1994. HSG/95/5*. London: Author.

Department of Health (1994b). *Guidance on the Discharge of Mentally Disordered People and Their Care in the Community. HSG/94/27*. London: Author.

Department of Health (1995) *Building Bridges*. London: HMSO.

Department of Health (1996) *The Spectrum of Care: Local Services for People with Mental Health Problems*. London: HMSO.

Department of Health (1998a). *A First Class Service*. London: Author.

Department of Health (1998b) *Modernising Mental Health Services*. London: HMSO.

Department of Health and Home Office (1992). *Review of health and social services for mentally disordered offenders and others requiring similar services: final summary report*. London: HMSO.

Denzin, N. K. & Lincoln, Y. S. (1994). *Handbook of Qualitative Research*. New York: Sage.

Dick, D., Shuttleworth, B. & Charlton, J. (1991). *Report of the Panel of Inquiry Appointed to Investigate the Case of Kim Kirkman* (Chair, Dr Donald Dick). Birmingham: West Midlands Regional Health Authority.

Dodge, K. A., Bates, J. E., & Pettit, G. S. (1990a). Mechanisms in the cycle of violence. *Science, 250*, 1678–1683.

Dodge, K. A., Price, J. M., Coie, J. D., & Christopoulos, C. (1990b). On the development of aggressive dyadic relationships in boys' peer groups. *Human Development, 33*, 260–270.

Dolan, B. & Coid, J. (1993). *Psychopathic and Antisocial Personality Disorder: Treatment and Research Issues*. London: Gaskell.

Douglas, K. S., & Hart, S. D. (submitted). Psychosis as a risk factor for violence: A quantitative review of the research.

Douglas, K.S., Ogloff, J.R.P., Nicholls, T.L. & Grant, I. (1998). Assessing risk for violence among psychiatric patients: The HCR-20 violence risk assessment scheme and the Psychopathy Checklist – Screening Version. Unpublished manuscript.

Douglas, K.S. & Webster, C.D. (1999). The HCR-20 violence risk assessment scheme: Concurrent validity in a sample of incarcerated offenders. *Criminal Justice and Behaviour, 26*, 3–19.

Dutton, D. G., & Hart, S. D. (1992). Evidence for long-term, specific effects of childhood abuse and neglect on criminal behaviour in men. *International Journal of Offender Therapy and Comparative Criminology, 36*, 129–137.

Dvoskin, J. A., & Steadman, H. J. (1994). Using intensive case management to reduce violence by mentally ill persons in the community. *Hospital and Community Psychiatry, 45*, 679–684.

DYG Corporation. (1990). *Public Attitudes Toward People with Chronic Mental Illness*. Elmsford, NY: Author.

Eastman, N. (1999). Public health psychiatry or crime prevention? *British Medical Journal, 318*, 549–551.

Edwards, J. G., Jones, D., & Reid, W. H. (1988). Physical assaults in a psychiatric unit in a general hospital. *American Journal of Psychiatry, 145*, 1568–71.

Eronen, M., Hakola, P., & Tiihonen, J. (1996a). Mental disorders and homicidal behaviour in Finland. *Archives of General Psychiatry, 53*, 497–501.

Eronen, M., Tiihonen, J., & Hakola, P. (1996b). Schizophrenia and homicidal behaviour. *Schizophrenia Bulletin, 22*, 83–89.

Estroff, S. E., & Zimmer, C. (1994). Social networks, social support, and violence among persons with severe, persistent mental illness. In J. Monahan & H. Steadman (Eds.), *Violence and Mental Disorder: Developments in risk assessment* (259–295). Chicago, IL, US: University of Chicago Press.

Estroff, S. E., Zimmer, C., Lachicotte, W. S., & Benoit, J. (1994). The influence of social networks and social support on violence by persons with serious mental illness. *Hospital and Community Psychiatry, 45*, 669–679.

Eysenck, H. J. (1977). Crime & Personality. (3rd Ed). St Albans, England: Paladin.

Fagan, J. (1990). Intoxication and aggression. In M. Tonry & J. Q. Wilson (Eds.), *Crime and Justice: A review of research: Vol. 13. Drugs and Crime* (241–314). Chicago: Chicago University Press.

Fallon, P., Bluglass, R., Edwards, B. & Daniels, G. (1999). *Report of the Committee of Inquiry into the Personality Disorder Unit, Ashworth Special Hospital*. London: The Stationary Office.

Falloon, I. (1988). Expressed emotion: Current status. *Psychological Medicine, 18*, 269–274.

Farrington, D. (1978). The family backgrounds of aggressive youths. In L. Hersov, M. Berger, & D. Shaffer (Eds.), *Aggression and Antisocial Behaviour in Children and Adolescence* (73–93). Oxford: Pergamon.

Farrington, D. (1991). Childhood aggression and adult violence: early precursors and later-life outcomes. In D. Pepler & K. Rubin (Eds.), *The Development and Treatment of Childhood Aggression*. Hillsdale, N.J.: Lawrence Erlbaum Associates.

Farrington, D. P., Gallegher, B., Morely, L., St Ledger, R. J., & West, D. J. (1988). Are there any successful men from criminogenic backgrounds? *Psychiatry, 50*, 116–130.

Farrington, D. P., Loeber, R., & Van Kammen, W. B. (1990). Long-term criminal outcomes of hyperactivity-impulsivity-attention deficit and conduct problems in childhood. In L. Robins & M.Rutter (Eds.), *Straight and Devious Pathways from Childhood to Adulthood* (62–81). Cambridge, UK: Cambridge University Press.

Ferguson, J. S., & Smith, A. (1996). Aggressive behaviour on an inpatient geriatric unit. *Journal of Psychosocial Nursing, 34*, 27–32.

Fergusson, D. M., & Lynskey, M. T. (1997). Physical punishment/maltreatment during childhood and adjustment in young adulthood. *Child Abuse Neglect, 21*, 617–30.

Field Institute. (1984). *In Persuit of Wellness: A Survey of California Adults.* (Vol. 4). Sacramento: California Department of Mental Health.

Fitch, F. J., & Papantonio, A. (1983). Men who batter: Some pertinent characteristics. *Journal of Nervous and Mental Disease, 171*, 190–192.

Fonagy, P., Leigh, T., Steele, M., Steele, H., Kennedy, R., Mattoon, G., Target, M., & Gerber, A. (1996). The relation of attachment status, psychiatric classification, and response to psychotherapy. *Journal of Consulting and Clinical Psychology, 64*, 22–31.

Fonagy, P., & Target, M. (1999). Towards understanding violence: The use of the body and the role of the father. In R. J. Perelberg (Ed.), *Psychoanalytic Understanding of Violence and Suicide* (51–72). London: Routledge.

Fonagy, P., Target, M., Steele, M., & Steele, H. (1997). The development of violence and crime as it relates to security of attachment. In J. Osojsky (Ed.), *Children in a Violent Society* (150–177). New York: Guildford Press.

Freeman, C., Brown, A., Dunleavy, D. & Graham, F. (1996). *Report of the Inquiry into the Care and Treatment of Shaun Anthony Armstrong.* (Chair, C.J. Freeman). Middlesborough: Tees District Health Authority.

Freud, S. (1914). Remembering, repeating and working through. In J.

Strachey (Ed.), *The Standard Edition of the Complete Psychological Works of Sigmund Freud, Vol. 12*. London: Hogarth Press.

Frith, U. & Blair, J. (1998). Does antisocial personality disorder have a neurological basis and can it be treated? *Criminal Behaviour & Mental Health, 8,* 247–250.

Fryers, T., Brugha, T., Grounds, A., & Meltzer, D. (1998). Severe mental illness in prisoners. *British Medical Journal, 317,* 1025–6.

Fulwiler, C., Grossman, H., Forbes, C., & Ruthazer, R. (1997). Early-onset substance abuse and community violence by outpatients with chronic mental illness. *Psychiatric Services, 48,* 1181–1185.

Galvin, S. W. & McCarthy, S. (1994) Multi-disciplinary teams: clinging to the wreckage. *Journal of Mental Health, 3,* 167–174.

Gardner, W., Lidz, C. W., Mulvey, E. P., & Shaw, E. C. (1996a). Clinical versus actuarial predictions of violence of patients with mental illnesses. *Journal of Consulting and Clinical Psychology, 64,* 602–9.

Gardner, W., Lidz, C., Mulvey, E., & Shaw, E. (1996b). A comparison of actuarial methods for identifying repetitively violent patients with mental illness. *Law and Human Behaviour, 20,* 35–48.

Geddes, J. (1999). Suicide and homicide by people with mental illness: We still don't know how to prevent most of these deaths. *British Medical Journal, 318,* 1225–6.

George, C., Kaplan, N., & Main, M. (1996). *Adult Attachment Interview* . Berkley, CA: Unpublished manuscript, Department of Psychology, University of California (3rd Edition).

George, C., & Main, M. (1979). Social interactions of young abused children: approach, avoidance and aggression. *Child Development, 50,* 306–18.

Gerbner, C., Gross, L., Morgan, M., & Signorielli, N. (1981). Health and medicine on television. *New England Journal of Medicine, 305,* 901–4.

Gilbert, L., El Bassel, N., Schilling, R. F., & Friedman, E. (1997). Childhood abuse as a risk for partner abuse among women in methadone maintenance. *American Journal of Drug and Alcohol Abuse, 23,* 581–595.

Gilders, I. (1997). Violence in the community: a study of violence and aggression in homelessness and mental health day services. *Journal of Community and Applied Social Psychology, 7,* 377–387.

Gilligan, J. (1996). *Violence: Reflections on a National Epidemic*. New York: Vintage.

Glasser, M. (1996a). The assessment and management of dangerousness: the psychoanalytical contribution. *Journal of Forensic Psychiatry, 7,* 271–283.

Glasser, M. (1996b). Aggression and sadism in the perversions. In I. Rosen (Ed.), *Sexual Deviation (3rd Edition)* (279–299). Oxford: Oxford

University Press.

Glasser, M. (1998). On violence: A preliminary communication. *International Journal of Psycho-Analysis, 79,* 887–902.

Goldberg, L.R. (1968). Simple models or simple processes? *American Psychologist, 23,* 483–496.

Goodman, L. A., Dutton, M. A., & Harris, M. (1995). Episodically homeless women with serious mental illness: Prevalence of physical and sexual abuse. *American Journal of Orthopsychiatry, 65,* 468–477.

Gottesman, I. I. & Shields, J. (1982). *Schizophrenia: The Epigenetic Puzzle.* Cambridge: Cambridge University Press.

Gottlieb, P., Cabrielsen, G., & Kramp, P. (1987). Psychotic homicide in Copenhagen from 1959 to 1983. *Acta Psychiatrica Scandanavia, 76,* 285–292.

Green, C. M. (1981). Matricide by sons. *Medicine, Science and the Law, 21,* 207–214.

Gray, J. A., Feldon, L., Rawlins, J. N. P., Hemsley, D. R. & Smith, A. D. (1979). The neuropsychology of schizophrenia. *Behavioural and Brain Sciences, 14,* 1–84.

Grisso, T., Davis, J., Vesselinov, R., Appelbaum, P.S. & Monahan, J. (in press). Violent thoughts and violent behaviour following hospitalisation for mental disorder.

Gross, A. B., & Keller, H. R. (1992). Long-term consequences on childhood physical and psychological maltreatment. *Aggressive Behaviour, 18,* 171–185.

Grubin, D. (1997). Inferring predictors of risk: Sex offenders. *International Review of Psychiatry, 9,* 225–231.

Gunn, J. (1993). Dangerousness. In J. Gunn & P. J. Taylor (Eds.), *Forensic Psychiatry. Clinical, Legal and Ethical Issues.* Oxford: Butterworth-Heinemann.

Gunn, J., Maden, T., & Swinton, M. (1991a). *Mentally Disordered Prisoners.* London: HMSO.

Gunn, J., Maden, T., & Swinton, M. (1991b). Treatment needs of prisoners with psychiatric disorders. *British Medical Journal, 303,* 338–340.

Guttridge, P., Gabrielli, W. F., Mednick, S. A., & Van Dusen, K. (1983). Criminal violence in a birth cohort. In K. T. V. Dusen & S. A. Mednick (Eds.), *Prospective Studies of Crime and Delinquency* (211–224). Boston: Kluwer-Nijhoff.

Haapasalo, J., & Kankkonen, M. (1997). Self-reported childhood abuse among sex and violent offenders. *Archives of Sexual Behaviour, 26,* 421–431.

Hafner, H., & Boker, W. (1973). *Crimes of Violence by Mentally Disorderd Offenders.* Cambridge, UK: Cambridge University Press. (Translated by

Helen Marshall, 1982).

Harbour, A., Brunning, J., Bolter, L. & Hally, H (1996). *The Report of the Independent Inquiry into the Circumstances Surrounding the Deaths of Robert and Muriel Viner* (Chair, Anthony Harbour). Dorset: Dorset Health Commission.

Hare, R. D. (1991). *Manual for the Hare Psychopathy Checklist-Revised.* Toronto: Multihealth Systems.

Hare, R. D., & Hart, S. D. (1993). Psychopathy, mental disorder, and crime. In S. Hodgins (Ed.), *Mental disorder and crime.* Newbury Park, CA, USA: Sage Publications.

Harpur, T. J., Hare, S. D., & Hakstian, A. R. (1989). Two-factor conceptualisation of psychopathy: Construct validity and assessment implications. *Psychological Assessment: A Journal of Consulting and Clinical Psychology, 1*, 6–17.

Harris, G., Rice, M., & Quinsey, V. (1993). Violent recidivism of mentally disordered offenders: The development of a statistical prediction instrument. *Criminal Justice and Behaviour, 20*, 315–335.

Harris, G. T., & Rice, M. E. (1997). Risk appraisal and management of violent behaviour. *Psychiatric Services, 48*, 1168–1176.

Harris, G. T., Rice, M. E., & Cormier, C. A. (1991). Psychopathy and violent recidivism. *Law and Human Behaviour, 15*, 625–37.

Harry, B., & Steadman, H. J. (1988). Arrest rates of patients treated at a community mental health centre. *Hospital and Community Psychiatry, 39*, 862–66.

Hart, S. D., Hare, R. D., & Forth, A. E. (1994). Psychopathy as a risk marker for violence. In J. Monahan & H. S. Steadman (Eds.), *Violence and Mental Disorder* (81–98). Chicago: University of Chicago Press.

Hart, S. D., Kropp, P. R., & Hare, R. D. (1988). Performance of male psychopaths following conditional release from prison. *Journal of Consulting and Clinical Psychology, 56*, 227–32.

Heads, T. C., Taylor, P. J., & Leese, M. (1997). Childhood experiences of patients with schizophrenia and a history of violence: A special hospital sample. *Criminal Behaviour and Mental Health, 7*, 117–130.

Hedlund, J. L., Sletten, I. W., Altman, H., & Evenson, R. C. (1973). Prediction of patients who are dangerous to others. *Journal of Clinical Psychology, 29*, 443–7.

Hemenway, D., Solnick, S., & Carter, J. (1994). Child-rearing violence. *Child Abuse Neglect, 18*, 1011–20.

Herman, J. L., Perry, J. C., & Van der Kolk, B. A. (1989). Childhood trauma in borderline personality disorder. *American Journal of Psychiatry, 146*, 490–495.

Herrenkohl, R. C., Egolf, B. P., & Herrenkohl, E. C. (1997). Preschool antecedents of adolescent assaultive behaviour: A longitudinal study. *American Journal of Orthopsychiatry, 67,* 422–432.

Hiday, V. (1995). The social context of mental illness and violence. *Journal of Health and Social Behaviour, 36,* 122–137.

Hiday, V. (1997). Understanding the connection between mental illness and violence. *International Journal of Law and Psychiatry., 20,* 399–417.

Hiday, V. A., Swartz, M. S., Swanson, J. W., Borum, R., & Wagner, H. R. (1999). Criminal victimisation of persons with severe mental illness. *Psychiatric Services, 50,* 62–68.

Hingley, S. M. (1997a). Psychodynamic perspectives on psychosis and psychotherapy I: theory. *British Journal of Medical Psychology, 20,* 301–312.

Hingley, S. M. (1997b). Psychodynamic perspectives on psychosis and psychotherapy: practice. *British Journal of Medical Psychology, 20,* 313–322.

Hinshelwood, R.D. (1999). The difficult patient. *British Journal of Psychiatry, 174,* 187–190.

Hodgins, S. (1992). Mental disorder, intellectual deficiency, and crime. Evidence from a birth cohort. *Archives of General Psychiatry, 49,* 476–83.

Hodgins, S., & Cote, G. (1993a). The criminality of mentally disordered offenders. *Criminal Justice and Behaviour, 20,* 115–129.

Hodgins, S., Mednick, S. A., Brennan, P. A., Schulsinger, F., & Engberg, M. (1996). Mental disorder and crime: Evidence from a Danish birth cohort. *Archives of General Psychiatry, 53,* 489–496.

Hodgins, S. C., & Cote, G. (1993b). Major mental disorder and antisocial personality disorder: A criminal combination. *Bulletin of the American Academy of Psychiatry and the Law, 21,* 155–160.

Hodgkinson, P. E., McIvor, L., & Phillips, M. (1985). Patient assaults on staff in psychiatric hospital: a 2–year retrospective study. *Medicine, Science and the Law, 25,* 288–294.

Holcomb, W. R., & Ahr, P. R. (1988). Arrest rates among young adult psychiatric patients treated in inpatient and outpatient settings. *Hospital and Community Psychiatry, 39,* 52–7.

Hollin, C.R. & Howells, K. (1989). An introduction to concepts, models and techniques. In K. Howells & C.R. Hollin (Eds.). *Clinical Approaches to Violence.* Chichester: John Wiley & Sons.

Holloway, F. (1998). Risk assessment. *British Journal of Psychiatry, 173,* 540–3.

Holtzworth-Munroe, A., Stuart, G. L., & Hutchinson, G. (1997). Violent versus nonviolent husbands: Differences in attachment patterns, dependency, and jealousy. *Journal of Family Psychology, 11,* 314–331.

Home Office, Department of Health and Welsh Office. (1995). *National Standards for the Supervision of Offenders in the Community.* London: Home

Office.

Howes, C., & Espinosa, M. P. (1985). The consequences of child abuse for the formation of relationships with peers. *Child Abuse and Neglect, 9,* 397–404.

Howlett, M. (1998). *Medication, Non-Compliance & Mentally Disordered Offenders.* London: The Zito Trust.

Hyde, A. P. (1997). Coping with the threatening, intimidating, violent behaviors of people with psychiatric disabilities living at home: Guidelines for family caregivers. *Psychiatric Rehabilitation Journal., 21,* 144–149.

Jackson, H. F. (1990). Biological markers in schizophrenia. In, R. P. Bentall (Ed) *Reconstructing Schizophrenia.* London: Routledge.

James, D. V., Fineberg, N. A., & Shah, A. K. (1990). An increase in violence on an acute psychiatric ward. *British Journal of Psychiatry, 156,* 846–52.

Janofsky, J. S., Spears, S., & Neubauer, D. N. (1988). Psychiatrists' accuracy in predicting violent behaviour on an inpatient unit. *Hospital and Community Psychiatry, 39,* 1090–4.

Jernigan, T. L. (1992). Neuroanatomical factors in schizophrenia. In, D. J. Kavanagh (Ed) *Schizophrenia: An Overview and Practical Handbook.* London: Chapman Hall.

Johns, A. (1997). Substance misuse: A primary risk and a major problem of comorbidity. *International Review of Psychiatry, 9,* 2–3.

Johnston, E., Crow, T., Johnston, A., & Macmillan, F. (1986). The Northwick Park Study of first episodes of schizophrenia. 1. Presentation of the illness and problems relating to admission. *British Journal of Psychiatry, 149,* 51–56.

Johnston, M. E. (1988). Correlates of early violence experience among men who are abusive toward female mates. In G. T. Hotaling & D. Finkelhor (Eds.), *Family abuse and its consequences: New directions in research* (192–202). Newbury Park, CA: Sage Publications.

Jordan, B. K., Schlenger, W. E., Fairbank, J. A., & Caddell, J. M. (1996). Prevalence of psychiatric disorders among incarcerated women. *Archives of General Psychiatry, 53,* 513–519.

Junginger, J. (1990). Predicting compliance with command hallucinations. *American Journal of Psychiatry, 147,* 245–7.

Junginger, J. (1995). Command hallucinations and the prediction of dangerousness. *Psychiatric Services, 46,* 911–914.

Junginger, J. (1996). Psychosis and violence: The case for a content analysis of psychotic experience. *Schizophrenia Bulletin., 22,* 91–103.

Kalmuss, D. (1984). The intergenerational transmission of marital aggression. *Journal of Marriage and the Family, 46,* 11–19.

Katz, P., & Kirkland, F. R. (1990). Violence and social structure on mental hospital wards. *Psychiatry, 53*, 262–277.

Kay, S., Wolkenfeld, F., & Murrill, L. (1988). Profiles of aggression among psychiatric patients: nature and prevalence. *Journal of Nervous and Mental Disease, 176*, 539–546.

Kemp, R., Hayward, P., & David, A. (1997). *Compliance Therapy Manual* . Cheshire, UK: Gardiner-Caldwell.

Kendell, R. E., Brockington, I. F. & Leff, J. S. (1976). Prognostic implication of six alternative definitions of schizophrenia. *Archives of General Psychiatry, 36*, 25–31.

Kessler, R. C., & Magee, W. J. (1994). Childhood family violence and adult recurrent depression. *Journal of Health and Social Behaviour, 35*, 13–27.

Klassen, D., & O'Connor, W. A. (1988a). A prospective study of predictors of violence in adult mental health admissions. *Law and Human Behaviour, 12*, 143–158.

Klassen, D., & O'Connor, W. A. (1988b). Crime, inpatient admissions, and violence among male mental patients. *International Journal of Law and Psychiatry, 11*, 305–312.

Klassen, D., & O'Connor, W. A. (1989). Assessing the risk of violence in released mental patients: A cross validation study. *Psychological Assessment, 1*, 75–81.

Klimes-Dougan, B., & Kistner, J. (1990). Physically abused preschoolers' responses to peers' distress. *Developmental Psychology, 26*, 599–602.

Kraemer, H. C., Kazdin, A. E., Offord, D. R., Kessler, R. C., Jensen, P. S., & Kupfer, D. J. (1997). Coming to terms with the terms of risk. *Archives of General Psychiatry, 54*, 337–343.

Krakowski, M., Volavka, J., & Brizer, D. (1986). Psychopathology and violence: a review of the literature. *Comprehensive Psychiatry, 27*, 131–48.

Krakowski, M. I., & Czobor, P. (1994). Clinical symptoms, neurological impairment, and prediction of violence in psychiatric inpatients. *Hospital and Community Psychiatry, 45*, 700–705.

Kraupl-Taylor, F. (1979). *Psychopathology: Its Causes and Symptoms*. Romney Marsh, UK: Quartermain House.

Kuipers, E., Garety, P., Fowler, D., Dunn, D., Bebbington, P., Freeman, D. & Hadley, C. (1997). London-East Anglia randomised controlled trial of cognitive-behavioural therapy for psychosis. *British Journal of Psychiatry, 171*, 319–327.

Kuperschmidt, J. B., Coie, J. D., & Dodge, K. A. (1990). The role of poor peer relationships in the development of disorder. In S. R. Asher & J. D. Coie (Eds.), *Peer Rejection in Childhood* (217–249). Cambridge: Cambridge University Press.

Lagos, J. M., Perlmutter, K., & Saexinger, H. (1977). Fear of the mentally ill: Empirical support for the common man's response. *American Journal of Psychiatry, 134,* 1134–1137.

Lake, E. S. (1993). An exploration of the violent victim experiences of female offenders. *Violence and Victims, 8,* 41–51.

Lake, E. S. (1995). Offenders' experiences of violence: A comparison of male and female inmates as victims. *Deviant Behaviour, 16,* 269–290.

Lam, D. (1991). Psychological family intervention in schizophrenia: a review of empirical studies. *Psychological Medicine, 21,* 423–441.

Larkin, E. P., Murtagh, S., & Jones, S. J. (1988). A preliminary study of violent incidents in a Special Hospital (Rampton). *British Journal of Psychiatry, 153,* 226–231.

Lavender, A. (1999). Schizophrenia. In, M. Power & L. Champion (Eds) *Adult Psychological Problems.* London: Falmer.

Lavender, A. & Holloway, F. (1988). *Community Care in Practice: Services for the Continuing Care Client.* Chichester: Wiley.

Layden, M.A., Newman, C.F., Freeman, A. & Morse, S.B. (1993). *Cognitive Therapy of Borderline Personality Disorder.* Boston: Allyn and Bacon.

Lehmann, L.S., McCormick, R.A. & Kizer, K.W. (1999). A survey of assaultative behaviour in Veterans Health Administration facilities. *Psychiatric Services, 50,* 384–389.

Levinson, A., & Fonagy, P. (submitted). Adult attachment patterns in forensic non-psychiatric patients.

Lewis, A. (1974). Psychopathic personality: A most elusive category. *Psychological Medicine, 9,* 133–140.

Lewis, D. O., Mallouh, C., & Webb, V. (1989). Child abuse, delinquency, and violent criminality. In D. Cicchetti & V. Carlson (Eds.), *Child maltreatment: Theory and research on the causes and consequences of child abuse and neglect* (707–721). New York, NY: Cambridge University Press.

Lewis, D. O., Shanock, S. S., Pincus, J. H., & Glaser, G. H. (1980). Violent juvenile delinquents: Psychiatric, neurological, psychological, and abuse factors. *Annual Progress in Child Psychiatry and Child Development,* 591–603.

Lidz, C. W., Mulvey, E. P., & Gardner, W. (1993). The accuracy of predictions of violence to others. *Journal of the American Medical Association, 269,* 1007–1011.

Lilienfeld, S.O. (1998). Methodological advances and developments in the assessment of psychopathy. *Behavioural Research and Therapy, 36,* 99–125.

Limentani, A. (1991). Neglected fathers in the aetiology and treatment of sexual deviations. *International Journal of Psycho-Analysis, 72,* 573–584.

Lindqvist, P., & Allebeck, P. (1990). Schizophrenia and crime: a longitudinal follow-up of 644 schizophrenics in Stockholm. *British Journal of Psychiatry, 157*, 345–350.

Link, B., Cullen, F., Frank, J., & Wozniak, J. (1987). The social rejection of former mental patients: understanding why labels matter. *American Journal of Sociology*, 1461–1500.

Link, B. G., Andrews, H. A., & Cullen, F. T. (1992). The violent and illegal behaviour of mental patients reconsidered. *American Sociological Review, 57*, 275–292.

Link, B. G., & Stueve, A. (1994). Psychotic symptoms and the violent/illegal behaviour of mental patients compared to community controls. In J. Monahan & H. Steadman (Eds.), *Violence and Mental Disorder* . Chicago: University of Chicago Press.

Link, B. G., & Stueve, A. (1995). Evidence bearing on mental illness as a possible cause of violent behaviour. *Epidemiologic Reviews, 17*, 172–81.

Litwack, T. R. (1994). Assessments of dangerousness: Legal, research, and clinical developments. *Administration and Policy in Mental Health, 21*, 361–377.

Livesley, W.J., Jang, K., Schroeder, M.L. & Jackson, D.N. (1993). Genetic and environmental factors in personality dimensions. *American Journal of Psychiatry, 150*, 1826–1831.

Loeber, R. (1982). The stability of antisocial and delinquent child behaviour: A review. *Child Development, 53*, 1431–1446.

Loeber, R., & Stouthamer-Loeber, M. (1986). Family factors as correlates and predictors of juvenile conduct problems and delinquency. In M. Tonry & N. Morris (Eds.), *Crime and Justice* (Vol. 7,). Chicago: University of Chicago Press.

Lowerstein, M., Binder, R. L., & McNeil, D. E. (1990). The relationship between admission symptoms and hospital assault. *Hospital and Community Psychiatry, 41*, 311–3.

Lundy, M. S., Pfohl, B. M., & Kuperman, S. (1993). Adult criminality among formerly hospitalized child psychiatric patients. *Journal of the American Academy of Child and Adolescent Psychiatry, 32*, 568–576.

MACA (1999). *Review of the Mental Health Act (1983). Consultation Exercise.* London: Author.

Mackenbach, J. P., Kunst, A. E., Lautenbach, H., Bijlsma, F., & Oei, Y. B. (1995). Competing causes of death: An analysis using multiple-cause-of-death data from the Netherlands. *American Journal of Epidemiology, 141*, 466–475.

MacKenzie, D. L. (1991). The parole performance of offenders released from shock incarceration (boot camp prisons): A survival time analysis. *Journal of Quantitative Criminology, 7*(3), 213–236.

Magnusson, D., & Bergman, L. R. (1990). A pattern approach to the study of pathways from childhood to adulthood. In L. Robins & M. Rutter (Eds.), *Straight and Devious Pathways from Childhood to Adulthood* (101–115). Cambridge: Cambridge University Press.

Main, M. (1991). Metacognitive knowledge, metacognititive monitoring, and singular (coherent) vs. multiple (incoherent) model of attachment: findings and directions for future research. In C. M. Parkes, J. Stevenson-Hinde, & P. Marris (Eds.), *Attachment Across the Life Cycle* . London: Routledge.

Main, M., & George, C. (1985). Response of abused and disadvantaged toddlers to distress in agemates: A study in the day care setting. *Developmental Psychology, 21*, 407–412.

Main, M., & Hesse, P. (1990). Parent's unresolved traumatic experiences are related to disorganised infant attachment status. In M. Greenberg, D. Cichetti, & E. M. Cummings (Eds.), *Attachment during the preschool years* (161–182). Chicago: University of Chicago Press.

Main, M., Kaplan, N., & Cassidy, J. (1985). Security in infancy, childhood and adulthood: A move to the level of representation. In I. Bretherton & E. Waters (Eds.), *Growing points of attachment theory and research. Mongraphs of the Society for Research in Child Development, 50*, 66–104 .

Mannuzza, S., Klein, R., & Bonagura, N. (1988). Hyperactive boys almost grown up. II: Status of subjects without mental disorder. *Archives of General Psychiatry, 45*, 13–18.

Marshall, E. L., Laws, D. R., & Barbaree, H. E. (1990). Issues in sexual assault. In E. L. Marshall, D. R. Laws, & H. E. Barbaree (Eds.), *Handbook of Sexual Assault: Issues, Theories, and Treatment of the Offender* . New York: Plenum Press.

Marshall, J. R. (1990). The genetics of schizophrenia. In, R. Bentall (Ed) *Reconstructing Schizophrenia*. London: Routledge.

Marshall, P. (1997). *A Reconviction Study of HMP Grendon Therapeutic Community*. London: HMSO.

Martell, D., & Dietz, P. (1992). Mentally disordered offenders who push or attempt to push victims onto subway tracks in New York City. *Archives of General Psychiatry, 49*, 472–5.

Martell, D. A., Rosner, R., & Harmon, R. B. (1995). Base-rate estimates of criminal behaviour by homeless mentally ill persons in New York City. *Psychiatric Services, 46*, 596–601.

Marzuk, P. M. (1996). Violence, crime, and mental illness. How strong a link? *Archives of General Psychiatry, 53*, 481–6.

Maughan, B. (1993). Childhood precursors of aggressive offending in personality-disordered adults. In S. Hodgins (Ed.), *Mental disorder and crime* (119–139). Newbury Park, CA, USA: Sage Publications.

Mayer, A., & Barry, D. D. (1992). Working with the media to

destigmatize mental illness. *Hospital and Community Psychiatry, 43,* 77–8.

McCann, J. T., & Dyer, F. J. (1996). *Forensic Assessment with the Millon Inventories.* New York: Guildford Press.

McCord, J. (1979). Some child-rearing antecedents of criminal behaviour in adult men. *Journal of Personality and Social Psychology, 37,* 1477–1486.

McCormack, A., Rokous, F. E., Hazelwood, R. R., & Burgess, A. W. (1992). An exploration of incest in the childhood development of serial rapists. *Journal of Family Violence, 7,* 219–228.

McFarland, B., Faulkner, L., Bloom, J., Hallaux, R., & Bray, J. (1989). Chronic mental illness and the criminal justice system. *Hospital and Community Psychiatry, 40,* 718–23.

McGuffin, P. (1988). Genetics of schizophrenia. In, P. Bebbington & P. McGuffin (Eds) *Schizophrenia: The Major Issues.* London: Heinemann.

McNeil, D., & Binder, R. (1991). Clinical assessment of the risk of violence among psychiatric inpatients. *American Journal of Psychiatry, 148,* 1317–1321.

McNeil, D., & Binder, R. (1994). Screening for risk of inpatient violence: Validation of an actuarial tool. *Law and Human Behaviour, 18,* 579.

McNiel, D. E. (1994). Hallucinations and violence. In J. Monahan & H. Steadman (Eds.), *Violence and Mental Disorder: Developments in Risk Assessment.* Chicago, IL, USA: Chicago University Press.

McNiel, D. E. (1997). Correlates of violence in psychotic patients. *Psychiatric Annals, 27,* 683–690.

McNiel, D. E., & Binder, R. L. (1994). The relationship between acute psychiatric symptoms, diagnosis, and short-term risk of violence [see comments]. *Hospital and Community Psychiatry, 45,* 133–7.

McNiel, D. E., & Binder, R. L. (1995). Correlates of accuracy in the assessment of psychiatric inpatients' risk of violence. *American Journal of Psychiatry, 152,* 901–6.

Mednick, S. A. (1977). A biosocial theory of learning and law abiding behaviour. In, S.

A. Mednick & K. O. Christiansen (Eds). Biosocial Basis of Criminal Behaviour. New York: Gardender.

Mednick, S. A., Brennan, P., & Kandel, E. (1988). Predisposition to violence. *Aggressive Behaviour, 14,* 25–33.

Megargee, E.I. (1982). Psychological determinants and correlates of criminal violence. In M.E. Wolfgang and N.A. Weiner (Eds.). *Criminal Violence.* Beverly Hills, CA: Sage Publications.

Melick, M. E., Steadman, H. J., & Cocozza, J. J. (1979). The medicalisation of criminal behaviour among mental patients. *Journal of Health and Social Behaviour, 20,* 228–37.

Meninger, K. A. (1968). *The Crime of Punishment.* New York: Viking.

Mental Health Act (1983). London: HMSO.

Milner, J. S., & Campbell, J. C. (1995). Prediction issues for practitioners. In J. C. Campbell (Ed.), *Assessing dangerousness: Violence by sexual offenders, batterers, and child abusers* (20–40). Thousand Oaks, CA, USA: Sage Publications.

Milner, J. S., Robertson, K. R., & Rogers, D. L. (1990). Childhood history of abuse and adult child abuse potential. *Journal of Family Violence, 5*, 15–34.

Mishcon, J., Dick, D., Milne, I. & Beard, P. (1996). *Report of the Independent Inquiry Team into the Care and Treatment of Francis Hampshire to Redbridge and Waltham Forest Health Authority* (Chair: Jane Mishcon). London: Redbridge and Waltham Forest Health Authority.

Mishcon, J., Dick, D., Welsh, N., Sheehan, A. & Mackay (1995). *Report of the Independent Inquiry Team into the Care and Treatment of Kenneth Grey to East London and the City Health Authority* (Chair, Jane Mischon). London: East London & the City Health Authority.

Modestin, J., & Ammann, R. (1995). Mental disorders and criminal behaviour. *British Journal of Psychiatry, 166*, 667–75.

Modestin, J., Berger, A., & Ammann, R. (1996). Mental disorder and criminality. Male alcoholism. *Journal of Nervous and Mental Disorder, 184*, 393–402.

Moffitt, T. E. (1993). Adolescence-limited and life course persistent antisocial behaviour. *Psychological Review*, 100, 674–701.

Moffit, T. E., & Silva, P. A. (1988). Self-reported delinquency, neuropsychological deficit and history of attention deficit disorder. *Journal of Abnormal Child Psychology, 16*, 553–569.

Moffitt, T. E. (1987). Parental mental disorder and offspring criminal behaviour: An adoption study. *Psychiatry, 50*, 346–360.

Monahan, J. (1973). The psychiatrization of criminal behaviour: A reply. *Hospital and Community Psychiatry, 24*, 105–7.

Monahan, J. (1981). *Predicting Violent Behaviour*. Newbury, CA.: Sage.

Monahan, J. (1988). Risk assessment of violence among the mentally disordered: Generating useful knowledge. *International Journal of Law and Psychiatry, 11*, 249–257.

Monahan, J. (1992). Mental disorder and violent behaviour: Perceptions and evidence. *American Psychologist, 47*, 511–521.

Monahan, J. (1993a). Mental disorder and violence: Another look. In S. Hodgins (Ed.), *Mental Disorder and Crime* (287–302). Newbury Park, CA, USA: Sage Publications.

Monahan, J. (1993b). Causes of Violence. In U.S.S. Commission (Ed.), *Drugs and Violence in America*. Washington, D.C.: U.S. Government Printing Office.

Monahan, J. (1993c). Limiting therapist exposure to Tarasoff liability: Guidelines for risk containment. *American Psychologist, 48*, 242–250.

Monahan, J. (1996). Violence prediction. *Criminal Justice and Behaviour, 23*, 107–120.

Monahan, J. (2000). Clinical and actuarial predictions of violence. In D. Faigman, D. Kaye, M. Saks, & J. Sanders (Eds.), *Modern Scientific Evidence: The Law and Science of Expert Testimony* (Vol. 1). St Paul, MN: West Publishing Company.

Monahan, J., & Steadman, H. (1983). Crime and mental disorder: an epidemiological approach. In M. Tonry & N. Morris (Eds.), *Crime and Justice: an annual review of research* (Vol. 4, 145–189). Chicago: Chicago University Press.

Monahan, J., & Steadman, H. (1994). Toward a rejuvenation of risk assessment research. In J. Monahan & H. Steadman (Eds.), *Violence and Mental Disorder: Developments in risk assessment* (1–18). Chicago, IL, USA: Chicago University Press.

Monahan, J., Steadman, H.J., Appelbaum, P.S., Robbins, P.C., Mulvey, E.P., Silver, E., Roth, L.H. & Grisso, T. (in press). Developing a clinically useful actuarial tool for assessing violence risk. *British Journal of Psychiatry*.

MORI (1997). *Attitudes towards Schizophrenia: A Survey of Public Opinion Conducted for Fleishman Hillard*. London: MORI.

Morrison, E. F. (1994). The evolution of a concept: Aggression and violence in psychiatric settings. *Archives of Psychiatric Nursing, 8*, 245–253.

Mossman, D. (1994). Assessing predictions of violence: Being accurate about accuracy. *Journal of Consulting and Clinical Psychology, 62*, 783–792.

Mueser, K. T., Bond, G. R., Drake, R. E. & Resnick, G. (1998). Models of community care for severe mental illness: A review of research on case management. *Schizophrenia Bulletin, 24*, 38–73.

Muetzell, S. (1995). Human violence in Stockholm County, Sweden. *International Journal of Adolescence and Youth, 6*, 75–88.

Mullen, P. E. (1997). A reassessment of the link between mental disorder and violent behaviour, and its implications for clinical practice. *Australian and New Zealand Journal of Psychiatry, 31*, 3–11.

Mulvey, E. P. (1994). Assessing the evidence of a link between mental illness and violence. *Hospital and Community Psychiatry, 45*, 663–668.

Mulvey, E. P., & Lidz, C. W. (1995). Conditional prediction: a model for research on dangerousness to others in a new era. *International Journal of Law and Psychiatry, 18*, 129–143.

Murdoch, D., Pihl, R. O., & Ross, D. (1990). Alcohol and crimes of violence: Present issues. *International Journal of the Addictions, 25*, 1065–1081.

National Mental Health Association. (1987). *Stigma: a lack of awareness and understanding*. Alexandria, VA: National Mental Health Association.

National Schizophrenia Fellowship. (1999). *Better Act Now! NSF's Views on the Mental Health Act Review*. London: Author.

Nelson, T. O., Stuart, R. B., Howard, C. & Crowley, M. (1999). Metacognition and clinical psychology: a preliminary framework for research and practice. *Clinical Psychology & Psychotherapy, 6 (2)*, 73–79.

Noble, P., & Rodger, S. (1989). Violence by psychiatric inpatients. *British Journal of Psychiatry, 155*, 384–90.

Novaco, R. W. (1994). Anger as a risk factor for violence among the mentally disordered. In J. Monahan & H. J. Steadman (Eds.), *Violence and Mental Disorder: Developments in risk assessment*. Chicago, IL, USA: Chicago University Press.

Nuechterlein, K. H. & Dawson, M. E. (1984). A heuristic vulnerability/stress model of schizophrenic episodes. *Schizophrenia Bulletin, 10*, 300–312.

Nuechterlein, K. H. (1987). Vulnerability models for schizophrenia: state of the art. In H. Hafner, W. F. Gattaz & W. Janarzik (Eds), *Search for the Causes of Schizophrenia*. Berlin, Heidleberg: Springer.

Oliver, J. E. (1993). Intergenerational transmission of child abuse: rates, research and clinical implications. *American Journal of Psychiatry, 150*, 1315–1324.

Onyett, S. R. (1999a). *An Exploratory Study of English Community Mental Health Teams*. Unpublished PhD Thesis: Liverpool University.

Onyett, S. R. (1999b). Community mental health team working on a socially valued enterprise. *Journal of Mental Health, 8*, 3, 245–251.

Onyett, S. R. & Ford, R. (1996). Community mental health teams – where's the wreckage? *Journal of Mental Health, 5*, 47–55.

Onyett, S. R., Heppleston, T. & Muijen, M. (1995). *Making Community Mental Health Teams Work*. London: Sainsbury Centre for Mental Health.

Ortmann, J. (1981). *Psykisk Afvigelse og Kriminel Adraerd*. Copenhagen, Denmark: Justitministeriet.

Owen, C., Tarantello, C., Jones, M., & Tennant, C. (1998a). Repetitively violent patients in psychiatric units. *Psychiatric Services, 49*, 1458–1461.

Owen, C., Tarantello, C., Jones, M., & Tennant, C. (1998b). Violence and aggression in psychiatric units. *Psychiatric Services, 49*, 1452–1457.

Padesky, C. A. (1994). Schema change process in cognitive therapy. *Clinical Psychology & Psychotherapy, 1, 5*, 267–278.

Paris, J. (1996). *Social Factors in the Personality Disorders*. Cambridge, USA: Cambridge University Press.

Patrick, M., Hobson, R. P., Castle, D., Howard, R. & Maughan, B.

(1994). Personality disorder and the mental representation of early social experience. *Development and Psychopathology, 6,* 375–388.

Patterson, G. R., & Yoerger, K. (1993). Developmental models of delinquent behaviour. In S. Hodgins (Ed.), *Mental disorder and crime* (140–172). Newbury Park, CA, USA: Sage Publications.

Peck, E. & Parker, E. (1998). Mental health in the NHS: policy and practice 1979–1998. *Journal of Mental Health, 7,* 241–260.

Perelberg, R. J. (1999). *Psychoanalytic Understanding of Violence and Suicide.* London: Routledge.

Performance Management Directorate (1993). *Health of the Nation: Mentally Disordered Offenders.* Leeds: NHS Management Executive.

Pescosolido, B. A., Monahan, J., Link, B., Stueve, A., & Kikuzawa, M. S. (in press). The public's view of the competence, dangerousness and need for legal coercion among persons with mental illness. *American Journal of Public Health.*

Petersson, H., & Gudjonsson, G. H. (1981). Psychiatric aspects of homicide. *Acta Psychiatrica Scandanavica, 64,* 363–372.

Philo, G., Henderson, L., & McLaughlin, G. (1994). *Mass Media Representations of Mental Health/Illness. Report for Health Education Board of Scotland.* Glasgow: Glasgow University Media Group.

Pihl, R. O., & Peterson, J. B. (1993). Alcohol/drug use and aggressive behaviour. In S. Hodgins (Ed.), *Mental disorder and crime* . Newbury Park, CA, USA: Sage Publications.

Piper, E. S. (1985). Violent recidivism and chronicity in the 1958 Philadelphia cohort. *Journal of Quantitative Criminology, 1,* 319–344.

Planansky, K., & Johnston, R. (1977). Homicidal aggression in schizophrenic men. *Acta Psychiatrica Scandanavica, 55,* 65–73.

Plomin, R., DeFries, J.C. & McClearn, G.E. (1990). *Behavioural Genetics: A Primer.* New York: Freeman.

Powell, G., Cann, W., & Crowe, M. (1994). What events precede violent incidents in psychiatric hospitals? *British Journal of Psychiatry, 165,* 107–112.

Prentky, R. A., Knight, R. A., Sims Knight, J. E., Straus, H., & al., e. (1989). Developmental antecedents of sexual aggression. *Development and Psychopathology, 1,* 153–169.

Pretzer, J. (1994). Cognitive therapy of personality disorders: the state of the art. *Clinical Psychology & Psychotherapy, 1, 5,* 257–266.

Prins, H. (1990). Mental abnormality and criminality – an uncertain relationship. *Medicine, Science and the Law, 30,* 247–258.

Prins, H. (1998). Inquiries after homicide in England and Wales. *Medicine, Science and the Law, 38,* 211–220.

Quinsey, V.L., Harris, G.T., Rice, M.E. & Cormier, C.A. (1998). *Violent*

Offenders: Appraising and Managing Risk. Washington, DC: American Psychological Association.

Quinsey, V. L., Rice, M. E., & Harris, G. T. (1995). The actuarial prediction of sexual recidivism. *Journal of Interpersonal Violence, 10,* 85–105.

Rabkin, J. (1974). Attitudes toward mental illness. *Schizophrenia Bulletin, 10,* 7–19.

Rabkin, J. (1979). Criminal behaviour of discharged mental patients: a critical appraisal of the research. *Psychological Bulletin, 86,* 1–27.

Rabkin, J. G. (1972). Opinions about mental illness: a review of the literature. *Psychological Bulletin, 77,* 153–71.

Raine, A., Brennan, P., Mednick, B., & Mednick, S. A. (1996). High rates of violence, crime, academic problems, and behavioral problems in males with both early neuromotor deficits and unstable family environments. *Archives of General Psychiatry, 53,* 544–549.

Raine, A., Brennan, P., & Mednick, S. A. (1994). Birth complications combined with early maternal rejection at age 1 year predispose to violent crime at age 18 years. *Archives of General Psychiatry, 51,* 984–988.

Raine, A., Brennan, P., & Mednick, S. A. (1997). Interaction between birth complications and early maternal rejection in predisposing individuals to adult violence: Specificity to serious, early-onset violence. *American Journal of Psychiatry., Vol 154,* 1265–1271.

Rasmussen, K., & Levander, S. (1996). Crime and violence among psychiatric patients in a maximum security psychiatric hospital. *Criminal Justice and Behaviour, 23,* 455–471.

Reber, A. (1985). *Dictionary of Psychology*. Harmondsworth, UK: Penguin Books.

Reed, J. (1997). Risk assessment and clinical risk management: The lessons from recent inquiries. *British Journal of Psychiatry, 170* (Suppl 32), 4–7.

Regier, D. A., Farmer, M. E., Rae, D. A., et al. (1990). Comorbidity of mental disorders with alchol and other drugs of abuse: results of the Epidemiologic Catchment Area (ECA) Study. *Journal of the American Medical Association, 264,* 2511–8.

Reid, W., Bollinger, M., & Edwards, G. (1985). Assaults in hospitals. *Bulletin of the American Academy of Psychiatry and the Law, 13,* 1–4.

Reiss, A., & Roth, J. (Eds.). (1993). *Understanding and Preventing Violence.*: National Academy Report.

Reith, M. (1998). Risk assessment and management: lessons from mental health inquiry reports. *Medicine, Science and the Law, 38,* 221–226.

Reynolds, G. P. (1983). Increased concentrations and lateral asymmetry of amygdala dopamine in schizophrenia. *Nature, 305,* 527–529.

Reynolds, G. P. (1987). Post-mortem neurochemical studies in human postmortem brain tissue. In, H. Hafner, W. F. Gattaz & W. Janzarik (Eds) *Search for the Causes of Schizophrenia.* Heidelberg: Springer.

Rice, M., & Harris, G. T. (1992). A comparison of criminal recidivism among schizophrenic and non-schizophrenic offenders. *International Journal of Law and Psychiatry, 15,* 397–408.

Rice, M. E., & Harris, G. T. (1995a). Psychopathy, schizophrenia, alcohol abuse, and violent recidivism. *International Journal of Law and Psychiatry, 18,* 333–342.

Rice, M. E., & Harris, G. T. (1995b). Violent recidivism: assessing predictive validity. *Journal of Consulting and Clinical Psychology, 63,* 737–748.

Rice, M. E., & Harris, G. T. (1997). Cross-validation and extension of the violence risk appraisal guide for child molesters and rapists. *Law Hum Behav, 21,* 231–41.

Rice, M.E., Harris, G.T. & Cormier, C. (1992). Evaluation of a maximum security therapeutic community for psychopaths and other mentally disordered offenders. *Law and Human Behaviour, 16,* 399–412.

Rice, M. E., Harris, G. T., & Quinsey, V. L. (1990). A follow-up of rapists assessed in a maximum security psychiatric facility. *Journal of Interpersonal Violence, 5,* 435–448.

Rice, M.E., Harris, G. T., & Quinsey, V. L. (1996). Treatment for forensic patients. In B.D. Sales & S.A. Shah (Eds.), *Mental Health and Law: Research, Policy and Services* (141–189). New York: Academic Press.

Richardson, J. T. E. (1996). *Handbook of Qualitative Research Methods.* Leicester: BPS Books.

Ritchie, J., Dick, D. & Lingham, R. (1994). *The Report of the Inquiry into the Care and Treatment of Christopher Clunis* (Chair, Jean Ritchie QC). London: HMSO.

Rivera, B., & Widom, C. S. (1990). Childhood victimization and violent offending. *Violence and Victims, 5,* 19–35.

Robertson, G. (1987). Mentally disordered offenders: manner of death. *British Medical Journal, 295,* 632–4.

Robertson, G., Pearson, R., & Gibb, R. (1995). *The Mentally Disordered and the Police. Home Office Research Findings No. 21.* London: HMSO.

Robins, L.N. (1991). Conduct disorders. *Journal of Child Psychology and Psychiatry, 32,* 193–212.

Robins, L.N. (1993). Childhood conduct problems, adult psychopathology, and crime. In S. Hodgins (Ed.), *Mental disorder and crime* (173–193). Newbury Park, CA, USA: Sage Publications.

Robins, L. N., Tipp, J., & Przybeck, T. R. (1990). Antisocial personality. In L. N. Robins & D. A. Reiger (Eds.), *Psychiatric Disorders in America* (258–290). New York, NY: Free Press.

Roff, J. D. (1992). Childhood aggression, peer status, and social class as predictors of delinquency. *Psychological Reports, 70,* 31–34.

Rogers, A. & Pilgrim, D. (1996). *Mental Health Policy in Britain: A Critical Introduction.* London: Croom Helm.

Rogers, R., Dion, K.L. & Lynett, E. (1992). Diagnostic validity of antisocial personality disorder: A prototypical analysis. *Law and Human Behaviour, 16,* 677–689.

Rogers, R., Gillis, J., Turner, R., & al., e. (1990). The clinical presentation of command hallucinations in a forensic population. *American Journal of Psychiatry, 147,* 1304–7.

Rogosch, F. A., & Cicchetti, D. (1994). Illustrating the interface of family and peer relations through the study of child maltreatment. *Social Development, 3,* 291–308.

Rogosch, F. A., Cicchetti, D., & Aber, J. L. (1995). The role of child maltreatment in early deviations in cognitive and affective processing abilities and later peer relationship problems. *Development and Psychopathology, 7,* 591–609.

Rosch, E. (1978). Principles of categorisation. In E. Rosch & B. Lloyd (Eds.), *Cognition and Categorisation* . Hillside: Lawrence Earlbaum Associates.

Rossi, A. M., Jacobs, M., Monteleone, M., Olser, R., Surber, R. W., Winkler, E. L., & Wommack, A. (1986). Characteristics of psychiatric patients who engage in assaultative behaviour or other fear inducing behaviours. *Journal of Nervous and Mental Diseases, 174,* 154–160.

Roth, L. (1980). Correctional psychiatry. In W. Curran, A. McGarry, & C. Petty (Eds.), *Modern Legal Medicine, Psychiatry and Forensic Science* . Philidelphia: Davis.

Rutter, M. (1987). Psychosocial resilience and protective mechanisms. *American Journal of Orthopsychiatry, 57,* 316–331.

Rutter, M. & Quinton, D. (1984). Long-term follow-up of women institutionalised in childhood. *British Journal of Developmental Psychology, 18,* 225–234.

Rutter, M. & Rutter, M. (1993). *Developing Minds: Challenge and Continuity Across the Life Span.* New York: Basic Books.

Ryan, G. (1989). Victim to victimiser. *Journal of Interpersonal Violence, 4,* 325–341.

Rycroft, C. (1968). *A Critical Dictionary of Psychoanalysis.* London: Penguin.

Rydelius, P. A. (1988). The development of antisocial behaviour and sudden violent death. *Acta Psychiatrica Scandinavica, 77,* 398–403.

Rydelius, P. A. (1994). Children of alcoholic parents: At risk to experience violence and to develop violent behaviour. In C. Chiland & J. G. Young

(Eds.), *Children and violence. The child in the family: The monograph series of the International Association for Child and Adolescent Psychiatry and Allied Professions, Vol. 11* (72–90). Northvale, NJ: Jason Aronson.

Ryle, A. (1997). The structure and development of borderline personality disorder: a proposed model. *British Journal of Psychiatry, 170,* 82–87.

Salekin, R. T., Roger, R., & Sewell, K. W. (1996). A review and meta-analysis of the Psychopathy Checklist and Psychopathy Checklist-Revised: Predictive validity and dangerousness. *Clinical Psychology: Science and Practice, 3,* 203–215.

Satterfield, J. K., Hoppe, C. M., & Schell, A. M. (1982). A prospective study of delinquency in 110 adolescent boys with attention deficit disorder and 88 normal adolescent boys. *American Journal of Psychiatry, 139,* 795–798.

Schuerman, L., & Kobrin, S. (1984). Exposure of community mental health clients to the criminal justice system. In L. Teplin (Ed.), *Mental Health and Criminal Justice* (pp. 87–118). Beverley Hills, CA: Sage.

Scott, P. D. (1977). Assessing dangerousness in criminals. *British Journal of Psychiatry, 131,* 127–142.

Sepejak, D. S., Menzies, R. J., Webster, C. D., & Jensen, F. A. (1983). Clinical predictions of dangerousness: Two year follow-up of 408 pre-trial forensic cases. *Bulletin of the American Academy of Psychiatry and the Law, 171.*

Serin, R. C., & Amos, N. L. (1995). The role of psychopathy in the assessment of dangerousness. *International Journal of Law and Psychiatry, 18,* 231–8.

Shah, A. K. (1993). An increase in violence among psychiatric inpatients: Real or apparent? *Medicine, Science and the Law, 33,* 227–30.

Shain, R., & Phillips, J. (1991). The stigma of mental illness: labelling and stereotyping in the news. In L. Wilkins & P. Patterson (Eds.), *Risky business: Communicating issues of science, risk, and public policy* (61–74). Westport, CN: Greenwood Press.

Shaw, J., Appleby, L., Amos, T., McDonnell, R., Harris, C., McCann, K., Kiernan, K., Davies, S., Bickley, H. and Parsons, R. (1999). Mental disorder and clinical care in people convicted of homicide: national clinical survey. *British Medical Journal, 318,* 1240–4.

Shaw, S. H. (1973). The dangerousness of dangerousness. *Medicine, Science and Law, 13,* 269–271.

Shepherd, G. (1995). Care and control in the community. In J. Crichton (Ed.), *Psychiatric Patient Violence – Risk and Response.* London Duckworth.

Shepherd, G. (1998). Models of community care. *Journal of Mental Health, 7,* 165–177.

Shepherd, M. & Lavender, T. (1999). Putting aggression in context: An investigation into contextual factors influencing the rate of aggressive incidents in a psychiatric hospital. *Journal of Mental Health, 8,* 151–162.

Sheppard, D. (1996). *Learning the Lessons.* London: Zito Trust.

Sheridan, M., Henrion, R., Robinson, L., & Baxter, V. (1990). Precipitants of violence in a psychiatric inpatient setting. *Hospital and Community Psychiatry, 41,* 776–780.

Shore, D., Filson, C. R., Johnson, W. E., Rae, D. S., Mueher, P., Kelley, D. J., Davis, T. S., Waldman, I. N., & Wyatt, R. J. (1989). Murder and assault arrests of White House cases: clinical and demographic correlates of violence subsequent to civil commitment. *American Journal of Psychiatry, 146,* 645–651.

Shore, D., Filson, R., & Rae, D. (1980). Violent crime arrest reates of White House case and match control subjects. *American Journal of Psychiatry, 147,* 746–50.

Signorielli, N. (1989). The stigma of mental illness on television. *Journal of Broadcasting and Electronic Media, 33,* 325–331.

Silver, E., Mulvey, E. P., & Monahan, J. (1999). Assessing violence risk among discharged psychiatric patients: Toward an ecological approach. *Law and Human Behaviour, 23,* 237–255.

Singleton, N., Meltzer, H., Gatward, R., Coid, J., & Deasy, D. (1998). *Psychiatric Morbidity Among Prisoners.* London: Stationary Office.

Smail, D. (1993). *The Origins of Unhappiness.* London, UK: Harper Collins.

Smith, J. A. (1996) Evolving issues for qualitative research. In J. T. E. Richardson (Ed), *Handbook of Qualitative Research Methods.* Leicester: BPS Books.

Smith, J., & Hucker, S. (1994). Schizophrenia and substance abuse. *British Journal of Psychiatry, 165,* 13–21.

Smith Report (1997). *Report of the Independent Panel of Inquiry into the Care and Treatment of Paul Smith* (Chair, Jane Mishcon). Peterborough: North West Anglia Health Authority.

Snowden, P. (1997). Practical aspects of clinical risk assessment and management. *British Journal of Psychiatry, 170* (Suppl 32), 32–34.

Solomon, P., Draine, J., & Meyerson, A. (1994). Jail recidivism and receipt of community mental health services. *Hospital and Community Psychiatry, 45,* 793–797.

Sontag, S. (1978). *Illness as Metaphor.* Toronto: McGraw-Hill Ryerson.

Sosowsky, L. (1974). The community approach to mental health in San Mateo County, *Putting State Mental Hospitals Out of Business* (34–73). Berkley: University of California.

Stalker, C. A., & Davies, F. (1995). Attachment organisation and adaption in sexually abused women. *Canadian Journal of Psychiatry, 40,* 3–10.

Stattin, H., & Magnusson, D. (1989). The role of early aggressive behaviour in the frequency, seriousness, and types of later crime. *Journal of Consulting and Clinical Psychology, 57,* 710–718.

Steadman, H. J. (1980). The right not to be a false positive: problems in the application of the dangerousness standard. *Psychiatric Quarterly, 32,* 84–99.

Steadman, H. J. (1983). Predicting dangerousness among the mentally ill: Art, magic and science. *International Journal of Law and Psychiatry, 6,* 381–390.

Steadman, H. J., Cocozza, J. J., & Melick, M. E. (1978). Explaining the increased arrest rate among mental patients: the changing clientele of state hospitals. *American Journal of Psychiatry, 135,* 816–20.

Steadman, H. J., Fabisiak, S., Dvoskin, J., & Holohean, E. (1987). A survey of mental disability among state prison inmates. *Hospital and Community Psychiatry, 38,* 1086–1090.

Steadman, H. J., Monahan, J., Robbins, P. C., Appelbaum, P., Grisso, T., Klassen, D., Mulvey, E. P., & Roth, L. (1993). From dangerousness to risk assessment: Implications for appropriate research strategies. In S. Hodgins (Ed.), *Mental disorder and crime* (39–62). Newbury Park, CA, USA: Sage Publications.

Steadman, H. J., & Morrissey, J. P. (1981). The statistical prediction of violent behaviour: measuring the costs of a public protectionist versus a civil libertarian model. *Law and Human Behaviour, 5,* 263–274.

Steadman, H. J., Mulvey, E. P., Monahan, J., Robbins, P. C., Appelbaum, P. S., Grisso, T., Roth, L. H., & Silver, E. (1998). Violence by people discharged from acute psychiatric inpatient facilties and by others in the same neighbourhoods. *Archives of General Psychiatry, 55,* 1–9.

Steadman, H. J., Monahan, J., Appelbaum, P. S., Grisso, T., Mulvey, E. P., Roth, L. H., Robbins, P. C., & Klassen, D. (1994). Designing a new generation of risk assessment research. In J. Monahan & H. J. Steadman (Eds.), *Violence and Mental Disorder: Developments in risk assessment* (101–136). Chicago, IL, USA: Chicago University Press.

Steadman, H.J., Silver, E., Monahan, J., Appelbaum, P.S., Robbins, P.C., Mulvey, E.P., Grisso, T., Roth, L.H., & Banks, S. (in press). A classification tree approach to the development of acturial violence risk assessment tools. *Law and Human Behaviour.*

Steering Committee of the Confidential Inquiry into Homicides and Suicides by Mentally Ill People (1994). *Preliminary Report.* London: Royal College of Psychiatrists.

Stevens, G.F. (1993). Applying the diagnosis antisocial personality to imprisoned offenders: Looking for hay in a haystack. *Journal of Offender Rehabilitation, 19,* 1–26.

Stoller, R. J. (1975). *Perversion: The Erotic Form of Hatred.* New York: Pantheon.

Strand, S., Belfrage, H., Fransson, G. & Levander, S. (1999). Clinical and risk management factors in risk prediction of mentally disordered offenders – more important than historical data? *Legal and Criminological Psychology, 4,* 67–76.

Strauss, J. S. & Carpenter, W. T. (1977). Predication of outcome in schizophrenia. III. Five year outcome and its predictions. *Archives of General Psychiatry, 34,* 154–163.

Straw, J. (1998). Letter to The Times. 31st October.

Straznickas, K. A., McNeil, D. E., & Binder, R. L. (1993). Violence toward family caregivers by mentally ill relatives. *Hospital and Community Psychiatry, 44,* 385–387.

Stueve, A., & Link, B. G. (1997). Violence and psychiatric disorders: Results from an epidemiological study of young adults in Israel. *Psychiatric Quarterly, 68,* 327–342.

Summit, R. (1983). The child sexual abuse accommodation syndrome. *Child Abuse and Neglect, 7,* 177–193.

Svanberg, P. O. G. (1998) Attachment, resilience and prevention. *Journal of Mental Health, 7,* 543–578.

Swanson, J., Estroff, S., Swartz, M., Borum, R., Lachicotte, W., Zimmer, C., & Wagner, R. (1997). Violence and severe mental disorder in clinical and community populations: The effects of psychotic symptoms, comorbidity, and lack of treatment. *Psychiatry: Interpersonal and Biological Processes, 60,* 1–22.

Swanson, J., Holzer, C., Gunju, V., & Jono, R. (1990). Violence and psychiatric disorder in the community: evidence from the epidemiological catchment area surveys. *Hospital and Community Psychiatry, 41,* 761–70.

Swanson, J. W. (1993). Alcohol abuse, mental disorder, and violent behaviour: An epidemiologic inquiry. *Alcohol Health and Research World, 17,* 123–132.

Swanson, J. W. (1994). Mental disorder, substance abuse, and community violence: An epidemiological approach. In J. Monahan & H. J. Steadman (Eds.), *Violence and Mental Disorder: Developments in risk assessment* (101–136). Chicago, IL, USA: Chicago University Press.

Swanson, J. W., Borum, R., Swartz, M. S., & Monahan, J. (1996). Psychotic symptoms and disorders and the risk of violent behaviour in the community. *Criminal Behaviour and Mental Health, 6,* 309–329.

Swanson, J. W., & Holzer, C. E. (1991). Violence and ECA data. *Hospital and Community Psychiatry, 42,* 954–955.

Swartz, M. S., Swanson, J. W., Hiday, V. A., Borum, R., Wagner, H. R.,

& Burns, B. J. (1998). Violence and severe mental illness: The effects of substance abuse and nonadherence to medication. *American Journal of Psychiatry, 155*, 226–231.

Tarasoff v. Regents of the University of California, 551 P. 2d 334 (1976).

Tardiff, K. (1984). Characteristics of assaultive patients in private hospitals. *American Journal of Psychiatry, 141*, 1232–1235.

Tardiff, K., Marzuk, P., Leon, A., & Portera, L. (1997). A prospective study of violence by psychiatric patients after hospital discharge. *Psychiatric Services, 48*, 678.

Tardiff, K., & Sweillam, A. (1980). Assault, suicide and mental illness. *American Journal of Psychiatry, 37*, 164–9.

Tardiff, K., & Sweillam, A. (1982). Assaultive behaviour among chronic inpatients. *American Journal of Psychiatry, 139*, 212–5.

Tarrier, N., Yusupoff, L., Kinney, C., McCarthy, E., Gledhill, A., Haddock, G. & Morris, J. (1998). Randomised controlled trial of intensive cognitive behaviour therapy for patients with chronic schizophrenia. *British Medical Journal, 317*, 303–307.

Taylor, P. J. (1985). Motives for offending among violent and psychotic men. *British Journal of Psychiatry, 147*, 491–498.

Taylor, P. J. (1987). Social implications of psychosis. *British Medical Bulletin, 43*, 718–40.

Taylor, P. J., Garety, P., Buchanan, A., Reed, A., Wessely, S., Ray, K., Dunn, G., & Grubin, D. (1994). Delusion and violence. In J. Monahan & H. J. Steadman (Eds.), *Violence and Mental Disorder: Developments in risk assessment* (161–182). Chicago, IL, USA: Chicago University Press.

Taylor, P. J., & Gunn, J. (1984). Violence and psychosis. I. Risk of violence among psychotic ment. *British Medical Journal, 288*, 1945–8.

Taylor, P. J., & Gunn, J. (1999). Homicides by people with mental illness: Myth or reality. *British Journal of Psychiatry, 174*, 9–14.

Taylor, P. J., Leese, M., Williams, D., Butwell, M., Daly, R., & Larkin, E. (1998). Mental disorder and violence: A special (high security) hospital study. *British Journal of Psychiatry, 172*, 218–226.

Taylor, P. J., & Parrott, J. (1988). Elderly offenders: a study of age with related factors among custodially remanded prisoners. *British Journal of Psychiatry, 152*, 340–6.

Teasdale, J. D. (1993). Emotion and two kinds of meaning: cognitive therapy and applied cognitive science. *Behaviour Research and Therapy, 31*, 339–354.

Teasdale, J. D. (1996). Clinically relevant theory: integrating clinical insight with cognitive science. In P. M. Salkovskis (Ed.), *Frontiers of Cognitive Therapy*. New York: Guildford.

Temple, N. (1996). Transference and countertransference: general and forensic aspects. In C. Cordess & M. Cox (Eds.), *Forensic Psychotherapy: Crime, Psychodynamics and the Offender Patient* . London: Jessica Kingsley Publishers.

Teplin, L. (1984). Criminalizing mental disorder: comparative arrest rate of the mentally ill. *American Psychologist, 39*, 794–803.

Teplin, L. (1990). The prevalence of severe mental disroder among male urban jail detainees: comparison with the Epidemiologic Catchment Area program. *American Journal of Public Health, 80*, 663–9.

Teplin, L. A., Abram, K. M., & McClelland, G. M. (1994). Does psychiatric disorder predict violent crime among released jail detainees? A six-year longitudinal study. *American Psychologist, 49*, 335–342.

Teplin, L. A., Abram, K. M., & McClelland, G. M. (1996). Prevalence of psychiatric disorders among incarcerated women. I. Pretrial jail detainees. *Archives of General Psychiatry, 53*, 505–12.

Teplin, L. A., McClelland, G. M., & Abram, K. M. (1993). The role of mental disorder and substance abuse in predicting violent crime among released offenders. In S. Hodgins (Ed.), *Mental Disorder and Crime* (86–103). Newbury Park, CA, USA: Sage Publications.

Tiihonen, J., & Hakola, P. (1995). Homicide and mental disorders. *Psychiatria Fennica, 26*, 125–129.

Tiihonen, J., Isohanni, M., Rasanen, P., Koiranen, M., & Moring, J. (1997). Specific major mental disorders and criminality: A 26–year prospective study of the 1966 Northern Finland birth cohort. *American Journal of Psychiatry, 154*, 840.

Timmins, N. (1996). *The Five Giants: A Biography of the Welfare State*. London: Harper Collins.

Tingle, D., Barnard, G. W., Robbins, L., Newman, G., et al. (1986). Childhood and adolescent characteristics of pedophiles and rapists. *International Journal of Law and Psychiatry, 9*, 103–116.

Torrey, E. F. (1994). Violent behaviour by individuals with serious mental illness. *Hospital and Community Psychiatry, 45*, 653–62.

Troy, M., & Stroufe, L. A. (1987). Victimisation among preschoolers: role of attachment relationship history. *Journal of American Academy of Child and Adolescent Psychiatry, 26*, 166–172.

Vaddadi, K. S., Soosai, E., Gilleard, C. J., & Adlard, S. (1997). Mental illness, physical abuse and burden of care on relatives: a study of acute psychiatric admission patients. *Acta Psychiatrica Scandinavica, 95*, 313–7.

Van Ijzendoorn, M. (1995). Adult attachment representations, parental responsiveness, and infant attachment: A meta-analysis on the predictive validity of the Adult Attachment Interview. *Psychological Bulletin, 117*, 387–403.

Van Ijzendoorn, M. H., Feldbrugge, J., Derks, F. C. H., De Ruiter, C.,

Verhagen, M. F. M., Philipse, M. W. G., Van der Staak, C. P. F., & Riksen Walraven, J. M. A. (1997). Attachment representations of personality-disordered criminal offenders. *Am J Orthopsychiatry, 67*, 449–459.

Vaughn, C. E. & Leff, J. P. (1976). The influences of family and social factors on the course of psychiatric illness: a comparison of schizophrenic and depressed neurotic patients. *British Journal of Psychiatry, 129*, 125–137.

Vaughn, C. E., Snyder, K. S., Jones, S., et al. (1984). Family factors in schizophrenic relapse. *Archives of General Psychiatry, 4*, 1169–1177.

Ventura, L. A., Cassel, C. A., Jacoby, J. E., & Huang, B. (1998). Case management and recidivism of mentally ill persons released from jail. *Psychiatric Services, 49*, 1330–1337.

Virkkunen, M. (1986). Insulin secretion during the glucose tolerance test among habitually violent and impulsive offenders. *Aggressive Behaviour, 12*, 303–312.

Virkkunen, M., DeJong, J., Bartko, J., Goodwin, F. K., & Linnoila, M. (1989). Relationship of psychobiological variables to recidivism in violent offenders and impulsive fire setters. *Archives of General Psychiatry, 46*, 600–603.

Wallace, C., Mullen, P., Burgess, P., Palmer, S., Ruschena, D., & Browne, C. (1998). Serious criminal offending and mental disorder. *British Journal of Psychiatry, 172*, 477–484.

Warner, R. (1994). *Recovery from Schizophrenia (2nd ed.)*. London: Routledge and Keegan Paul.

Webster, C. D., & Cox, D. (1997). Integration of nomothetic and ideographic positions in risk assessment: Implications for practice and the education of psychologists and other mental health professionals. *American Psychologist, 52*, 1245–1246.

Webster, C. D., Douglas, K. S., Eaves, D., & Hart, S. D. (1997). *HCR – 20: Assessing risk of violence to others (Version 2)*. Burnaby, BC: Mental Health Law and Policy Unit, Simon Fraser University.

Webster, C. D., Eaves, D., Douglas, K., & Wintrup, A. (1995). *The HCR – 20 Scheme: The Assessment of Dangerousness and Risk (Version 1)*. Burnaby, BC: Mental Health Law and Policy Unit, Simon Fraser University.

Weiler, B. L., & Widom, C. S. (1996). Psychopathy and violent behaviour in abused and neglected young adults. *Criminal Behaviour and Mental Health, 6*, 253–271.

Weiss, B., Dodge, K. A., Bates, J. E., & Pettit, G. S. (1992). Some consequences of early harsh discipline: Child aggression and a maladaptive social information processing style. *Child Development, 63*, 1321–1335.

Weiss, G., & Hechtman, L. T. (1986). *Hyperactive Children Grown Up.* New York: Guildford Press.

Werner, P. D., Rose, T. L., Yesavage, J. A., & Seeman, K. (1984). Psychiatrists' judgements of dangerousness on an acute care unit. *American Journal of Psychiatry, 141,* 263–6.

Wessely, S. (1993a). Violence and psychosis. In C. Thompson & P. Cowen (Eds.), *Violence: basic and clinical science* (119–34). Oxford, UK: Butterworth-Heinemann.

Wessely, S., Buchanan, A., Reed, A., Cutting, J., Everitt, B., Garety, P., & Taylor, P. (1993b). Acting on delusions: I. Prevalence. *British Journal of Psychiatry, 163,* 69–76.

Wessely, S., & Castle, D. (1998). Mental disorder and crime. *Archives of General Psychiatry, 55,* 86–87.

Wessely, S., & Taylor, P. J. (1991). Madness and crime: Criminology versus psychiatry. *Criminal Behaviour and Mental Health, 1,* 193–228.

Wessely, S. C., Castle, D., & Douglas, A. J. (1994). The criminal careers of incident cases of schizophrenia. *Psychological Medicine, 24,* 483–502.

Widom, C. S. (1989a). Child abuse, neglect, and adult behaviour: Research design and findings on criminality, violence, and child abuse. *American Journal of Orthopsychiatry, 59,* 355–367.

Widom, C. S. (1989b). The cycle of violence. *Science, 244,* 160–166.

Widom, C. S. (1989c). Does violence beget violence? A critical examination of the literature. *Psychological Bulletin, 106,* 3–28.

Wilson, D. & Ashton, J. *Crime & Punishment.* London: Blackstone Press Ltd.

Wintrup, A. (1996). *Assessing Risk of Violence in Mentally Disordered Offenders with the HCR-20.* Unpublised Master's Thesis, Simon Fraser University, Burnaby, British Columbia, Canada.

Wittgenstein, L. (1953). *Philosophical Investigations.* Oxford: Basil Blackwell.

Wittington, R. (1994). Violence in psychiatric hospitals. In T. Wykes (Ed.), *Violence and Health Care Professionals.* London, UK: Chapman and Hall.

Wittington, R., & Wykes, T. (1994). The prediction of violence in a health care setting. In T. Wykes (Ed.), *Violence and Health Care Professionals* . London, UK: Chapman and Hall.

Woodley, L., Dixon, K., Lindow, V., Oyebode, O., Sandford, T. & Simlet, S. (1995). *The Woodley Team Report* (Chair, Len Woodley QC). London: East London & the City Health Authority & Newham Council.

World Health Organisation. (1992). *The ICD-10 Classification of Mental and Behavioural Disorders: Clinical Descriptions and Diagnostic Guidelines.* Geneva: World Health Organisation.

Yesavage, J. A. (1983). Bipolar illness: Correlates of dangerous inpatient behaviour. *British Journal of Psychiatry, 143*, 554–7.

Yesavage, J. A., Becker, J. M., Werner, P. D., Patton, M. J., Seeman, K., Brunsting, D. W., & Mills, M. J. (1983). Family conflict, psychopathology, and dangerous behaviour by schizophrenic inpatients. *Psychiatry Research, 8*, 271–280.

Zitrin, A., Hardesty, A., Burdock, E., & Drossman, A. (1976). Crime and violence among mental patients. *American Journal of Psychiatry, 133*, 142–149.

Zubin, J. & Spring, B. (1977). Vulnerability : a new view of schizophrenia. *Journal of Abnormal Psychiatry, 86*, 260–266.

INDEX